Hegel and Aesthetics

SUNY Series in Hegelian Studies
William Desmond, editor

Hegel and Aesthetics

edited by
William Maker

State University of New York Press

Quotations from *Aesthetics: Lectures on Fine Art,* by G. W. F. Hegel
and translated by T. M. Knox reprinted by permission of
Oxford University Press © 1975, Oxford University Press.
Chapter 12, "The Logic of Art: Beauty and Nature" by Edward Halper,
© Edward Halper.

Published by
State University of New York Press, Albany

Printed in the United States of America

For information, address State University of New York Press
State University Plaza, Albany, New York 12246

Production by Dana Foote
Marketing by Fran Keneston

Library of Congress Cataloging-in-Publication Data

Hegel and aesthetics / edited by William Maker.
p. cm. — (SUNY series in Hegelian studies)
Essays first presented at the 14th Biennial Meeting of the Hegel Society of America.
held Oct. 18–20, 1996 in Keystone, Colo.
Includes bibliographical references and index.
ISBN 0-7914-4551-8 (hc : alk. paper) — ISBN 0-7914-4552-6 (pb : alk. paper)
1. Hegel, Georg Wilhelm Friedrich, 1770–1831 — Aesthetics. I. Maker, William. II.
Hegel Society of America. Meeting (14th : 1996 : Keystone, Colo.) III. Series.

B2949 A4 H44 2000

111′.85092–dc21 00-027467

10 9 8 7 6 5 4 3 2 1

Contents

Introduction

William Maker

But what *we* want to consider is art which
is *free* alike in its ends and its means.
—Hegel

Hegel was preeminently a *systematic philosopher*. His work addresses its subjects in a manner markedly informed by their location in and relation to his whole project and the conception of philosophy it articulates. So, understanding and evaluating his aesthetics require that we pay attention to his idea of a system. In addition, Hegel was deeply involved with freedom and with what has come to be known as the problem of modernity. His aesthetics need to be located within the field of these concerns as well. In this introduction I shall present a brief overview of Hegel's aesthetics, followed by considerations of his systematic approach and its treatment of freedom and modernity (I). Next I shall address the location and understanding of art in this systematic orbit (II), the contemporary significance of his aesthetics (III), and give an overview of the collected essays (IV).

In his *Lectures on Aesthetics,* Hegel presents art not only as capable of rational comprehension, but as being an embodiment of our free rationality in the sensible. As free rational beings—as Spiritual—humans strive to objectify, express, and comprehend ourselves. Art is one way in which we do this. In art the outer world of objective reality is shaped in accordance with human subjectivity, imbued with meaning and purpose, rendered intelligible, and thereby transfigured with beauty. Like religion and philosophy, art is centrally concerned with ultimate truth. Its business is to realize and to bring to consciousness who and what we are as creatures engaged in attaining our freedom. Thus, rather than being ephemeral, ethereal, or otherworldly, art according to Hegel addresses the very core of our being. In art fundamental truths about humanity are discovered and brought to understanding.

As comprehended philosophically, art appears as a manifestation of Spirit's historical development toward freedom. The philosophy of art is a grand historical narrative depicting the stages of the development and transformation of the forms and styles of art, with changes in art reflecting the progress in humanity's realization and understanding of its freedom. The narrative ends with Spirit's completion in modernity, revealing, not only that art is subordinate to religion and philosophy, but that the time of art's greatest glory is past. According to Hegel, art no longer occupies the central place it once did in human experience in that it is no longer the paramount medium through which we display the essential truths of the human condition. In this sense, Hegel's philosophy of art proclaims, not the death, but the diminution of art's role in our self-understanding. While still pursued and appreciated, art in the modern world has become secondary to other human endeavors.

What are we to make of Hegel's view of art in today's posteverything era where the culture of high theory has rejected, not only the legitimacy of grand narratives, but also the fundamental conceptions of reason, truth, modernity, freedom, and philosophy from out of which Hegel's aesthetics emerge? In a variety of ways, the essays collected here address this central question. But before considering the issue of the contemporary location and significance of Hegel's philosophy of art, and how these essays deal with it, it is crucial first to locate the aesthetics in the context of his philosophical project. What was Hegel up to in his systematic philosophy?

I. System and Modernity

Hegel's overriding concern was to attempt to comprehend and critically legitimate modernity as the historical triumph of Spirit, the human self-creation of freedom. Modernity and its institutions emerge as the culmination of humanity's realizing the truth of its being as freedom to the extent to which the modern world is one in which we can be at home because we have succeeded in creating and understanding the conditions for our freedom. Thus, Hegel sought to articulate the definitive features of all the central aspects of the modern world insofar as they are required by and accord with rationally intelligible freedom. His philosophy asks the twofold question: can we comprehend freedom as rationally legitimate and humanly attainable, and if we can, what various institutions and activities are necessary in order that humans can fully attain freedom? So the Hegelian project is both normative and descriptive.

It is fundamentally normative in that its conceptual presentation of freedom is articulated and defended on strictly rational, a priori grounds. Taking an important step beyond his predecessors Kant and Fichte, Hegel realized that neither the legitimacy nor the normative authority of freedom can be presupposed as given. According to Hegel, if freedom is to be defended and understood as the norm against which the given world is to be judged, our normative concept of freedom must be articulated independent of any determinative foundation in any given (and irreducibly arbitrary) conditions whatsoever: even the notion of a spontaneous subjectivity cannot be assumed as paradigmatic. To begin with such a notion, even in the transcendentally purified versions of Kant and Fichte, is to commence with an ungrounded given and thereby also with an acknowledgment of the authority of givenness in a project which would reject the heteronomy of the given in the name of the supreme authority of autonomy.

When Hegel rejects this approach of grounding or founding freedom in something antecedently given and other than itself, freedom—autonomy—emerges in a new light. Most distinctive about Hegel's conception of foundationless freedom is that it is consummately rational, neither a groundless spontaneity nor an arbitrary caprice. Both of these contemporary, purportedly postfoundational notions of an ungrounded freedom revert to foundationalism by using subjectivity as a given, determinative, model for freedom: only if human willing is taken as an ineliminable model can postmodernists confidently assert that an ungrounded freedom must reduce to a capricious, irrational, agency. Abjuring these and *all* such models altogether, and holding that freedom must and can determine itself in a non-arbitrary fashion, Hegel presents foundationless freedom as irreducibly rational. The Hegelian link between freedom and reason is twofold.

First (as Hegel argues in the *Phenomenology of Spirit* and the *Science of Logic*) reason requires freedom. Philosophically critical rationality and its demand for a thorough account of truth are themselves incoherent except insofar as reason is thoroughly constituted in an autonomous fashion: rationality and autonomy must coincide in the conceptual self-determination of an autonomous reason which all attempts at rational justification finally demand. For, if reason is grounded in some given—if it is heteronomous—that given must always remain unjustified, compromising reason's claim to establish unconditional truth. The only thing that may legitimately condition or determine reason is what reason itself establishes.

Second, freedom requires reason. From its own side, freedom is inseparable from reason because (as he argues in the philosophy of Spirit) attempts to sever it from rationality, from autonomous self-determination, end up reducing freedom to domination. The detachment of freedom from rational self-determination leads to the collapse of autonomy into some form of heteronomy. For, (paralleling what we saw with reason) if freedom is understood as grounded in some antecedently given condition, that given must then determine—rule—freedom. However, the state of being determined by an other is not freedom, but heteronomy. The only thing that may legitimately condition or determine freedom is what freedom itself requires. So both rationality *and* freedom require the renunciation of the determinative authority of the given. Thus, reason and freedom alike are only finally intelligible as self-determination. At the core of Hegel's whole philosophical project are the crucial insights that philosophical rationality can only give an account of itself insofar as it is autonomous, and that only autonomous reason can comprehend and legitimate the normative authority of freedom. Put differently, both truth and justice need to be construed non-foundationally, in terms of autonomous self-determination.

Hegel realized then that, rather than precluding philosophical rationality and objectivity altogether, it is precisely the absence of foundations, and the discovery of what that means, which makes philosophy possible as the knowledge of objective truth in which normative conditions for truth and justice are set forth. So what postmodernists present as the fatal flaw of modernity and its philosophy—their lack of any final given or postulatable foundations in subjectivity, nature, language, being, etc.—Hegel recognized and proclaimed as the initial key to, and the first step in understanding, modernity's and philosophy's triumph. In Hegelian terms, it is only postmodernists' tacit foundationalism, their obdurate and otiose attachment to the belief that freedom and reason must be grounded in some givens, that leads them to the illicit conclusion that the absence of such given foundations must result in the nihilistic victory of arbitrary caprice and irrational subjectivism. (Of course, if Hegel is right—if freedom is not a given, if it is not guaranteed, and if its attainment presupposes understanding its nature as such—the persistence of such philosophical misunderstandings could have consequences that threaten freedom.)

Looked at in historical terms, modernity's practical assertion of the normative authority of freedom makes possible philosophy's theoretical completion by opening the way for philosophy's discovery that freedom—as autonomous conceptual self-determination—is the basis for attaining a philosophical discourse capable of legitimating itself because it is not founded on heteronomous givens incapable of final justification. Correlatively, the fact of modernity's assertion of the right of freedom calls for a philosophical legitimation of that right—a legitimation which can establish the unprecedented normative authority of freedom unfounded in anything given. Philosophy and freedom are inseparable co-conspirators in the project of modernity. As even modernity's harshest critics recognize (albeit inchoately), just this sort of foundationless freedom is presupposed by modern institutions and practices in their rejection of given customs and traditions in the name of the rightful authority of individual self-determination. Unlike Hegel, what those critics fail to see is that the absence of foundations for modernity's freedom need not necessarily lead to a nihilistic will-to-power as some sort of "postfoundational foundation." Paradoxically endorsing some version of Nietzsche's cryptofoundationalism, they miss, or ignore, Hegel's discovery that the conceptual and practical legitimacy of modernity can be demonstrated by a systematic philosophy that originates in the liberating discovery that the foundational assumption is itself without foundations.

Hegel's philosophy of freedom is secondarily (but necessarily) descriptive in that its idea of rational freedom insists that a rational freedom must be a thoroughly attainable one. A freedom that cannot be realized is incoherent, it is not freedom at all. Thus, Hegel endeavors to indicate just what actual features of the world may satisfy the requirements of a rational, actualizable freedom, a freedom that is not a utopian ideal whose perpetually postponed realization demands a striving incapable of satisfaction. This descriptive component does not compromise the normative one. It is absolutely crucial to understand that Hegel's concept of freedom does not entail that freedom has been fully actualized, but only that it be actualizable. Were freedom vouchsafed to us of historical necessity it would not be freedom at all, as Hegel understands freedom: as a free human creation. Thus, Hegel's descriptive account of those features of the modern world that enable freedom does not amount to surrendering the authority of autonomous reason to judge this world in its givenness. On the contrary.

For one thing, and as the continuing debates about modernity which have marked post-Hegelian history show, far from being a given, the legitimacy of modernity stands in need of a philosophical accounting. The unprecedented character of its claims means that the sheer fact of modernity, its givenness, is not enough to establish its legitimacy. (Hegel appreciated that this legitimation must be one of the most radical sort, that is, one that rejects the authority of giveness thoroughly and completely.) The widespread (albeit still contended) acceptance of modern institutions and practices implicitly presupposes a philosophical account capable of demonstrating the normative legitimacy of the rational freedom they may embody. So Hegel's conception of the nature of freedom, of modernity, and of philosophy are all predicated on recognizing the normative authority of freedom over facticity. Thus, while the descriptive component of his philosophy attends to given facts, this in no way indicates that facticity grounds normativity.

For another thing, it is Hegel's oft-repeated dictum that the mere existence of something, its factual givenness, neither guarantees, nor is, as such, evidence of its rationality. What is rational must be actualizable (and *may* have been actualized) but to comprehend this philosophically—to grasp what rational freedom is and requires—is not proof that the rational has been actualized. Making the rational actual requires more than philosophical thought. It requires human action in which philosophical, conceptual labor is only one part.

Thus, Hegel was neither a right-wing nor a left-wing Hegelian. He demands that we reject equally the conservative propensity to endorse the given, just because it is given, as well as the radical propensity to reject the given, just because it is given. Only autonomous reason can determine what is to be accepted and rejected in the world we find given. Hegel's philosophy is not a Panglossian theodicy or a quietistic endorsement of the status quo. Nor, at the opposite extreme, does it afford a distopian view in which freedom is always denied by the present. Hegel rejects both postmodernist visions of freedom: the neo-Marxist view, where freedom is an ever-evanescent hope, demanding perpetual rebellion against the status quo (but forever projected into a never-attainable and indeterminate future state) and the neo-Nietzschean view, where freedom is relegated to the private, asocial interiority of an egotistic subjectivism of self-referential self-discovery. Rather, by demanding both that the given world accord with self-determining reason and that what reason conceives must be actualizable, achievable through human self-determination, Hegel's is the critical philosophy par excellence.

II. Freedom and Art Systematically Conceived

In his philosophy of Spirit where he treats aesthetics, Hegel works to demonstrate which types of human activity and which institutions are required for the actualization of Spirit, the full human self-realization of freedom. His approach is systematic, which is to say it looks at freedom developmentally, multidimensionally, and comprehensively.

Hegel conceptualizes freedom in historically developmental fashion by examining how different stages and different forms of freedom emerge over time. He articulates freedom in a conceptually developmental fashion by indicating how the abstract and incomplete character of one mode of freedom logically requires ever more concrete and fully developed modes. (For example, the abstract freedom of property right is inherently unstable and unrealizable without the institution of civil society which incorporates and complements the freedom of property.)

Additionally his approach is multidimensional in that assessing how one form of freedom requires another for its fulfillment means seeing that freedom has diverse dimensions. (For example, the freedom realized in the market is not the same as political freedom and yet requires the latter in order both to secure economic freedom and to have its limitations ameliorated.) And finally, Hegel's systematic conception of freedom is comprehensive in that thinking through the interdependent and interrelated aspects of differing forms of freedom which are incomplete in their own right makes possible a thorough consideration of the topic. An important feature of the Hegelian understanding of freedom is the comprehensive and multidimensional account he provides. Unlike the conception of freedom as liberty, which still predominates in the anglophone world, Hegel does not restrict freedom to the political and economic realms. Nor does he conceive it solely in negative terms, as a matter of the minimum of humanly imposed restrictions on a solitary individual who would be fully free in a state of nature if only others were absent. He refuses to regard human plurality as leading to the "necessary evil" of societies and states which compromise a purportedly ideal liberty attainable only in the fictional isolation of a Robinson Crusoe. While Hegel acknowledges the importance of this sort of "freedom from," he refuses to absolutize it. For him, freedom encompasses the full range of human modes of self-realization. It is not a gift of nature but requires development and education. And freedom importantly includes positive, cooperative interactions with others.

So the basic Hegelian outlook is that we can best render the human condition, human history, and our contemporary place in it intelligible when they are considered from the point of view of rational freedom, *sub species libertatis*. As freedom is not a natural given but a human attainment, our understanding of freedom plays a crucial role in its realization. Philosophy, religion, and art are decisive as distinctive achievements through which we both realize and come to understand different aspects of our freedom. In what ways is freedom central to art in Hegel's view?

Art is a product of Spirit, it is part of the effort to craft our freedom, and in contemplating works of art we also come to understand something distinctive about that effort and its realization. Through art we attain a particular kind of freedom and we also learn about what we are as creatures capable of striving to realize our humanness as autonomous beings. As involving both creative thought and the material world, art is a way of resolving the immediate, restrictive opposition between the inner, private domain and the outer, initially alien domain of nature. In that works of art are transformations of given, sensible materials in accordance with a free play of individual imagination which finds harmonious expression in those materials, art both is and celebrates an independence from nature and natural necessity even while recognizing and affirming our sensible and sensuous nature. And since artworks are appreciated for what they are, allowed to stand free, in their own right, art is also liberatory in that through art we rise above merely consumptive and desirous relations to material things. Thus the human capacity for realizing a distinctive type of freedom—the pleasing, uncoerced unity of an inner subjectivity with an outer world of material objectivity—is both attained and proclaimed in works of art.

Yet true art, beautiful art, is not merely the sensible manifestation of a free subjective creativity. In genuine art something universally true about humanity is expressed in and radiates itself through the unique features and details of the particular artwork. Beautiful art speaks to and about the human condition. Since for Hegel "to be" in the fullest sense is to be individual, since the highest truth is the synthesis of the particular and the universal in individuality, beautiful artworks are a distinctive mode in which this reality and this truth are actualized and made comprehensible. Successful works of art stand alone in an individuality of form as well as content. In terms of form, each is a unique creation in which a particular artist has made universal truths manifest in the manifold particulars of the specific materials and styles of the artwork. Artworks also attain a distinctive mode of individuality in their content: successful works of art depict the ways in which universal features of our humanness are individuated in an endless variety of particular human circumstances, conditions, times, and places.

Thus, because art resonates a sensuous intelligibility, because in art we engage in sensorially meaningful acts of fashioning, discovering, and understanding ourselves and our world, art is fundamentally capable of rational comprehension. This is the case according to Hegel even though works of art are unique and are the expression of particular artists, styles, times, and places, and even though philosophical, conceptual intelligibility is of a different order than the sensuous intelligibility of art. Art can be rendered conceptually intelligible in philosophy while not being reduced to a mere adjunct of philosophical rationality and without having its uniqueness—its freedom—compromised, because of Hegel's distinctive notion of rationality. For Hegel, philosophically rational comprehension is nonreductive (and does not succumb to panlogicism) because it is not a matter of purging concrete particulars from a given subject in order to reach the formal husk of abstract generality in an empty universal. Rather, Hegelian conceptualizing (*Begreifen*) is a matter of thinking through the manifold nature of autonomous self-determination, the attainment of individuality, in all its guises and modes. Rational comprehension according to Hegel involves seeing how universality may concretize itself in a variety of substantive individualities. Each of these will be distinctive and self-subsistent, irreducible, just because it is an individual. To paraphrase Aristotle, individuality may be said in many ways. But each is still philosophically intelligible because we have come to understand the general features of individuality, including how it attains its irreducible character through a relation of self-identification and self-differentiation with other individuals: individuals are all alike in being individual through the fact that each attains its self-determination in a different way.

And yet, while for Hegel art is an expression of the deepest truths about human being and human beings, he is opposed to and critical of views of art that regard it from a predominantly pragmatic or utilitarian perspective, as intelligible and worthwhile because it serves some end outside of itself. Like science, indeed, like thought, art may well serve other ends, but the true understanding of art must allow art to stand free, a unique activity with its own ends. Hegel's philosophy of art allows art this freedom by explaining art not just as manifesting truth in a particular way, but also as having its *own* unique truth to express; art is not just a means for, or a manifestation of, something other than itself which could be articulated or communicated in another fashion. It is insofar as Hegel's aesthetics succeeds in doing this—bringing to philosophical, conceptual clarity what is genuinely essential and distinctive about art as art—that it lays claim to being *the* philosophy of art.

But while Hegel appreciates art as a distinctive expression of humanness, his understanding of *ars gratia artis* is not one which precludes objective critical judgments. Hegel's conception of "art which is *free* alike in its ends and its means" leads neither to a hermeticism in which art is so radically self-contained and self-sufficient that no external criteria or standpoints for judgment are attainable, nor to a subjectivism in which art is nothing but the expression of individual creative genius where anything goes. Because art in general is a distinctive expression of Spirit, free rationality, we can judge the adequacy of works of art in terms of how well the universally rational is individuated by being given sensuous configuration in them. Furthermore, because Spirit, the process of the realization of freedom, is historically developmental, we can understand art's mode of realizing Spirit not only as having a history, but as having one period in which art is the preeminent mode in which truth is made manifest. According to Hegel, that period has gone by. First religion, and now philosophy have superseded art as the best means through which Spirit can now comprehend itself. So for Hegel, the essence of what we moderns are is no longer best rendered comprehensible in art.

III. Hegel's Aesthetics Today

What are we to make of his views in our contemporary context? At first glance it seems that Hegel presents a view of art that appears to have been thoroughly refuted by the received view of post-Hegelian history. The contemporary posture on such matters asserts an ironic reversal of the key Hegelian notions which link rationality, freedom, truth, and modernity in a philosophical grand narrative ending with the ascension of philosophy over art. The postmodern condition has long since proclaimed rationality and its pretensions toward understanding as illusory masks of an omnipresent drive, not toward freedom, but domination and terror. Religion and philosophy have been disclosed as false idols. And rather than art's waning, postmodernism heralds an arational artistic creativity, not only as the essence of art, but as the only possible hope for liberation and an authentic existence; a groundless and capricious creativity is touted as the ultimate ground and the final truth of all human activity, including philosophy. In their correction of Hegel, postmodernists tell us that "reason" does not underlie, emerge in, render comprehensible, and validate art. Rather, a khthonic drive whose model is art underlies, emerges in, renders incomprehensible, and invalidates "reason." "Art," it would seem, has triumphed to proclaim the death of philosophy. If then, in the spirit of Croce, we are to ask "What is living and what is dead in Hegel," may we confidently assert that certainly his aesthetics are dead? Before we sign the death certificate, let us take a closer look at the alleged corpse.

A key feature of what postmodernism regards as its post-Hegelian displacement of philosophy by art is the proclamation of an ironic detachment which questions the reality of the objective world even as it calls attention to and mocks the authority of the subject; a displacing which continually moves to displace itself, lest it be caught in a foundational move. As many of the essays here point out, rather than being ignorant of this mode of subjective self-understanding, Hegel was among the first to analyze this posture as reflective of art in the modern world. Further inspection of the postmodern situation discloses other ironies that may lead us to wonder just how post-Hegelian postmodernity really is. A further irony of the postmodernist reversal of Hegel is that the proclamation of "the death of philosophy in the spirit of art" is everywhere made by philosophers, or by self-styled "post-philosophical thinkers" (some of whom labor in philosophy departments). The purported triumph of arational art is announced in discourses that are for the most part conventionally "rational" and nonartistic. Whether it is called "philosophy" or not, something very like it remains regnant even while proclaiming its own dethronement.

And it is in such discourses (where theses are put forward, arguments made, and evidence adduced) that disputes about the nature of art continue to take place. The activity of art criticism proceeds apace and often challenges the centrality and importance of its subject, art, in the name of its own philosophical authority. When everything is a text, it is not the artist, but the philosophical critic (who knows everything knowable about textuality) who attains prominence: in postmodernity interpretation is *the* point, and the object of interpretation becomes secondary to what the all-knowing interpreter makes of it, so much grist for the playful interpretive act smugly intimating its own superior consciousness by its pseudo-self-deprecation. If works of art (like everything else) are truly what postmodernist post-philosophers assert, just instances of subjective self-expression, then a curious dialectic seems to have ensued: a shift of the locus of attention from the art object and the artist to the theorizing critic who reaches a higher level of subjective self-expression—a higher level of art, that is—in creative criticism. If everything is a creative fiction, then acts of self-consciously creative fiction about creative fiction are the highest expression of "truth," as Nietzsche observed. So the post-Hegelian theories that purport to glorify art (or certain models of artistic creativity) may actually end up confirming Hegel's contention that ours is an age when philosophy, not art, is prominent.

When we consider, then, that the postmodern glorification of artistic discovery which is found everywhere has brought into question traditional distinctions between what is and is not art, and bids fair to raise theorizing itself to the level of a purported art form, Hegel's questioning of the end of art, and his notion that ours is an age in which philosophical theory dominates, take on a new resonance. The recent publication of Arthur Danto's unabashedly neo-Hegelian *Art After the End of Art* may herald a reconsideration of Hegelian themes and approaches. Is philosophy dead? Is art dead? Is Hegel's philosophy of art dead? In a variety of ways and from different perspectives, the essays collected here are concerned with these questions. Some offer an overview of Hegel's aesthetic project. Others focus on his treatment of particular art forms, such as poetry, music, painting, and architecture. Still others concern themselves with the relation between Hegel's views on art and those of his contemporaries. If the authors do not arrive at a consensus about how these questions are to be answered, they do concur that Hegel's philosophy of art is important, relevant, unjustly ignored, and deserving of a voice in contemporary debates.

IV. The Essays

In "Art and the Absolute Revisited: The Neglect of Hegel's Aesthetics," William Desmond explores the contemporary neglect of Hegel's aesthetics, asking why it is ignored, and whether the disdain is justified. Hegel is not much regarded in contemporary aesthetic considerations, Desmond explains, because he subordinates art to philosophy and intimately associates it with religion. This runs counter to the prevailing post-Nietzschean orthodoxy which disparages religion and, in its place, absolutizes artistic creativity as an end-in-itself, relegating philosophy to a subordinate position as a merely derivative form of artistic creation. Much of contemporary thought deifies artists and artworks: in the godlike originality of genius, art appears as the embodiment of absolute power; it is in artworks that transcendence is said to emerge in immanence.

Hegel is neglected, not only because he rejects this aestheticism and refuses to make art absolute, but because his notions of the supersession of art and his critique of romantic genius are tellingly applicable to contemporary attempts to absolutize art. As Desmond presents the Hegelian perspective, the absolutization of art in the romantic cult of subjective creativity makes art incomprehensible and impotent by making everything into art and rendering everything permissible: if everything is permitted in art and as art, art loses all distinctiveness and becomes trivial, rather than absolute. Yet if Desmond sees an important place for Hegel's aesthetics today, his is by no means an unequivocal endorsement. He is somewhat sympathetic to the postmodernist charge that Hegel tends to absorb everything into rationally self-determining thought. Thus Hegel is partly to blame for his neglect. But if absolutizing thought is an erroneous move which Hegel may not have thoroughly avoided, the contemporary absolutization of art is not a proper corrective. Despite its failings, Desmond feels that Hegel's approach is more nuanced than aestheticism and offers us more prospects for further questioning.

If Desmond is concerned with explaining why Hegel's aesthetics are largely, but unjustly ignored today, Carl Rapp makes a further case for the relevance of these aesthetics for diagnosing and criticizing the same post-Nietzschean condition which rejects them. In "Hegel's Concept of the Dissolution of Art," Rapp argues provocatively that Hegel's conception of romantic art proleptically grasps the central motifs of the post-Hegelian, postromantic movements of realism, symbolism, and abstractionism. Discussing Eliot, Stevens, Bloom, Derrida, Foucault, and Rorty, Rapp argues for the continuing relevance of Hegel's insight that art in modernity is overcome in a romantic irony which proclaims itself triumphant over all cultural productions.

As Rapp explains, much of contemporary art and philosophy exhibit precisely the condition associated with what Hegel described as the self-dissolution of art: a central focus on subjectivity itself as the creative source of all meaning and truth. In Hegel's diagnosis of romantic irony, this triumphant subjectivity moves even to question its own supremacy, continually displacing itself. This leads to art in a state of self-dissolution because (echoing Desmond) no artwork can ever adequately express the ever-mutating creative genius which is now the sole legitimate subject of art. The artwork becomes secondary to the artist's personality in the face of which all fixities of form and content dissolve. Anything and everything can be used to express the truth of radical subjectivity. Deconstruction too, with its notion that truth is fiction and that neither art nor philosophy have any truth to reflect, is modeled after romantic subjectivity. Now the thinker adopts the stance of destabilizing all fixed notions, even including the notion of the thinker. According to Rapp, Hegel has provided a telling vision of modernity after his own time. Art and philosophy modeled after art occupy themselves with a ceaseless self-dissolution which has no goal or conceivable endpoint.

Brian K. Etter's essay, "Hegel's Aesthetic and the Possibility of Art Criticism," also takes up a broad consideration of the contemporary relevance of Hegelian approaches to art. In Etter's view the prevailing post-Nietzschean orthodoxy is fundamentally historicist and thus endorses a presentism according to which there are no transcendent truths or values beyond those of an ever-changing now which continually consumes the past. The predominant aesthetic theories glimmering in today's post-Nietzschean twilight reflect this stance and preclude critical assessment. When art is understood as the expression of the self it stands in need of no justification, and as long as art is of the moment there is no basis for criticism of it.

But while he agrees with the broader features of Desmond's and Rapp's analysis of the contemporary situation, Etter's view of Hegel's relation to it is rather different from both, although certainly closer to Desmond's than Rapp's. According to Etter, Hegel's endorsement of modernity as the end of history involves a sort of presentism, and the stress he places on subjectivity and individuality prefigure the contemporary glorification of self-expression. Yet Hegel's aesthetics are critical of this situation, and Etter wants to know how this is possible. Hegel can maintain a critical stance toward art in modernity, despite his historicist and presentist endorsement of modernity generally, because of ambiguities in his heterodox conception of the divine. What enables Hegel to sustain a critical perspective is what Etter sees as his equivocation about Spirit: it is the fulfillment of the divine without fully incorporating it. Thus Hegel's endorsement of the present and of subjectivity are equivocal because, even as the triumph of Spirit, there is still something transcendent present as a basis for his critique of the spiritual poverty of the modern world. In disagreement with Rapp, and taking a more explicit position than Desmond, Etter holds however that an orthodox conception of the divinely transcendent is needed to overcome what he regards as Hegel's confusion on this point.

Jere Surber takes up the topic of the contemporary relevance of Hegel's aesthetics from yet another vantage point. "Art as a Mode of Thought: Hegel's Aesthetics and the Origins of Modernism" directly challenges recent readings that see Hegel's treatment as thoroughly locked in the past, incapable of being meaningfully applied to the arts beyond his own time. Surber disputes the notion that his work merely completes a tradition from which the present is radically cut off, arguing that Hegel can do more than help us understand and appreciate art of the past. Like Rapp, Surber applies Hegel's aesthetics to modernist art, contending that Hegel managed to anticipate later developments.

Considering Hegel's musical aesthetics and a variety of modernist composers, Surber's thesis is that, rather than failing to understand art's philosophical potential, Hegel's treatment of art helped to make it possible for subsequent art to address philosophical issues directly and to take philosophical positions. Hegel allows for art as a mode of philosophical thought and, by doing so, offers the first theory of modern art. Hegel's linkage of art, religion, and philosophy in Absolute Spirit shows that they share an absolute content, thus philosophy can be represented in art and art can have philosophical import. Hegel's assertion of the supremacy of philosophy over art does mean that art can no longer be autonomous, but the Hegelian joining of philosophy and art may be seen to relate positively to modern and postmodern efforts to eliminate traditional distinctions between art and philosophy. Considering some disputed issues in modernist music through Hegel's musical aesthetics, Surber argues that his rational and linguistic approach fits post-Hegelian music by providing an appropriately postromantic and nonemotivist understanding of what music is about and what it can accomplish.

In his Presidential Address, "Hegel and the Art of Painting," Stephen Houlgate directs our attention to Hegel's treatment of another art form, arguing vigorously for the importance of Hegel's analysis of painting in spite of the general indifference with which it has been met. Again, a case is made for the continuing worth of Hegel's treatment. Houlgate contends that Hegel may be said not only to have grasped the nature of painting as such, but that this treatment can help us to understand and criticize post-Hegelian developments in painting. According to Houlgate, Hegel sees painting as the artistic medium in which our inner subjectivity is first adequately expressed materially. What is crucial to and distinctive of painting as an expression of this aspect of spirituality is its artificial and illusory character. The immediate and real spaciality and materiality of the objective world, which sculpture directly manifests, is transformed in painting, subjectivized, by being rendered two-dimensional and artificial. The inescapably illusory character of painting's representation of the real makes possible the expression of the inwardness of subjectivity and of its primacy: everything in painting is manifestly an artifice, a human product in which the natural objects represented have been transformed in accordance with the free spirit of the artist. Thus inner freedom becomes directly and concretely visible in representational paintings which manifest the larger human capacity to transform objectivity according to its own lights.

What about abstract art then? Houlgate argues that the primary justifications for it do not stand up to Hegelian analysis. On the one hand, abstract art does not succeed in being the best expression of the inner subjectivity and freedom of the artist. Its abandonment of representation cannot really make the inner life intelligibly manifest to another. And sheer abstraction misses the essence of freedom because it turns its back on the real world, rather than displaying the transformative capturing of objectivity by the subject which is evident in representation. On the other hand, neither does abstract art realize the true essence of art by making the materiality of painting its sole focus. Doing that actually brings art closer to sculpture, rather than articulating its unique character as painting. What painting can do better than any other art form is to be honestly illusory: naturalistic illusion manifests Spirit as capable of expressively transforming the world in its own guise.

Turning to yet another art form, David Kolb's "The Spirit of Gravity: Architecture and Externality" offers a detailed consideration of the Hegelian notion that architecture is the art of the external, probing into the specific ways in which architecture works with, in, through, and as the external. Holding that art is a way in which Spirit moves from inwardness to express itself in objectivity, Hegel regards architecture as essential because it deals directly and transformatively with what is manifestly other than Spirit: inorganic nature as ruled by gravity and devoid of inherent meaning and purpose. As Kolb explains, in architectural construction sheer externality is overcome in and through its own nature and domain. Architecture works in and with spaciality and in and with materials that occupy space; and in building, these modes of externality are used to effect a transformation of externality. Externality is effused with Spirit but in such a way that its own nonspiritual character is not eradicated, but illuminated. In buildings, gravity is defied by being obeyed in ways that manifest its nature, and inert materials take on form and meaning in ways that still disclose their resistance to them. In architecture, even in being transformed, externality is displayed as what it is. Although other art forms are better expressions of Spirit, architecture is art, and an essential art because architecture makes art out of what is most unartistic and spacializes Spirit in a way no other art can.

Yet as the most basic expression of Spirit, Hegel sees architecture as limited, incapable of adequately expressing in a fully reflective way its own fundamental character of being the art of the external. As functional, buildings have their meaning and purpose outside themselves, another dimension of the externality of architecture. Kolb asks whether this self-externality can actually be asserted *in* architecture? From Hegel's perspective it would seem that the meaning unique to architecture, that its meaning lies external to itself, is something architecture cannot convey. It can never fully articulate the truth of its own nature as an art, and would thus appear to be inadequate according to Hegel's demand that Spirit, and art, reflexively postulate—be and also *say*—what they are.

Raising again the question of the relevance of Hegel's aesthetics today, Kolb doubts, though, whether this Hegelian stricture can capture contemporary developments. Looking at the work of various contemporary architects who try to make architecture's own externality their subject, Kolb asks whether they may not have moved toward doing what Hegel ruled out. Might architecture work through the Hegelian conceptions of its own limits to transcend those limits, and Hegel's philosophy of architecture as well? In Kolb's view, architecture may be able to do what Hegel wanted better than he understood. The tensions immanent in Hegel's treatment of architecture take us beyond that treatment.

Richard Dien Winfield also treats the question of the artistic status of architecture raised by the externality of its meaning and function. Can an aesthetics which stresses the self-sufficiency of art and art's role in providing human self-understanding comprehend architecture, with its distinctively functional and nonrepresentational character? Locating architecture is especially a problem for Hegel's aesthetics because of its insistence that artworks radiate and realize human individuality and freedom while attaining their own individuality and freedom independent of externally imposed meanings and goals. Architecture does not seem capable of depicting anything and appears locked into a utilitarian servitude to other ends. Winfield surveys Hegel's treatment of symbolic, classical, and romantic architecture to show how he goes about resolving these problems and providing a coherent understanding of architecture as an art.

Crucial to Hegel's approach is the historically differentiated and developmental view he takes both of Spirit and of art as a medium for spiritual self-realization and self-understanding. Different historical periods are marked by different ways in which subjective autonomy is understood and appreciated. Winfield argues that the particular, historically located understandings of form, function, and of their relation to one another which are manifested in symbolic, classic, and romantic architecture are convincingly linked to the spiritual development and self-understandings of subjectivity found in the ancient, classical, and modern eras. In each period we find a different perception of the nature and value of autonomous subjectivity, and correlatively different ways of realizing how subjective inwardness may be related to and expressed in the external world of space and materiality which is architecture's medium and milieu.

While Kolb sees contemporary architecture as pushing beyond a

Hegelian limit prescribed by architecture's restriction to working in and with externality, Winfield's view of today's architecture finds its inventive restlessness congruent with the larger Hegelian schema of modernity. On this issue of a Hegelian overview of contemporary art, he is more in agreement with Surber and Rapp in reading Hegel as providing a conciliatory comprehension of these movements, than with Desmond and Etter, who are uncomfortable with the subjectivism they find in these movements and, ambiguously, in Hegel as well. In Winfield's reading of Hegel, modernity seeks to express the truth of a subjective autonomy that recognizes only self-imposed limits, not limits imposed by nature or the past. Appropriately, and like abstract art and atonal music, modernist minimalist architecture expresses a self-understanding that focuses on subjective creativity beyond those confines, displaying how both nature and tradition can be transcended. Postmodernist architecture takes this spiritual development another step by showing how past styles can be playthings for the unbounded creative self which can never be reduced to any external embodiment. In the anything goes spirit of contemporary architecture where any style serves as well as another and in which no particular sensuous configuration has ultimate meaning, Winfield sees a recognition of Hegel's modernist assertion of the universal validity of free agency.

Stephen C. Law returns to the contentious issue of the overcoming of art, exploring the reasoning behind Hegel's assertion that comedy is the ultimate aesthetic experience and the self-dissolution of art, the art that transcends the limits of artistic expression.

Comedy is the art in which pleasure is derived by negation, through seeing things come apart. This is appropriate, freedom is served according to Hegel, when what gets undone in comedy are things antithetical to Spirit. But comedy is also capable of exercising its dissolutive force on any number of worthy things; it can be destructive rather than transcendent. Comedy emerges to prominence in the last, romantic stage of art when art has passed its empyrean and turned more away from its proper sphere of the outer sensuous world, to the inwardness of subjectivity, the domain of ideas. Comedy is a subset of poetry, whose linguistic medium is ideal for the fabrication of a thoroughly subjective world released from the confines of objectivity. As Law presents Hegel's historical overview, art progresses as the development of the sensuous expression of our increased realization of our nature as free, culminating in comedy: while tragedy represents a struggle between freedom and necessity, in comedy, restraints and constraints are set aside as inessential and the objective world emerges as a subjective creation; freedom is asserted through our ability to laugh at that world as something which cannot really threaten us. In comedy human beings, rather than natural or divine necessity, determine the outcome; we become the gods who dispense justice; and failure is punished only by laughter. The ability to laugh at circumstances that thwart our hopes and expectations, and at oneself, indicates a spirit who is autonomous in taking nothing too seriously.

Law argues that important in Hegel's appreciation of comedy is the distinction he draws between the comic and the ironic. In irony even the noble and worthwhile are nullified by a radical subjectivity. What he calls subjective comedy is criticized by Hegel because it heralds a subjectivity that has become quasi-divine, intent on dissolving the world without proffering any replacement.

If Desmond, Rapp, and Etter endorse the core of Hegel's critique of the romantics and romantic irony, and see his views as remaining applicable today, Judith Norman's dissection of Hegel's critique of Schlegel offers a defense of the romantics and their notion of the fusion of art and philosophy. In "Squaring the Romantic Circle: Hegel's Critique of Schlegel's Theories of Art," she questions, not the connection between the romantics and the present, but the force of a Hegelian critique of both.

According to Norman, Hegel has failed to understand Schelegel and the romantics. He wrongly read Schlegel's notion of genius as rooted in Fichte's absolute ego and thus failed to see that irony in Schlegel is not simply self-conscious value positing. Schlegel in fact recognizes something independent of artistic genius as informing the artist, so Hegel is wrong in attacking his notion of genius as willful, unrestrained self-expression. In fact, Norman argues, Schlegel recognized a link between art and philosophy which Hegel missed. Schlegel's elevation of art over philosophy is rooted in a conception of art as capable of completing the whole project of critical philosophy in a way not open to philosophy proper. Critique calls for a critique of itself, but this leads to philosophical paradoxes which a reflective or philosophical art can avoid by its notion of irony. Irony recognizes the subjective, fabricated character of reality, but unlike philosophy, it also discloses the ungrounded, incomprehensible nature of the world-making subject presupposed by critique. Art is thereby raised to philosophy, or unified with it.

While Hegel was right in attributing to Schlegel the notion that the world is subjective and illusory, Norman argues, he was wrong in seeing this irony as rooted in the subject. In fact, irony is that whereby the object indicates its illusory status. In sharp disagreement with Surber, Norman sees romanticism and its effort to unify art and philosophy providing possibilities Hegel missed owing to the incompatible roles he assigned to art and philosophy.

If Desmond and Etter question what they regard as Hegel's overly conceptual approach to and ambiguous position on the divine, and if Norman defends, against Hegel, romantic (and by implication, postromantic) attempts to synthesize philosophy and art, Martin Gammon explores the young Hegel's preoccupation with both these issues. At stake in "Modernity and the Crisis of Aesthetic Representation in Hegel's Early Writings" is the still disputed authorship of "The Earliest *Systemprogramm* of German Idealism."

That work postulates an aesthetic philosophy in which reason and the sensible are synthesized in the presentation of divinity. Looking closely at works of the period known to have come from Hegel's pen, Gammon disputes the attribution of the *Systemprogramm* to him. His richly detailed consideration of Hegel's earliest views on art offers insights into how Hegel came to the position that art in the modern world could not achieve what many of his contemporaries believed it could, the mediation of truth by beauty in an aestheticized philosophy. For Hegel, Gammon argues, art was now unable to perform this central function for two reasons. On the one hand, the contemporary ethical truth of Christianity is too intellectual for art; the infinite Christian God cannot be adequately captured in readily accessible images. On the other hand, art too has become overly intellectualized, subservient to the conceptual nature of Spirit in modernity. Thus, the synthesis of art and philosophy proclaimed in the *Systemprogramm*'s call for a new mythology of reason ought not to be attributed to Hegel. The early Hegel had already moved beyond seeking an aesthetic solution to the spiritual problems of modernity.

Like all the authors, Andrew G. Fiala examines the related issues of the appropriate character of an aesthetic response to modernity and the proper relation between art and philosophy. In "Aesthetic Education and the Aesthetic State: Hegel's Response to Schiller," Fiala focuses on Hegel's response to Schiller, whose *Letters on the Aesthetic Education of Man* influenced Hegel and have recently received renewed attention from those critical of modernity's allegedly dehumanizing, logocentric rationalization of the life-world and the political.

What is at stake for Schiller is how social alienation may be ameliorated by an aesthetics that can serve both as a means to mediate divisions, and as an end in itself in which aesthetic experience effects the unity of sensuousness and rationality, thereby overcoming alienation altogether. For Schiller, attaining the latter goal would consist in the attainment of an aesthetic state of absolute freedom. Beauty will lead to political freedom and thus art is subservient to political goals. Art can makes this possible because it synthesizes the two seeming opposing poles of humanity, the rational and the sensuous. Art reconciles the intellect to the sensual world while it also lifts us out of our immediate immersion in the sensible.

Fiala points out that Hegel is sympathetic to the basic features of this conception of art as a synthesis of sensuality and spirituality, to Schiller's notion that art can have a positive educative function, and to his association of art with freedom. Yet, Hegel's aesthetics refuses to accept the idea of art as a mere tool, arguing that whatever its instrumental value, aesthetic experience is fundamentally an end in itself. But the real disagreement between Schiller and Hegel according to Fiala concerns the issue of a utopian aesthetic state, conceived by Schiller as one in which humans interact in free play, governed by the natural harmony of beauty. Here the highest freedom is attained and humans' alienation from one another and from the state is overcome. So for Schiller aesthetic experience is both means and ultimate end, and the harmonious play realized in aesthetic experience becomes the determinative model for freedom and ideal humanness; art triumphs over all. For Hegel however, art and the political are and ought to be decidedly distinct spheres of human experience; while politics and art are both modes of human freedom, they are nonetheless different.

Furthermore, Fiala indicates, Hegel is opposed to Schiller's collapse of the ethical into the aesthetic. Art cannot be a substitute for the forms of ethical activity; and the ethical state, with its own distinctive type of freedom, is not to be overcome in an aesthetic state. In Hegelian terms, Schiller has misunderstood the character of the political and its relation to aesthetics. Politics, located in the sphere of objective Spirit, involves interaction to create a world. By contrast, art, located in the sphere of Absolute Spirit, involves attaining freedom from and in the natural and social worlds, a freedom realized in art's sensuous comprehension and representation of the truths of those worlds. And, Fiala points out, Hegel is adamantly opposed to utopian projections, which he regards as resulting from the displacement of subjective imagining into an arena where objective truth is needed. According to Fiala, Hegel is a refreshing contrast to Schiller's utopianism, realizing that problems of political and social alienation require political and social, not aesthetic solutions. Yet he feels Hegel's systematic approach precludes him from saying anything about how art might play a role in transforming politics.

In "The Logic of Art: Beauty and Nature," Edward Halper presents a schematic overview of the location of the aesthetics in Hegel's system. His aim is to elucidate the nature of aesthetic categories and the transitions between them by showing how they relate to and depend upon the systematic logic that Hegel presents as the scientific foundation of his philosophy.

According to Halper, a crucial issue for Hegel, as for Plato, is the problem of the reality of art: both philosophers assign the highest being to thought and thus for both, art, as sensuous, becomes problematic. The Hegelian solution is to disclose art's rational dimension, to comprehend it as participating in the rational. Philosophically, this means grasping its location in the rational totality of systematic philosophy, seeing it as a manifestation of the Absolute. Yet this means that we also must differentiate art from the other entities considered in the system. Thus Halper asks what the distinctive nature of aesthetic reality is, what sort of conceptual category art is, how the categories of aesthetics are different from the others', and how the categorial transitions in aesthetics are different from those of logic.

The basis for Halper's answers to these question is rooted in his claim that Hegel's is a panlogicist idealism which forbids him from introducing new, nonlogical categories, and commits him to reusing logical categories. As his system enters into its consideration of reality beyond logic, this development is effected by what Halper describes as the addition of earlier logical categories to later ones. His view is that, for Hegel, everything is literally an idea. Thus he analyzes the concept of art in terms of the Absolute Idea with an added logical concept of actuality. Halper contends that the appropriate concept to be added is that of Life, as the type of self-contained unity Hegel ascribes to Life is most appropriate for understanding the distinctive synthetic unity of parts in a whole that belongs with artistic beauty. Yet art, artistic beauty, must be distinguished from natural life, and is so in virtue of being animated by a higher unifying principle than that simply found everywhere in organic nature.

How are conceptual transitions brought about in aesthetics? Referring to different modes of categorial transition in different parts of the system, Halper analyzes the transitions in the opening of the aesthetics as variations on those in the *Philosophy of Right.* His goal is to demonstrate both that the conceptual content of Hegel's opening aesthetic categories and their mode of transition are based in and consistent with concepts and modes of development presented at the end of the *Logic.*

In recent years more and more scholars have contributed to a resurgence of interest in Hegel. The essays collected here serve to call attention to the coherence, power, and relevance of Hegel's philosophy of art. They can help to give his voice the role it deserves in contemporary debates. The essays were first presented at the Fourteenth Biennial Meeting of the Hegel Society of America, held at Keystone Colorado, October 18–20, 1996. I would like to thank Jere Surber for handling the local arrangements for that meeting and the University of Denver for its generous support.

I

Art and the Absolute Revisited: The Neglect of Hegel's Aesthetics

William Desmond

I. The Neglect of Hegel's Aesthetics

My reference to the neglect of Hegel is ambiguous, hence twofold. The first neglect concerns the character of interest in Hegel's aesthetics. This interest is surprisingly less than what one would expect both in his sympathizers and antagonists, even those who consider art to be of the greatest moment. The second neglect refers to ambiguities in Hegel's own occupation with art, namely, his dialectical repudiation of any meaning in excess of explicit philosophical conceptualization. Both neglects, as I hope to indicate, have to do with the relation of art and the Absolute, and each is full of complexities, not all of which I can explore here. I shall speak of the first neglect in the main, and make some concluding suggestions on the second. The two neglects cannot be entirely separated.

While many areas of Hegelian thought have been extensively explored, we cannot say this confidently about Hegel's aesthetics. This area of his thought has been one of the less well explored.[1] Sometimes half-hearted passion is roused by the question of the end of art, but for the most part the aesthetics does not command the same close attention as other parts of Hegel's corpus. You might think that this is due to Hegel's own consignment of art to a position subordinate to religion and philosophy, his demotion of the aesthetic image in relation to the concept. Yet Hegel himself did not neglect the aesthetic. By any standard his work is extraordinary, in terms of extensiveness of reach, of systematic organization of a multitude of topics, of hermeneutical finesse, as well as insightful and intensive penetration of so many specific issues connected with art and culture. Still, for many of his admirers the aesthetics is of secondary importance.

What of Hegel's critics? You might expect today, in the surge of post-Nietzschean aestheticism, that a more robust renewal of interest in Hegel's philosophy of art would be forthcoming. We have pieces dedicated to little fragments from Nietzsche, or to Heidegger, and yet so much of this surge remains ignorant of the wealth in Hegel. Is the neglect due to the anti-Hegelianism of much of this aestheticism? This is true to some extent. But I think there is a deeper reason turning on art's relation to the Absolute, and this I want to explore. Hegel's concept of art does not fit easily with post-Kantian aestheticism, of which post-Nietzschean aestheticism is one heir. In particular, Hegel's sense of art cannot in the end be art for art's sake; art's relation to the Absolute brings it into affiliation with the religious.

I want to focus below on the fact that *after* Hegel art was itself often seen in a quasi-religious light. We find, so to say, an equivocal longing for some sort of transcendence but this has migrated from religion into art. Paradoxically, Hegel's high view of art leads to a critique of art which is not consonant with this equivocal longing. If we properly follow Hegel's point, we cannot follow that migration. We have become too grey.

In some ways what I am saying has a stress divergent from my emphasis elsewhere in relation to art and the Absolute.[2] There I went more softly softly, more in a mood to affirm the still unspent promise of art, than to name harshly the equivocal relation to transcendence harbored since Hegel in quite a lot of talk about art. Relevant here is the theme of the so-called death of art. Hegel is ambiguous but I am convinced that this matter cannot be addressed without reference also to the problematic status of religion and indeed philosophy itself. Let me develop my remarks in respect to the following three points: first, the ambiguity in demands made of art after Hegel; second, in relation to Hegel's clairvoyance in relation to these demands; third, in relation to disagreements between Hegel and his successors.

II. After Hegel: Art's Equivocal Place

The first point concerns the demands made on art after Hegel. This is something that seems to tell against Hegel's claim that art, on its highest side, is for us a thing of the past.[3] One might claim indeed the contrary: that after Kant, and with Hegel the odd man out, there is a far stronger emphasis placed upon art in terms of its metaphysical import. It is clear already in Schelling that, in a crucial respect, art stands higher than philosophy: art brings the whole human being, philosophy brings but thought, to the standpoint of the Absolute. So also with Schopenhauer, a claimant to Kant's mantle, who has nothing but abuse for Hegel: he places art and especially music at an extraordinarily high level of metaphysical revelation. Art reveals the thing-in-itself, the Will beyond phenomena. While the other arts are copies of the Will—Schopenhauer's word for the ultimate—music is a direct expression and revelation of the ultimate. It is interesting to note an affiliation here between Schopenhauer and his hated other, Hegel, in so far as both put art at an absolute level, even if that level is differently understood. The metaphysical seriousness of the aesthetic is evident in both.[4]

Likewise with Nietzsche, we may say that the quarrel between philosophy and poetry, "Plato versus Homer,"[5] is resolved against Plato, and thus also against Hegel: the poet is a more ultimate figure than the philosopher, art stands higher than all other human activities. Between philosophy and art the hierarchy suggested by Hegel in Absolute Spirit is inverted. Again the differences of detail are immense, but the intensive significance of art is the matter at issue. In this case of Nietzsche, it is less art being behind us on its higher side, but more that life without art would have no meaning at all. Nietzsche is quite straightforward here. Were there not art, he would have found life hardly tolerable, so he confesses. Life is absurd, humans lie, philosophers lie, but the artist, so to say, lies honestly, and so makes life bearable.

Points of details aside,[6] I mean to underscore that for Nietzsche, if there is any "absoluteness," any solace in a world stripped of intrinsic intelligibility, the "absoluteness" belongs to art. In that regard we live in the age of Nietzsche: the poet seems to be repeatedly triumphing over the philosopher, repeatedly denying the respective evaluations Hegel ascribed to the two as approaches to ultimacy. A number of thinkers in our time could be cited: Heidegger, Adorno, Derrida in his own way. At the end of the line, with the potential for greatness finally wrung out of the theme, the *reductio ad absurdum* comes along in the grey last man, the chirpy ironist Richard Rorty.

I do not forget Hegel, whose ambiguous judgment on art stands out as different from this search for some refuge in art in our spiritless times. I connect this with Hegel's acknowledgment of the third member of the triad of Absolute Spirit, namely religion. The above-mentioned thinkers, with the exception of Schelling, either are diffident about mentioning the religious, or debunking, or snide, when not overtly hostile. The equivocity here is that art itself assumes a kind of quasi-religious role. Two citations: one, tragic art in Nietzsche is impossible to understand without religious pathos, understood albeit in terms of pagan myth instead of claims to monotheistic revelation; two, Heidegger's poet, especially in the figure of Hölderlin, is sacerdotal, a desolate mourner of the departed god, an unthanked priestly herald of the coming god.

In a way, the situation here is more Kantian than Hegelian. The transcendental unity of apperception, as a synthetic and productive power, is connected more and more with imagination, whose most powerful, original, and creative embodiment is said to be the artistic genius. Hence great art becomes the aesthetic embodiment, that is, the concrete sensuous incarnation of the absolute power. This is very evident in Schelling, but I think it is in the background in many of the others too. Art becomes the privileged place in immanence where transcendence can come to creative manifestation. Art is made to assume the burden of being *the* revealer of transcendence, transcendence previously named within the sanctuary of the religious, and ascribed first to God and not to the godlike originality of the genius. Far from art being a thing of the past, more is asked of it than ever before: it is asked to bear a religious function, even as overtly religious life seems to go into decline, and especially among the intellectual as heirs, in various ways, of the enlightenment debunking of religion.

An enormous amount is asked of art, a task that Hegel acknowledges was appropriate in former epochs when the sense of the Absolute came to expression in the images of art.[7] There is a new reconfiguration of this role of art, in wake of the so-called transcendental revolution of Kant in which original power passes into the immanence of subjectivity, and is most concretely incarnate in the great genius or original work of aesthetic greatness. Instead of the death of art, there is a reconfiguration of the absoluteness of art in light of the *perceived death of religion.* What seems to die in religion is being resurrected in art, thus reversing the kind of movement of death and resurrection we find in Hegel.

I will come to Hegel more directly but I want to suggest that all this still leaves art in a decidedly equivocal place. Can art be the revealer of the Absolute, or the bearer of transcendence, such as religion is? I think not, if religion itself is undergoing a death, or is wasted by hemorrhage of spirit. The reason why in the Greek world art could be this bearer was precisely because religion had not yet suffered the kind of decline associated with the onslaught of enlightenment debunking.[8] Because the religious fermented in art, then it could be the bearer of the Absolute. Because now the religious is said no longer to ferment, the aesthetic can no longer be that bearer, even if it wills it with the best of intentions of finding some sanctuary for the Absolute in a world falling into the idolatries of the merely finite.

You might exclaim: Hurrah for those defenders of art, and those who ask much of art! You might add: Hegel is unhelpful, since he sings an elegy to greatness but does not represent creative renewal of greatness. He mourns what is gone, does not herald what will come, or as the ardent Nietzschean will ejaculate, what must come. Yes and no. It is a question of ascription of absoluteness, and the wrong ascription of absoluteness to something that has some *promise* of absoluteness may actually result in the deformation of that promise, and hence in the deeper loss of just the absoluteness desired. I think you can claim that the equivocal position of art in post-Kantian aesthetics *between* religion and art comes to ruin in the long run.

I take no joy in the following dialectical reversal. After Kant art is elevated into a kind of absoluteness, but that very elevation comes to ascribe creative power to all. Everyone is a genius if he or she only taps into the creative power of their own originality. Philosophy and science are themselves but different forms of artistic creation. All is art, and in an act of generosity indistinguishable from flattening, all are said to be potentially creative. But if everything is art, nothing is really art, nothing really great with the greatness of spiritual seriousness we associate with great art. Art is made to be the carrier of transcendence, but it now ends up stripped of transcendence.

Elevated into absolute position, it suffers reversal in the depreciation of the present.

Put somewhat differently: after Hegel too much was asked of art, but now almost nothing is asked of it; and nothing is asked just because too much was asked of it. For the asking was improper. Art was treated as a god, but it is not a god, and when treated as such, it is an idol. When devotees lose faith in the power of their god, the spell of the bewitchment breaks, and before them stands a dead idol, and of the idol nothing at all is asked. We see bricks lined up in a museum, and we are not sure whether a puckish humor winks at us, as if to slyly suggest, the emperor has no clothes, or whether this is the last gasp of futile devotion to the fruitless idol.

Why not draw Hegel the aesthetician into this community of devotees of art? I think one of the reasons Hegel's aesthetics is neglected is because he does not worship at this post-Nietzschean shrine, and there is nothing more difficult to tolerate than the one who announces the death of one's beloved idol. The irony here is that Hegel prefigures this announcement *before* this idol came into the fullness of its temporal *parousia*. The one who might have been a herald was already an apostate of the god yet to come. This is unforgivable. And of the apostate we must be silent. Hence the neglect.

III. Hegel and Art's Equivocal Place

I now want to argue that Hegel's nuanced view would give one to anticipate something of the following ironical outcome: the asking too much of art ends with us asking almost nothing of art; art is made absolute such that everything is permitted of art, permitted as art, and hence nothing is absolute in art any more. Concerning Hegel's view I will focus first on art's ability to be the revealer of the Absolute, and secondly the characteristic mode of manifestation art allows. I will then connect these two points respectively with Hegel's view of art and religion, and then with some consequences for art of the romantic turn to inwardness.

To the first point, it is clear that for Hegel art can manifest the Absolute, but only in an epoch wherein the sense of the divine is taken with absolute seriousness. Lose this seriousness and not only is religion evacuated of ultimacy, so also is art, and art cannot be the sanctuary in which the evacuation of the religious is to be remedied.

I am not claiming that Hegel wants to subordinate art to an extrinsic purpose.[9] Art, he insists, is an end in itself. This idea, of course, easily leads to an aestheticism that makes art for itself alone. Hegel does not subscribe in any simple way to such an aestheticism. Great art is the manifestation of Spirit, hence also embodies the richest expression of a culture's or a people's or a nation's sense of what is most ultimate and high. A great strength of Hegel's aesthetics as a whole, in my view, is just his refreshing freedom from the aestheticist view of art. The freedom of art is not its separation unto itself and from all else. It is rather a freeing of Spirit into its own being for itself, and a freeing that comes to sensuous articulation in the great work of art. What is freed may include reference to the fullness of the human spirit, and indeed must do so in great works of art. The work of art is an end in itself because it is just the sensuous concretization of the freedom of the Spirit, as it takes on its most rich embodiments. Art concretizes a sensuous space for freedom that itself is inclusive of, or that shines through, so-called nonaesthetic concerns. It does not lie to one side of the nonaesthetic, but is a transformation that works in and through the nonaesthetic, and lifts it up to its own divine freedom.

This is especially evident with respect to the three formations of art, the symbolic, classical, and romantic. They refer to fundamental configurations of our understanding of being at its most ultimate, most fully expressed in the sense of the divine that finds representation in the mythologies and religions of different epochs and peoples. While the inseparability of art and religion is clearly evident in the classical world, the same holds for the other formations of art for Hegel. A brief reminder will be helpful here.

All art deals with the Ideal. The Ideal is the sensuous showing of the Idea, but the relation of Idea and its sensuous manifestation varies with the character of Spirit in its self-development.[10] In the symbolic formation of art there is an indeterminacy to the spiritual content and a certain predominance of the sensuous or material embodiment. In this regard, Hegel's discussion of the Egyptian pyramids and the sphinx shows this massiveness of the material embodiment dominating the still relatively indefinite spiritual content that is struggling to emerge into the light of day. The riddling sphinx embodies this doubleness of nature and nurture: the claws of the lion, massive claws, hence powerful as nature is powerful, but capable of tearing and twisting and effortlessly killing; the breasts of the woman that give suck and gently nurture the child. These architectural structures show the spiritual condition of the people, and most especially in relation to the meaning of death. And it is not possible to separate purely aesthetic concerns from the religious and spiritual culture of this formation.

The classical formation yields the Ideal: the ideal form wherein an individualized and determinate unification of Spirit and sensuous embodiment is found.[11] Generally we find this in Greek art, most especially in its sculpture of the gods. It makes no sense entirely to separate art and religion in classical art, even though the divine is shaped more to the measure of human form, especially human embodiment, rather than to the sometimes exceeding formlessness of nature. Here we have the acme of art for Hegel, where it is most fully the vehicle of the Absolute, and in the form of the religion which is *Kunstreligion*.[12] *Kunstsreligion* is religion and not any art that could be detached from the inspiring spiritual impulse that informs its works of art as a whole.[13] Analogous points could be made for Greek drama, which is sacred drama. One might also consult what Hegel has to say about the Greek temple as serving to house the god, embodied there in the sculpture.

The romantic formation is one where a sense of the Idea begins to transcend what can be incorporated into any sensuous manifestation. Like the symbolic there is here an excess but in a kind of reverse: it is the excess of Spirit over the sensuous, rather than the dominance of sensuous materiality over Spirit. The accent is not on the immediate harmonious embodiment of Spirit, but on the surpassing of Spirit, beyond every determinate embodiment. The meaning is then on transcending. This is evident not only in the turn to a deeper inwardness but in, say, the Gothic cathedral as the embodiment of the romantic form of architecture, as a spiritual transcending in massive materiality itself: the massiveness of materiality is itself made to soar.[14] It is true that in the romantic formation we have the emergence of the more *equivocal* position of art, as between religion and something that, in principle, allows an *unfixing* from the sense of the Absolute as religious. The advent of the Christian, postclassical world brings about an equivocal position of art with respect to transcendence, and the relativization of its formation of the appearance of the Absolute. Hegel means this especially in connection with the turn to inwardness, specific to the Christian religion and democratized and secularized in the modern West. The issue is less one of the ultimate no longer appearing in artistic form, or perhaps even of its disappearance, but rather the form it now must take such as to include the truth of Spirit as inwardness.

Notice that this very turn to the subject is the second point I mentioned above. Here we see Hegel to be in the same field of concerns as the post-Hegelians but with a different accentuation of the factors involved. The turn to the self as inwardness is manifest with the aesthetic of romantic art, and it takes many forms in the long history of its shaping of the human spirit. But the crux, of course, is that this turn to inwardness for Hegel leads to the surpassing of art's tie to the Absolute. Something is manifested that is always in excess of expression in terms of a sensuous form, such as is necessary for the aesthetic. The aesthetic deals with the sensuous show of the Idea; but there is something here transcending sensuous show, in that the latter is finite, the former infinite. If the Idea is shown, it is not shown adequately in aesthetic form. This is why religion in a more thoroughgoing inwardized form must be a more adequate vehicle for its manifestation.[15]

In a way, art can continue only if it keeps its bond with the religious, but the turn to inwardness yields also the turn to the creative selves who want, as artists, to assert their difference to anything other. And the self-assertion of art as for itself alone leads it to break its ties with the religious which would sustain its absolute seriousness. So its price of freedom, despite the initial celebrations of glorious liberations from the heavy hand of the religious, must be a hollowing out of its tenuous tie to the ultimate. One might rejoice at this, but this will be to concede the point, since it means the covert acquiescence in the self-chosen trivialization of art. Its freedom to pursue its own creative power means its freedom to be everything, and hence its reality, finally, as not counting for anything. Being everything in the end amounts to being nothing at all. We come round again to our previous conclusion: Asking too much of art in the wrong way leads to asking nothing in a proper way, in the end.

Consider the aesthetic turn to inwardness in others by contrast with Hegel. Consider the romantic glorifications of genius: where others dance a jubilee in the name of genius, Hegel utters his excoriation. For Hegel this individualism of creative originality reveals the unanchoring of subjectivity from its ontological and communal moorings. We might say it fulfills the destiny of the beautiful soul which is to become the ugly soul. The genius, we now know, squanders his self-proclaimed originality with technical gimmicks, on the one hand, with shocking outrage, on the other. Once spiritual seriousness has flown, these present the empty squibs of impotent originality.

I find it interesting that Kant had also a very ambiguous attitude to genius.[16] Many of those who read him did so with different ears, and as prepared to hear something different, namely, the glorification of a certain type of originality. Closer listening to Kant shows his contempt for this, and indeed his fear of the unruly. Others looked into Kant and saw themselves as those geniuses who would will to resurrect the Absolute aesthetically. Hegel's diffidence regarding some of these claims did not make him endearing to them. Kant is often endorsed as supposedly proclaiming the freedom of the aesthetic; but the endorsers read Kant as if he were one of their company, which he was not. Kant wanted to moralize art, in the end, and in order to bring back to it the power of the ultimate. For it is the moral ideal that is the ultimate for Kant. Art for art's sake cannot do this job.

I think that Hegel has the longer hermeneutical perspective than Kant here.[17] For instance, Hegel knows far more about the concrete religious traditions in which the turn to inwardness—also driving romantic art, and hence also the major thought of Kant and post-Kantian aesthetics—is inseparable from a concept of Spirit or God. He is in a better position to understand, to discriminate and to judge. Hence his lectures on art proceed on a track that reverberates back and forth with his lectures on the philosophy of religion, the philosophy of history, and also the history of philosophy. The lectures on aesthetics could be as much an introduction to philosophy of religion and philosophy of history, both seen from the side of the dominant images of the formations of Spirit. It could also be seen as mirroring the development of philosophy also, as, for instance, the way the classical world cannot be understood, both in its art and philosophy, without taking both together, and each also in light of dominant religious conceptions.

Think of his interpretation of Socrates here—it is as much to be viewed through the light of tragic action, as through the immanent development of concepts in antiquity, as through the development of *Vorstellungen* of the divine. Not Plato versus Homer, but Socrates with Homer and the tragedians, and this "with" does not exclude the happening of tragic conflict, and the war of opposition in the development of Spirit. I think it is the fertile togetherness of these many possibilities that makes Hegel's reflections on aesthetics so powerful. Note it is in the history of philosophy that, for instance, we have his best reflections on Aristophanes![18]

Just Hegel's immunity from scholastic or bureaucratic separations makes him more powerful than Kant. The latter is the thinker of *Verstand*, as Hegel suggests. His formalist view of art as in a class of its own reflects this. Those who neglect Hegel for the Kantian legacy are also partakers of this type of *verstandlich* separateness. It may all be with the view to treat art with its own inherent respect, but it leads to a kind of poverty in the long run. Of course, this separation is not Kant's last word, for he wants to bring art back to the moral. Hegel does not moralize art in that sense, but he does not separate it either. He has a richer sense of mediation of art and what is other.

Again I find it strange that it is the Kantian formalist/aestheticist strain that is found more congenial here than Hegel. Surely Hegel's sense of the togetherness of art, religion, and philosophy is fertile for those wishing to break out of the sterility of the aestheticist view of art, and the separation of art into its own self-sufficiency: art for art's sake as the aesthetic version of a self-enclosed thought for thought's sake, or a closed thought thinking itself, out of which the so-called postmodern thinkers would emerge. Hegel offers more resource for rethinking the community of art, philosophy, and religion than these others. Why then the diffidence about Hegel?

I think because of unresolved ambiguities about the closeness of art and religion, as well as alarm when Hegel, after all, does subordinate art to philosophy. The first brings us too close to the exigence of religion that the self-image of many philosophers as post-Enlightenment thinkers cannot brook. As if they were being asked to go down on their knees again, having learned the unbowed capacity to demand their own autonomy against all hated priestcraft and obscurantism. This attitude to the latter Enlightenment cliché shows in itself the legacy of the same Enlightenment they affect to despise.

The second view, namely the subordination of art to philosophy, seems to bespeak the dreaded tyranny of the concept which the postmodern thinker also affects to despise, though you might say there is a peculiar tyranny in the way the deconstruction of philosophy has itself been exercised. Suffice it to say that the claim regarding rank, namely, the imputation of superiority to philosophy, is as offensive as the secret threat of submission, regarding the affiliation of the artistic and the religious. Rank is alarming, even intolerable, since from the side of philosophy it too seems to put the beloved art in a finally subordinate position. There is an irony here, of course, since it is rank that insists on difference, difference that cannot all be homogenized.

IV. Hegel's Neglect?

At the outset I suggested that there is another side to the neglect of Hegel, and not the neglect of Hegel in the above respects. In some ways, it is Hegel's own neglect that contributes to this above neglect. I mean that many of the post-Hegelian aestheticians mentioned are in tension with Hegel so far as they claim that some form of resistant otherness, perhaps even transcendence, needs to be affirmed against Hegel. Hegel's subordination of art and religion to philosophy seems to suggest that all forms of otherness and transcendence must take their place within the autonomous immanence of self-determining thought. Neither art nor religion are finally self-determining in the fullest sense: art so far as the sensuous medium and the expression of the inexpressible, religion so far as the mystery of the holy, remain recalcitrant to dialectical conceptualization. Hegel and his opponents agree on that resistance but in the case of art give a different interpretation: Hegel as limiting art, the other as seeing its challenge to philosophy at philosophy's own limit. An other thinking of this resistance of transcendence to dialectic also deserves to have its day.

One might think here of the symbol in relation to artistic meaning in Hegel, and in some others after Hegel.[19] There is in the latter a willingness to call us towards the return of something like the excess of the symbolic, understood as an indeterminate origin that in Hegel's scheme is progressively appropriated to the immanence of self-determining thought. Thus, to cite but two instances, the Will of Schopenhauer is said to be beyond the principle of sufficient reason, while Nietzsche's Dionysian origin is also placed on the other side of dialectical reason and beyond its mastery.[20] Nor is it surprising that music is the art deemed most metaphysical, in comparison with poetry in both Kant and Hegel. Music seems to be an art which, even in its determinacy, draws on an indeterminate power that remains in excess of conceptual, perhaps even artistic determination.

Excess is a word for transcendence, even when anxieties about religion will prevent these thinkers from invoking the name of transcendence. Thinkers such as I have mentioned can be taken to represent a kind of countermovement to the apotheosis of thought thinking itself. It seems to me that the return to the excess of transcendence is often couched in aesthetic terms that are finally unable to bear the burden, especially given the equivocation on the religious. I also think that even though Hegel relativizes the symbol, and the sublime, the context he offers us is often more nuanced relative to the many sides of the question: the question of art is as much connected with the religious sense of mystery, as with philosophical clarity concerning the ultimate.

Nevertheless, I have some sympathy for the tack in a non-Hegelian direction, and find myself wary about Hegel's dialectically ambiguous relation to any notion of mystery. That said, dialectical clarity is just what is lacking in other celebrations of the excess of the indeterminate. In his ambiguous clarity Hegel offers us help to face the neglect of something essential. I mean the explicit affiliation of art, religion, and philosophy is rich with resources for thinking, without the pulling of punches about the question of the ultimate, or the Absolute. Hegel, I think, would be more in agreement than disagreement relative to the foolishness of asking of art what it cannot do. Art cannot be asked to bear the burden of the Absolute, or the freedom of transcendence, on its own, if the religious is hemorrhaging and philosophy is tempted to commit hari kiri. The orientation of any dialectical philosophy, or any reorientation beyond dialectic, demands this agreement as helping forward any project of rethinking the relations of art, religion, philosophy—and this against the equivocal relation between art and religion, and any Nietzschean repudiation of truth. To want to make art the privileged site is finally to break art under a burden art cannot completely bear on its own.

Notes

1. If in the last ten years we find a spate of books in English on many aspects of Hegel's thought, on his aesthetics we find S. Bungay's, *Beauty and Truth* (Oxford; Oxford University Press, 1984) and W. Desmond's *Art and the Absolute* (Albany, SUNY Press, 1986). Recently Robert Wicks's monograph appeared, *Hegel's Theory of Aesthetic Judgment* (New York: Peter Lang, 1994). Two recent works of Richard Winfield offer a neo-Hegelian aesthetics: *Systematic Aesthetics* (Gainesville: University of Florida Press, 1995) and *Stylistics* (Albany: SUNY Press, 1996). Stephen Houlgate in *Freedom, Truth and History: An Introduction to Hegel's Philosophy* (London: Routledge, 1991) is sensitive to the importance of Hegel's insights concerning the aesthetic and the religious. See Werner Koepsel, *Die Rezeption der Hegelschen Ästhetik im 20 Jahrhundert* (Bonn: Bouvier, 1975).

2. In *Art and the Absolute.*

3. G. W. F. Hegel, *Vorlesungen über die Ästhetik,* ed. E. Moldenhauer and K. M. Michel, *Werke in zwanzig Bänden,* 20 vols. and Index (Frankfurt am Main: Suhrkamp Verlag, 1969ff), 13: 24, 23; English translation, G. W. F. Hegel, *Aesthetics: Lectures on Fine Art,* trans. T. M. Knox, 2 vols. (Oxford: Clarendon Press, 1975), 1: 11, 9–10. Further references will be given in the form: *Werke,* 13 24; *A,* 1:11.

4. See my "Schopenhauer, Art and the Dark Origin," in *Schopenhauer,* ed. Eric von der Luft (Lewistown, N.Y.: Mellen Press, 1988), 101–22.

5. F. Nietzsche, *On the Genealogy of Morals,* trans. W. Kaufmann and R. J. Hollingdale (New York: Vintage Books, 1969), 154.

6. "Rethinking the Origin: Hegel and Nietzsche," to appear in *Hegel History and Interpretation,* ed. Shaun Gallagher (Albany: SUNY Press, 1997), 71–94.

7. Art achieves its highest task when "it has placed itself in the same sphere as religion and philosophy, and when it is simply one way of bringing to our minds and expressing the *Divine,* the deepest interests of mankind, and the most comprehensive truths of the spirit. In works of art the nations have deposited their richest inner

intuitions and ideas, and art is often the key, and in many nations the sole key, to understanding their philosophy [*Weisheit*] and religions." *Werke,* 13:20–21; *A,* 1:7.

8. On this in relation to *Kunstreligion,* see G. W. F. Hegel, *Phänomenologie des Geistes* (Hamburg: Felix Meiner, 1952), 490ff.; *Phenomenology of Spirit,* trans. A.V. Miller (Oxford: Clarendon Press, 1977). Hereafter *PhG,* and *PS.*

9. On the internal teleology of art that Hegel terms *Selbstzweck,* see *Werke,* 13:44, 65ff.; *A,* 1:25, 41ff.

10. On the ideal, see *Werke,* 13:104ff.; *A,* 1:73 ff.; also G. W. F. Hegel, *Enzyklopädie der philosophischen Wissenschaften im Grundrisse* (Hamburg: Felix Miener, 1959), section 556.

11. See *Werke,* 13:60–61; *A,* 1:38–39, on the general requirement of the Ideal that there be both a sensuous showing of Spirit, and a spiritualization of the sensuous.

12. See note 8 above; and also *PhG,* 506ff.; *PS,* 439ff. See also *Werke,* 13:111; *A,* 1:79, where Hegel says that the limit of classical art is the limit of art as such.

13. We philosophers tend to think of the Greeks as a philosophical people, but they were an aesthetic people, such that Hegel would agree with Hölderlin's description of Greece as *ein Reich der Kunst.* "Aesthetic" here means something very different from its meaning in post-Kantian aesthetics. Nietzsche was trying to recover something of that meaning in, say, *The Birth of Tragedy.*

14. See my "Gothic Hegel," *The Owl of Minerva,* 30:2, (Spring, 1999), 237–252. I make some remarks on the differences of Hegel and Heidegger in relation to the Greek temple.

15. On the inwardizing of the infinite in romantic art, see *Werke,* 14:128ff.; *A,* 1:518ff.

16. See my "Kant and the Terror of Genius: Between Enlightenment and Romanticism," *Kant's Aesthetics,* ed. Herman Parret (Berlin: De Gruyter, 1998), 594–614.

17. See my "Art, Origins, Otherness: Hegel and Aesthetic Self-Mediation," in *Philosophy and Art,* ed. Dan Dahlstrom, (Washington: Catholic University of America Press, 1991); also *Art and the Absolute,* ch. 3.

18. For extended discussion of Hegel and Aristophanes, see my *Beyond Hegel and Dialectic* (Albany: SUNY, 1992), ch. 6.

19. See my remarks on what I call a postromantic symbol in *Desire, Dialectic and Otherness* (New Haven: Yale University Press, 1987), 237–38, 246; *Being and the Between* (Albany: SUNY Press, 1995), 216–22, especially 220; also remarks on "Art, Origins, Otherness," as cited in note 16 above.

20. One also thinks of Heidegger's being as origin beyond logocentric reason in "On the Origin of the Artwork."

II

Hegel's Concept of the Dissolution of Art

Carl Rapp

For many contemporary students of art, the most surprising thing in Hegel's lectures on fine art is the judgment that art has come to the end of its development, that "for us art counts no longer as the highest mode in which truth fashions an existence for itself," since, though "we may well hope that art will always rise higher and come to perfection," the truth is that "the form of art has ceased to be the supreme need of the spirit."[1] This judgment often comes as a shock, and, to students of nineteenth- and twentieth-century art especially, it must seem both mistaken and perverse. Could it not be taken as simply another piece of evidence that Hegel was compelled by his system to imagine his own time and place as the culmination of history? Surely art has gone on developing throughout the various periods and movements that have come along since Hegel's time. There have been schools and programs almost without number, and in the modern period particularly the intention of being profoundly experimental or radically new was frequently proclaimed. How then is it possible to take Hegel's judgment seriously? How can it be taken as expressing anything other than narrowness of mind?

Heidegger, we know, took it very seriously. Writing in 1935, he says

> The judgment that Hegel passes in these statements cannot be evaded by pointing out that since Hegel's lectures in aesthetics were given for the last time during the winter of 1828–29 at the University of Berlin, we have seen the rise of many new art works and new art movements. Hegel never meant to deny this possibility. But the question remains: is art still an essential and necessary way in which that truth happens which is decisive for our historical existence, or is art no longer of this character? . . . The truth of Hegel's judgment has not yet been decided; for behind this verdict there stands Western thought since the Greeks, which thought corresponds to a truth of beings that has already happened. Decision upon the judgment will be made, when it is made, from and about this truth of what is. Until then the judgment remains in force.[2]

Heidegger, of course, believed that the judgment would collapse as soon as "Western thought" was discerned to be a sort of wrong turn, or digression, away from the truth of Being. Accordingly, he worked hard to outflank the entire tradition on which, it seemed, Hegel's judgment depended. Despite his implicit hostility to the judgment, he was right, I think, to suspect that there are depths within it that need to be examined, if it is to be rightly understood. In fact, I shall argue in this paper that Hegel's description of the end stage of art (his description, that is, of the dissolution of the romantic form of art) was uncannily prophetic of future developments. Moreover, it is precisely these developments, many of which seek to get around philosophy or to go beyond it (as did Heidegger), that bear out the judgment and keep it "in force."

To begin with, it is necessary to understand what Hegel means when he says that art is no longer "the highest mode" of truth, no longer "the supreme need" of the Spirit. This implies that art can still be one mode of truth or one need of the Spirit, just not the highest mode or the supreme need. It also implies that there was a time when things were different. There was a time when art was the focal point of Spirit and truth. The whole of Hegel's *Aesthetics* is, in fact, an account of the constantly shifting ratios between the requirements of Spirit and truth, on the one hand, and the capacities of sensuous configuration, on the other. In terms of this account, with its broad categories of symbolic, classical, and romantic art, art becomes intelligible first as a quest for form, then as the achievement of form, and finally as the repudiation of form. In a sequence of phases or stages, the Spirit first seeks its reflection, then attains its reflection, and finally scorns its reflection, in the various configurations of which art is capable. Each configuration attests to, or makes possible, a particular type, or a particular degree, of self-consciousness on the part of Spirit. Thus the development of art bears witness to a corresponding development in spiritual self-consciousness. At the beginning of its development, Spirit can express itself only by means of art or in terms of art. There is, as yet, no other form of consciousness, no other medium for thinking. Such thinking as is possible makes its appearance as art. Art waxes as the expressive possibilities of sensuous configuration are more and more realized. Eventually, after it attains a sufficient degree of self-consciousness, thinking begins to detach itself from the limitations inherent in such configuration, passing first into the form of religion and ultimately into the form of philosophy. In short, as Hegel sees it, there was a time when thinking struggled to raise itself up to the level of art, a time when it might be said to have achieved all that can be achieved on the level of art, and finally a time when it is something more or something other than can be made to appear on that particular level. The crucial thing to notice here is that, according to Hegel, the entire process of these spiritual developments is itself reflected in art. Thus the inability of the Spirit to achieve an adequate reflection of itself in art is precisely that which is reflected, eloquently or pathetically, in symbolic art. Similarly, the achievement of the Spirit's reflection of itself in the representation of natural or physical forms, either of gods or of men, is that which is reflected, beautifully, in classical art. And finally, in the last stage of the process, the insufficiency of sensuous configuration to the requirements of Spirit is exactly that which is reflected, or at least suggested, in the configurations of romantic art. The paradox, then, of the romantic form of art is that it strikingly expresses in actual works of art the fact that the Spirit can no longer express itself completely or satisfactorily by means of artistic representations. Hence, in Hegel's formula, "romantic art is the self-transcendence of art but within its own sphere and in the form of art itself."[3]

If Hegel's account of these matters is followed closely enough, it becomes clear that art "ceased to be the supreme need of the Spirit" when religion first, and then philosophy, appeared on the scene. It ceases to be the supreme need of the Spirit, not by passing out of existence, but by becoming subordinate to these later forms of Spirit. As soon as art is willing to be didactic or allegorical with respect to religious truth or moral truth, at that very moment it is "no longer . . . the highest mode in which truth fashions an existence for itself." In later antiquity after Aristotle, and throughout the whole of the Christian era, this is the position in which art finds itself. Whatever positive truths it may illustrate or inculcate, it is all the while, simultaneously, reflecting the fact that it has gone into service and that, by virtue of its new function, which is to point "beyond itself,"[4] it exists after all in a state of "self-transcendence." Since it has been exhibiting this fact about itself for more than two thousand years now, there is no reason to infer from Hegel's judgment concerning its limits that art has come at last to the end of its tether. There is indeed no reason to suppose that it might not remain indefinitely in the state Hegel calls the state of "self-transcendence."

But, if that is the case, why does Hegel speak as though the art of his own time were bearing witness to the dissolution of the romantic form of art in general? If even romantic art is capable of reaching a final moment of disintegration, a sort of climactic conclusion beyond which no further development seems possible, does not this portend that art is over and done with? One way to answer this last question would be to say that even the dissolution of romantic art itself is something that might well go on forever. Virtually all the art movements since Hegel's time have exhibited, in one way or another, tendencies or attitudes that Hegel himself described as belonging to the dissolution of romantic art. This is just as true in the case of modern "experimental" art as it is in the case of nineteenth-century "realist" or "symbolist" art. It is equally true with respect to the various gestures attributed to postmodern art. And since one of the principal gestures of this last kind of art has been to roam freely over the history of art in search of previous styles that might be recycled into new works of art, there is no reason to assume that the future of art may not consist of an endless series of appropriations of what has gone before, or an endless repetition of previous artistic gestures, undertaken in a spirit of sympathy or even in a spirit of irony. Thus, I would argue, we are still moving through the process Hegel refers to as the dissolution of romantic art.

In order to understand what Hegel means by this dissolution, it is necessary to realize that what he was looking at primarily was the phenomenon of German romanticism. The break-up of what he called the romantic form of art was, in fact, occurring through the agency of what later scholars would refer to as the romantic movement, with which Hegel was exactly contemporary. The effect of romanticism (in this sense of the term) was, as Hegel saw it, to intensify the already-existing subordination of art to the higher spiritual interests it could never hope to mirror adequately. But, at the same time, this intensified subordination was associated with a new concept of Spirit, which demanded that a new set of artistic gestures be made in proper deference to Spirit. The old way of being subordinate was no longer adequate now that a new idea of Spirit had evolved.

The intensification of the subordination of art to higher spiritual interests was, in Hegel's view, an achievement of what he calls "humor" or "caprice," which "could make every determinacy waver and dissolve and therefore made it possible for art to transcend itself."[5] "Humor" was a mode of expression completely consonant with "the free development of the spirit," whose duty it was to liberate itself from "all faith which remains restricted to determinate forms of vision and presentation."[6] Hegel's contempt for the anarchistic implications of this attitude is unmistakable in his account of the famous irony, which had been theorized by Friedrich von Schlegel as a display of the Fichtean concept of "the *ego* as the absolute principle of all knowing, reason, and cognition."[7] Hegel's description of the various attitudes and postures associated with this kind of irony is, in effect, a description of what happens when the artist arrogates to himself supreme intellectual authority. In such a case, says Hegel, "nothing is treated *in and for itself* and as valuable in itself, but only as produced by the subjectivity of the *ego*."

> But in that case the *ego* can remain lord and master of everything, and in no sphere of morals, law, things human and divine, profane and sacred, is there anything that would not first have to be laid down by the *ego*, and that therefore could not equally well be destroyed by it. Consequently everything genuinely and independently real becomes only a show, not true and genuine on its own account or through itself, but a mere appearance due to the *ego* in whose power and caprice and at whose free disposal it remains. To admit or cancel it depends wholly on the pleasure of the *ego*, already absolute in itself simply as *ego*.[8]

There is both delight and terror in such self-consciousness on the part of the ego. On the one hand, it is exhilarating for the artist to feel that the world around him is essentially the product of his own imagination, that it is always necessarily a reflection of his own conceptions and interests, and that it can be completely transformed or even annihilated by simply altering these same conceptions and interests, or by performing a new exercise of imagination. On the other hand, it is terrifying to realize that, for this very reason, the ego is essentially isolated in a world without substance or content so that there is nothing essential to which the ego can relate itself or with which it can identify. The result, says Hegel, is that the artist becomes ironical or ambivalent about the worth of the reality he makes for himself and about his own reality-making consciousness.

It is exciting, for example, for "an ironical artistic life" to apprehend itself

> as a divine creative genius for which anything and everything is only an unsubstantial creature, to which the creator, knowing himself to be disengaged and free from everything, is not bound, because he is just as able to destroy it as to create it. In that case, he who has reached this standpoint of divine genius looks down from his high rank on all other men, for they are pronounced dull and limited, inasmuch as law, morals, etc., still count for them as fixed, essential, and obligatory.[9]

At the same time, however, it may also be depressing to contemplate "the vanity of everything factual, moral, and of intrinsic worth, the nullity of everything objective and absolutely valid." In one sense, it appears that the ego "can live only in the bliss of self-enjoyment."

> But, on the other hand, the *ego* may, contrariwise, fail to find satisfaction in this self-enjoyment and instead become inadequate to itself, so that it now feels a craving for the solid and the substantial, for specific and essential interests. Out of this comes misfortune, and the contradiction that, on the one hand, the subject does want to penetrate into truth and longs for objectivity, but, on the other hand, cannot renounce his isolation and withdrawal into himself or tear himself free from this unsatisfied abstract inwardness. Now he is attacked by the yearning which also we have seen proceeding from Fichtean philosophy. The dissatisfaction of this quiescence and impotence—which may not do or touch anything for fear of losing its inner harmony and which, even if pure in itself, is still unreal and empty despite its desire for reality and what is absolute—is the source of yearning and a *morbid* beautiful soul. For a *truly* beautiful soul acts and is actual. That longing, however, is only the empty vain subject's sense of nullity, and he lacks the strength to escape from this vanity and fill himself with a content of substance.[10]

Not here, but elsewhere (in his lectures on the history of philosophy), Hegel mentions Novalis as a poet who sets forth the "yearnings of a lofty soul," which desires "a firm and steady basis" but which finds itself enmeshed in "the extravagances of subjectivity": "This subjectivity does not reach substantiality, it dies away within itself, and the standpoint it adopts is one of inward workings and fine distinctions; it signifies an inward life and deals with the minutiae of the truth."[11]

In the twentieth century, it was T. S. Eliot who presented this condition as the fate of modern subjectivity, and for years it was not clear to his readers whether he himself shared in the condition or merely analyzed it as the hallmark of twentieth-century angst. Nearly all of Eliot's early personae exhibited a hyper-self-consciousness that was capable of ironizing itself by grasping itself immediately as a spectacle of infinitely various possibilities. These personae paralyzed themselves as they viewed themselves, and knew that they were paralyzing themselves, and laughed at themselves for doing what they were doing, and suffered deeply at the same time for doing it. Every contortion in the process was simultaneously experienced and ironized. This condition was superbly defined by Sir Henry Harcourt-Reilly in *The Cocktail Party* as "the final desolation / Of solitude in a phantasmal world / Of imagination, shuffling memories and desires." The later characters (and Eliot himself) escaped into religion, finding there the "firm and steady basis" sought in vain by the early characters. This was, of course, in keeping with one of the possible outcomes of romantic irony, as Hegel had indicated when he observed

> The utter despair in respect of thought, of truth, and absolute objectivity, as also the incapacity to give oneself any settled basis or spontaneity of action, induced the noble soul to abandon itself to feeling and to seek in Religion something fixed and steadfast. . . . This instinct impelling us towards something fixed has forced many into positive forms of religion, into Catholicism, superstition and miracle working, in order that they may find something on which they can rest, because to inward subjectivity everything fluctuates and wavers.[12]

Many of Eliot's readers sympathized deeply with the exquisite sufferings exhibited by the early personae and did not wish to see them resolved by a plunge into religion. Consequently, they refused to follow Eliot's own example after 1927. For these readers, Eliot's display of paralyzed inwardness was their "truth" and indeed the "truth" for modern man. Almost none of them considered that the character of this "truth" had been examined critically by Hegel in the 1820's, and even earlier in the *Phenomenology*.

Although Eliot's version of romantic irony was immensely popular from about 1920 to about 1960, it appeared thereafter to many critics, such as Harold Bloom, that the truly central, truly indispensable, poet had all along been Wallace Stevens. Eliot had been peerless in his representation of the consciousness that "lives in dread of besmirching the splendour of its inner being by action," and that "flees from contact with the actual world, and persists in its self-willed impotence."[13] Stevens, on the other hand, wavered with a minimum of pain between "the bliss of self-enjoyment" and "a craving for the solid and the substantial." In half of his poetry, he celebrated the Creative Imagination as an absolute, unconditioned power. In the other half, he mused speculatively on what it would be like if one could encounter Reality itself apart from all imaginings, "not ideas about the thing but the thing itself."[14] In a relatively early poem, "The Comedian as the Letter C," Stevens treated both the discovery of subjectivity and the quest for "the veritable ding an sich, at last," as an ironical comedy, in which a proliferating series of visions and revisions ended inconclusively as a result of the hero's collapse back into ordinary life. But, in fact, the poem gave memorable expression (at once magnificent and mocking) to the various attitudes and postures that Stevens himself would continue to strike as he fluctuated throughout the rest of his career between allegiance to Imagination and allegiance to Reality. For the most part, Stevens enjoyed his inwardness, and he inspired generations to regard the deliberate act of fiction making as the ultimate exercise of self-awareness. "In the long run," said Stevens, "the truth does not matter"[15] and "God is a postulate of the ego."[16] "Reality is not what it is," he said. "It consists of the many realities which it can be made into."[17] Similarly, "life is a composite of the propositions about it."[18] Since subjectivity had at last turned out to be the truth of objectivity, a deliberate acceptance of the burden and the glory of subjectivity seemed the ultimate guarantee of authenticity. Thus, "in an age of disbelief, when the gods have come to an end, when we think of them as the aesthetic projections of a time that has passed, men turn to a fundamental glory of their own and from that create a style of bearing themselves in reality. They create a new style of a new bearing in a new reality."[19] In place of objective truth, there was what Stevens called the "supreme fiction": "The final belief is to believe in a fiction, which you know to be a fiction, there being nothing else. The exquisite truth is to know that it is a fiction and that you believe in it willingly."[20] This was the very quintessence of irony. Orwell had called it *doublethink* in *1984,* denouncing it as deliberate self-deception or as the willing suspension of disbelief in what one knows to be false, but, to Stevens's admirers, it was the ultimate act of honesty. "Reality," they agreed, "is an activity of the most august imagination."[21]

But it was ever the privilege of irony to cancel its own constructions, and thus Stevens could say, without impropriety, that "eventually an imaginary world is entirely without interest."[22] This sent the poetry hurtling either towards a new imagination of the world or, alternatively, towards "the world without imagination," "a starker, barer world."[23] In this mood, Stevens could see how small a thing the imagination really was. "Poetry," he would then observe, "has to be something more than a conception of the mind. It has to be a revelation of nature. Conceptions are artificial. Perceptions are essential."[24] Or, "In the presence of extraordinary actuality, consciousness takes the place of imagination."[25] He tried to think of what it would be like to go "beyond the last thought,"[26] and he imagined himself, not imagining, but beholding, "nothing that is not there and the nothing that is."[27] Unlike Eliot, who had made irony seem, at least for a time, unendingly hellish, Stevens made it seem unendingly adventurous, replete with nuances yet to be recorded. There was no longing for escape, only a more and more deliberate pursuit of the various possibilities and implications. The ultimate consistency of Stevens's irony had to do with the fact that he never particularly concerned himself in his poetry with "the solid and the substantial," or with "specific and essential interests," but he did concern himself with his craving for these things and with the import that a contact with them might be supposed to have. Thus there was never an actual departure from the life of reflexive self-consciousness.

The position Hegel describes as irony was certainly not confined to the theories and expressions of the German romantics, nor was it, in its later appearances, confined only to avowed artists, like Eliot and Stevens. In the second half of the twentieth century, it had become practically the dominant position of literary and philosophical intellectuals alike. Richard Rorty and Harold Bloom both agreed that a postreligious, postphilosophical culture had been emerging ever since the early nineteenth century, and, without explicitly saying so, they both subscribed to the principles laid out in "The Oldest Systematic Program of German Idealism." Rorty understood that there was an analogy to be made between nineteenth-century idealism and twentieth-century textualism,[28] but at first he did not press the analogy because he interpreted idealism as a particular set of arguments or theories to be promulgated as dogma rather than as the absolute egotism exhibited by the followers of Fichte and described by Hegel under the rubric of irony. Bloom, on the other hand, by concentrating his attention on the literary intellectuals instead of on the technical philosophers, saw clearly that the triumph of autonomous sensibility in the late twentieth century had been announced, or prepared for, by a host of nineteenth-century writers whom he called "the Prophets of Sensibility."[29] These "precursors of modern cultural thought" included such figures as Ruskin, Arnold, Carlyle, and Pater (along with many others), and they created what Bloom describes as a "blend" of "moral reflection, prose poetry, psychological portraiture, art and literary criticism, cultural history and a curious kind of mythopoeic fiction . . . an amalgam that defies conventional description." Such writing, says Bloom, "mixes perception and sensation into a new kind of sensibility, one that is still with us today."

> Difficult to describe, this sensibility emphasizes a continuum haunted by intimations of mortality punctuated by brief bursts of radiance-privileged moments in which a peculiar vividness gives the illusion of redeeming life. It may be the stigma of the nineteenth-cen-

> tury Prophets of Sensibility that (except for Pater) they sought to combat this climate of the spirit but oddly fostered it implicitly (even as Pater did so overtly). The increasing internalization of the self depended upon an augmentation of estrangement from the object world, and what was intended as prophetic warning and lament as to this estrangement became instead a subtle suggestion of an inevitable movement in elite sensibility.

Thus it was a "strange anomaly" to Bloom that Nietzsche should now be given so much credit for fathering the future at the expense of these other precursors.

> They could not save or even preserve the post-Christian spirituality they sought to imbue in society, but they fostered in its place a pragmatic triumph of literary culture, beyond religion and beyond speculative philosophy. Psychoanalysis, despite its scientism, is only another form of that literary culture. So, in another way, are the textualist literary criticism and the language-oriented "human sciences" that are vivid parts of Structuralist and post-Structuralist formulations.

The "pragmatic triumph of literary culture" over science, philosophy, and religion was eventually explicated at some length by Rorty, who even revived the term "irony" in order to designate the new self-consciousness of thinkers in relation to their own projects and the projects of others. Rorty explained that what Bloom had described as "an inevitable movement in elite sensibility" was, in fact, the steadily growing acceptance, by intellectuals, of the arbitrariness, or groundlessness, of "final vocabularies." A "final vocabulary" was a particular way of conceiving and expressing one's sense of oneself or one's sense of the world. There were many such vocabularies, and there was no way to justify them or to resolve their differences. They did not correspond to anything objective but were themselves instead the basis for claims about objectivity. Thus Rorty defined the "ironist" as "someone who fulfills three conditions":

> (1) She has radical and continuing doubts about the final vocabulary she currently uses, because she has been impressed by other vocabularies, vocabularies taken as final by people or books she has encountered; (2) she realizes that argument phrased in her present vocabulary can neither underwrite nor dissolve these doubts; (3) insofar as she philosophizes about her situation, she does not think that her vocabulary is closer to reality than others, that it is in touch with a power not herself. Ironists who are inclined to philosophize see the choice between vocabularies as made neither within a neutral and universal

> metavocabulary nor by an attempt to fight one's way past appearances to the real, but simply by playing the new off against the old.[30]

Ironists, in Rorty's sense, shared an elite realization "that anything can be made to look good or bad by being redescribed." They had in common the fact that they were "never quite able to take themselves seriously" because they were "always aware that the terms in which they describe themselves are subject to change, always aware of the contingency and fragility of their final vocabularies, and thus of their selves."[31]

The world as Rorty described it was composed of individuals who either knew the vanity of all possible conceptions (including their own) or else failed to know it. Those who failed to know it were still, as Hegel would say, in earnest about what they considered to be true or important.

> For genuine earnestness enters only by means of a substantial interest, something of intrinsic worth like truth, ethical life, etc.,—by means of a content which counts as such for me as essential, so that I only become essential myself in my own eyes in so far as I have immersed myself in such a content and have brought myself into conformity with it in all my knowing and acting.[32]

Earnestness, in this sense, was precisely what was banished by the new ironical sensibility. The only project left for such a sensibility, according to Rorty, was the project of "self-creation," undertaken in terms "necessarily private, unshared, unsuited to argument," and rooted in beliefs and desires acknowledged to be "ungroundable."[33] Society would be saved, implied Rorty, by the freely extended kindness or benevolence or condescension of ironist intellectuals to those engaged in rival projects and to those who were otherwise impaired by material or intellectual disadvantages. In all of these activities, the beliefs and desires of the ironists would not be supported by knowledge or understanding; rather, whatever passed for knowledge and understanding would be supported by belief and desire, regarded as irreducible and absolutely primal. Right spirits—those who knew the true nature of spirit—would work tirelessly for the liberation of all spirits, especially those in physical or intellectual bondage, and they would do so on the basis of their own inexplicable power to envisage "an endless, proliferating realization of Freedom"[34] through the cultivation of imagination and sympathy. It was almost a perfect revival of "The Oldest Systematic Program of German Idealism," and yet, to intellectuals in the 1980s, it seemed fresh and new. The very fact that there was no way to reconcile theoretically the demands of self-creation and the demands of human solidarity became, in Rorty's account, a testimony to the power of the spirit to will the simultaneous establishment of both self and community, by "[dropping] the demand for a theory which unifies public and private, and [being] content to treat the demands of self-creation and of human solidarity as equally valid."[35] The decision to drop theory and to be content with apparent contradictions was, at bottom, an expression of ironic freedom and therefore appropriately, and gloriously, arbitrary.

In France, Jacques Derrida and Michel Foucault were among the age's chief ironists, and their influence was considerable, particularly with respect to literary intellectuals. Derrida labored to show how an interest in the processes of signification might be substituted for an interest in objectivity, with the result that the agonistics of writing and reading became more important than the signified contents of books, which were accordingly reduced to the level of being considered virtual realities or mere appearances. It was not appropriate from Derrida's point of view to regard writing as a reflection or representation of anything prior to itself, whether it be some actually existing situation or an idea in the writer's mind. Thus there was no access to, no contact with, a reality over and beyond what writing itself produced. "To write," said Derrida, was "to be incapable of making meaning absolutely precede writing."[36] "To write [was] to know that what has not yet been produced within literality has no other dwelling place, does not await us as prescription in some *topos ouranios,* or some divine understanding."[37] Writing thus became, for Derrida, the supreme spiritual gesture whereby the ordinary self of the writer and the world of reality were simultaneously generated out of nothing, *ex nihilo.* "The literary act thus recovers its true power at its source."[38] And, because it "is *inaugural,* in the fresh sense of the word," it is also, with respect to the writer, "dangerous and anguishing," even risky: "There is . . . no insurance [remarked Derrida] against the risk of writing."[39] Significations were "always enveloped within the regional limits of nature, life and the soul," but in the moment that Derrida calls "the moment of the attempt-to-write," "the play of meaning can overflow signification," eluding its regional limits.

> The attempt-to-write cannot be understood on the basis of voluntarism. The will to write is not an ulterior determination of a primal will. On the contrary, the will to write reawakens the willful sense of the will: freedom, break with the domain of empirical history, a break whose aim is reconciliation with the hidden essence of the empirical, with pure historicity. The will and the attempt to write are not the desire to write, for it is a question here not of affectivity but of freedom and duty. In its relationship to Being, the attempt-to-write poses itself as the only way out of affectivity. A way out that can only be aimed at, and without the certainty that deliverance is possible or that it is outside affectivity.[40]

In passages like these, Derrida imagined a Fichtean world of spiritual shadow-boxing, full of romantic drama. It was a place where the willful sense of the will might be reawakened, where deliverance from affectivity might be hoped for, and where a reconciliation with Being might be conceived.

None of these things could be said to make a direct appearance in the literary works which proceeded from them. They could not be objectified "without becoming absurdities, and the structure proper to them must escape all classical categories."[41] Instead, they were to be understood as belonging "to the internal historicity of the work itself, in its relationship to a subjective origin that is not simply psychological or mental."[42]

Terms like "danger," "risk," "deliverance" (from affectivity), "reconciliation" (with the hidden essence of the empirical), "uncertainty," and "anguish" seemed to suggest the hellish spirituality of Eliot's ironic personae, but in fact Derrida turned more in the direction of the endless adventurousness of Wallace Stevens. He greeted the overflow of the play of meaning in the works he interpreted with a spiritual affirmation of his own playfulness. He called it "the Nietzschean *affirmation,*" which he defined as "the joyous affirmation of the play of the world and of the innocence of becoming, the affirmation of a world of signs without fault, without truth, and without origin which is offered to an active interpretation," and he contrasted it with "the saddened, *negative,* nostalgic, guilty, Rousseauistic side of the thinking of play," which "dreams of deciphering a truth or an origin which escapes play and the order of the sign, and which lives the necessity of interpretation as an exile."[43] Curiously, he admitted, "we live [these two interpretations of interpretation] simultaneously and reconcile them in an obscure economy," even though they are "absolutely irreconcilable."[44] The more one read Derrida the clearer it was that he was constantly tracking a spiritual drama or a morality play wherein nostalgia for "the lost or impossible presence of the absent origin" was in the position of either mastering, or being mastered by, the acceptance of "absolute chance" through a surrender "to *genetic* indetermination" and "the *seminal* adventure of the trace."[45] These were absolutely primary, absolutely fundamental, spiritual gestures. Writers and readers were finally to be judged in terms of which gesture had been predominant in the works they produced. The will to meet the play of the world with a corresponding gesture of playfulness was constantly, however, being subverted by the tendency of its own structured expressions to suggest, in spite of themselves, "the lost or impossible presence of the absent origin." Just as constantly, then, this will-to-play, this Nietzschean affirmation, would be required to resist all definitions or determinations of itself, including those made previously on its own behalf or by its own agency. This was the reflux action of irony, the action whereby it canceled its constructions or returned them to the genetic indetermination of its own infinite spontaneity. All concepts were required to be volatilized or, by fiat, declared to be nonconcepts. All designations of the infinitely proliferating power of dissemination were to be interpreted by the adept as non-designations thereof, and so on. When Derrida sounded like Heidegger, he was, as his translator explained, not "simply adopting Heidegger's ideas," rather he was "gradually putting Heidegger into question."[46] Irony permitted, or required, a constantly mutating formula whereby former positions might be abandoned or discarded as restrictions of the playfulness of the spirit.

Foucault's irony took the form of an exposé of the fake objectivity of modern science. Like Derrida, he wished to pass beyond man and humanism, and he spoke of the arbitrary nature of the concept of "man," which had almost run its course and whose disappearance would betoken "the death of man." Consequently, he made it his ambition to produce a criticism of the "discursive practices" which were responsible for creating the illusion that man could be known objectively or that man could be regarded appropriately as the "object" of the human sciences. If the determinations produced by these sciences could be shown to be arbitrary or political at their point of origin, then the intellectual and social institutions that leaned upon, and gave currency to, the determined knowledge of man would be deprived of their own legitimacy. It was for freedom that Foucault fought, the freedom from being pinned down or categorized. If he renounced essentialism, it was only because he believed that man was not an object. As a romantic ironist, he knew that it was man's glory and agony to be an infinite spirit, never to be known but always in the process of becoming "other" than itself, "different" from itself, "more" or even "less" than itself. As he explained to Duccio Trombadori in 1978, in the entire course of their history,

> men had never ceased constructing themselves, that is, to shift continuously the level of their subjectivity, to constitute themselves in an infinite and multiple series of different subjectivities that would never place us in the presence of something that would be "man." Man is an animal of experience, he is involved *ad infinitum* within a process that, by defining a field of objects, at the same time changes him, deforms him, transforms him and transfigures him as a subject.[47]

In fact, Foucault was fascinated by Bataille's theme of the "limit-experiences" wherein "the subject reaches decomposition, leaves itself, at the limits of its own impossibility." That was "the way out," said Foucault, "the chance to free myself from certain traditional philosophical binds."[48] To be always in a state of transition was exactly the ironist's method of being truly spiritual. Thus

> the books I write constitute an experience for me that I'd like to be as rich as possible. . . . I write precisely because I don't know yet what to think about a subject that attracts my interest. In so doing, the book transforms me, changes what I think. As a consequence, each new work profoundly changes the terms of thinking which I had reached with the previous work. . . . When I write, I do it above all to change myself and not to think the same thing as before. . . . I don't construct

> a general method of definitive value for myself or others. What I write does not prescribe anything, neither to myself nor to others. At most, its character is instrumental and visionary or dreamlike.[49]

Experience was not sought after so that knowledge could be built up but so that the subject or the self could be torn down and thus acquire a new shape. The subject, said Foucault, must be torn away from itself

> in such a way that it is no longer the subject as such, or that it is completely "other" than itself so that it may arrive at its annihilation, its dissociation.
>
> It is this de-subjectifying undertaking, the idea of a "limit-experience" that tears the subject from itself, which is the fundamental lesson that I've learned from these authors [Nietzsche, Blanchot, and Bataille]. And no matter how boring and erudite my resulting books have been, this lesson has always allowed me to conceive them as direct experiences to "tear" me from myself, to prevent me from always being the same.[50]

The infinite malleability of human nature meant that humanism had to go, even Marxist humanism. Marx had said that man produces man, but "it's all in how you look at it," retorted Foucault. There were spirits who imagined that man ought to be faithful to the limitations or requirements of his own nature, and there were other spirits who realized that it was man's nature to be limitless and self-creating.

> For me, what must be produced is not man identical to himself, exactly as nature would have designed him or according to his essence; on the contrary, we must produce something that doesn't yet exist and about which we cannot know how and what it will be.[51]

Irony, as practiced by Derrida and Foucault, became (as Hegel predicted) a perpetual undermining of anything that offered itself as an objective determination of the Spirit, including all cultural formations and all pretended "knowledge." This was to be accomplished by "showing forth what has worth and dignity for mankind as null in its self-destruction," or by showing "that there is nothing in what is lofty and best, since, in its appearance in individuals, characters, and actions, it contradicts and destroys itself and so is ironical about itself."[52] The self-annihilation or deconstruction of all determinations and distinctions was sometimes imagined semi-idolatrously as a tendency within Being itself always to be something "other" than itself (Derrida's "play of the world"), but more often it was conceived along the lines of Rorty's insight that "anything can be made to look good or bad by being redescribed." As Hegel said, "Irony loves this irony of loss of character."[53]

Writing on Orwell in *Contingency, Irony, and Solidarity,* Rorty demonstrated the subversive power of redescription by constructing a new interpretation of *1984,* according to which doublethink became good and the pursuit of truth became bad. When it came to truth, Rorty observed that there was nothing in the nature of it that might prevent it from being used to any end or purpose. Orwell convinced us, said Rorty, that "all the intellectual and poetic gifts which had made Greek philosophy, modern science, and Romantic poetry possible might someday find employment in the Ministry of Truth."[54] But if the truth could not save us, what could save us was invincible rationalization. To have a self, in Rorty's reading of the novel, was to be capable "of weaving a coherent web of belief and desire."[55] To become irrational was not to lose contact with reality, it was to lose the ability to rationalize or justify oneself and one's actions by losing the capacity to go on weaving a coherent (or self-gratifying) web of belief and desire. The fact that Winston cannot "weave a story" around his betrayal of Julia, the fact that his betrayal of her *is* a fact, which he cannot permanently forget or conveniently redescribe, is interpreted by Rorty, not as a vindication of the truth over all evasions, but as a consequence of Winston's having lost, through torture, the power to sustain a face-saving rationalization of his own behavior, the power to go on weaving for himself a coherent web of belief and desire. Doublethink would save Winston from facing the truth, allowing him to retain his coherence. Thus, in Rorty's interpretation, the point Orwell is trying to make in *1984* is that the worst thing that can happen to one is that one's capacity for doublethinking (or supreme fiction making) should be disrupted. That doublethink, in Rorty's view, should turn out to be a good thing after all, and that the spirit of Greek philosophy should turn out to be fully employed in the Ministry of Truth (and thus a bad thing after all), was a brilliant piece of virtuoso irony and a perfect demonstration of irony's power to make every determinacy waver and dissolve, not unworthy of the Ministry of Truth itself.

For his own part, Foucault admitted to Trombadori that the coherence of his own project of being always other than himself had not been incompatible, at least for a time, with Stalinism. The attractiveness of Stalinism for Foucault, during his brief stint in the Communist Party, had been the very fact that it required continuous and unremitting doublethinking in order to stay abreast of official Party policy and thus permitted one to be constantly changing.

> No matter how unconvinced we were, we still forced ourselves into believing what they told us. This was part of an attitude—I'd call it disastrous, but it was mine and it was my way of staying in the Party—of being obligated to sustain the opposite of what's believable; this was part of that exercise of 'the dissolution of the self' and of the search for a way of being 'other'.[56]

In this way, the complete loss of character might be ironically construed as the perfect achievement of character. Foucault's later attitude towards politics was characterized by avoidance of commitment to particular programs or schemes of action, largely because ordinary politics required a narrow single-mindedness or a holding fast to a particular set of aims and purposes, which promoted sameness of character rather than the volatilization of character.

The success of irony in the twentieth century was nothing short of spectacular. The chief ironists of the age followed Heidegger in imagining that the Hegelian judgment concerning art might be set aside, or indeed had already been set aside, by their own artistic manipulation of intellectual and cultural materials. In fact, the judgment remained in force precisely because it had predicted and accounted for, in advance, all the gestures of which the ironists were capable. The judgment was not exactly that art should not be this; it was more nearly that this is what art has come to, this is what art will be henceforth. The more irony shows itself to be capable of making mincemeat out of philosophy in general (or out of Hegel's philosophy in particular), the more the judgment locks into place as an accurate description of the range and extent of ironic spirituality, already placed, by philosophy, within a larger, more comprehensive range of spiritual possibilities.

Notes

1. G. W. F. Hegel, *Vorlesungen über die Ästhetik, Werke in zwanzig Bänden,* ed. E. Moldenhauer and K. M. Michel, 20 vols. and Index (Frankfurt am Main: Suhrkamp Verlag, 1969ff), 13:141–42; English translation, G.W.F. Hegel, *Aesthetics: Lectures on Fine Art,* trans. T. M. Knox, 2 vols. (Oxford: Clarendon Press, 1975), 1:103. Further references will be given in the form: *Werke,* 13:141; *A,* 1:103.

2. Martin Heidegger, *Poetry, Language, Thought,* trans. Albert Hofstadter (New York: Harper and Row, 1971), 80.

3. *Werke,* 13:113; *A,* 1:80.

4. *Werke,* 13:141–42; *A,* 1:103.

5. *Werke,* 14:237; *A,* 1:607.

6. *Werke,* 14:236; *A,* 1:606.

7. *Werke,* 13:93; *A,* 1:64.

8. *Werke,* 13:94; *A,* 1:64–65.

9. *Werke,* 13:95; *A,* 1:66.

10. *Werke,* 13:96; *A,* 1:66–67.

11. G. W. F. Hegel, *Lectures on the Philosophy of History,* trans E.S. Haldane and Frances H. Simson (Atlantic Highlands, NJ: Humanities Press, 1983), 3:510.

12. *Lectures on the Philosophy of History,* 3:507–8.

13. G. W. F. Hegel, *Phenomenology of Spirit,* trans. A. V. Miller (Oxford: Oxford University Press, 1979), 400.

14. Wallace Stevens, *Collected Poems* (New York: Knopf, 1968), 534.

15. Wallace Stevens, *Opus Posthumous,* ed. Milton J. Bates (New York: Random House, 1990), 183.

16. Stevens, *Opus Posthumous,* 197.

17. Stevens, *Opus Posthumous,* 202.

18. Stevens, *Opus Posthumous,* 197.

19. Stevens, *Opus Posthumous,* 262.

20. Stevens, *Opus Posthumous,* 189.

21. Stevens, *Opus Posthumous,* 135.

22. Stevens, *Opus Posthumous,* 200.

23. Stevens, *Collected Poems,* 27, 29.

24. Stevens, *Opus Posthumous,* 191.

25. Stevens, *Opus Posthumous,* 191.

26. Stevens, *Opus Posthumous,* 141.

27. Stevens, *Collected Poems,* 10.

28. See Richard Rorty, "Nineteenth-Century Idealism and Twentieth-Century Textualism," in *Consequences of Pragmatism: Essays, 1972–1980* (Minneapolis: University of Minnesota Press, 1982), 139–59.

29. Harold Bloom, "Prophets of Sensibility: Precursors of Modern Cultural Thought," an unpaginated, three-page preface used to introduce numerous volumes of reprints of the most influential classics of nineteenth-century literary thought, published as a series in the 1980s by Chelsea House Publishers under the general editorship of Bloom. All quotations from Bloom are taken from this general preface to the series.

30. Richard Rorty, *Contingency, Irony, and Solidarity* (Cambridge: Cambridge University Press, 1989), 73.

31. Rorty, *Contingency, Irony, and Solidarity,* 73–74.

32. *Werke,* 13:94; *A,* 1:65.

33. Rorty, *Contingency, Irony, and Solidarity,* xiv–xv.

34. Rorty, *Contingency, Irony, and Solidarity,* xvi.

35. Rorty, *Contingency, Irony, and Solidarity,* xv.

36. Jacques Derrida, *Writing and Difference,* trans. Alan Bass (Chicago: University of Chicago Press, 1978), 10.

37. Derrida, *Writing and Difference,* 11.

38. Derrida, *Writing and Difference,* 11.

39. Derrida, *Writing and Difference,* 11.

40. Derrida, *Writing and Difference,* 12–13.

41. Derrida, *Writing and Difference,* 14.

42. Derrida, *Writing and Difference,* 14.

43. Derrida, *Writing and Difference,* 292.

44. Derrida, *Writing and Difference,* 293.

45. Derrida, *Writing and Difference,* 292.

46. Derrida, *Writing and Difference,* 305.

47. Michel Foucault, *Remarks on Marx: Conversations with Duccio Trombadori,* trans. R. James Goldstein and James Cascaito (New York: *Semiotext(e),* 1991), 123–24.

48. Foucault, *Remarks,* 48.

49. Foucault, *Remarks,* 27, 29.
50. Foucault, *Remarks,* 31–32.
51. Foucault, *Remarks,* 121.
52. *Werke,* 13:96; *A,* 1:67.
53. *Werke,* 13:96; *A,* 1:67.
54. Rorty, *Contingency, Irony, and Solidarity,* 175–76.
55. Rorty, *Contingency, Irony, and Solidarity,* 178.
56. Foucault, *Remarks,* 52.

III

Hegel's Aesthetic and the Possibility of Art Criticism

Brian K. Etter

Jacques Barzun begins his book, *The Use and Abuse of Art,* by considering "Why Art Must Be Challenged." There is something odd, he thinks, about the way the world today uses the arts, and something odd about the nature of the arts themselves: they are both contemptuous of the social world in which they exist, and contemptuous of their own status as art. Their apparent nihilism, however, contrasts strangely with the way in which the modern world idolizes artistic creativity.[1] How the arts developed from the conscious effort to create beauty—as in the work of Botticelli, Michelangelo, and Palestrina—to the modernist contempt for all beauty or sensuous pleasure, is a question which demands asking. Why the modern world esteems the ugly and revolting as the only genuinely creative art is a question even more worth being asked. These are critical questions, and Barzun is one of the few academicians to have the courage to raise them. They lead him necessarily to a critical examination of the history of art and aesthetics in the past two centuries, in which the arts today appear as products of the dissolution of the culture established in the Renaissance. Barzun's conclusion is pessimistic: art has become disposable, like the social institutions that form the context of our daily lives.[2] Indeed, belief in reason, a publicly shared morality, individual obligation and responsibility all have largely vanished since Barzun perceived their impending demise over twenty years ago. The arts have in no small measure helped to precipitate the disintegration of Western societies.

Such an assessment of the intellectual, moral, and institutional framework of today's world is by no means unfamiliar. Indeed, as regards the general sense of the course of history, Barzun's perception of the dissolution of "the culture of the Renaissance" is echoed by many thinkers, most (like Barzun himself) profoundly influenced by Nietzsche. Hence, for instance, Gianni Vattimo describes the present as "The End of Modernity," taking modernity as the entire period from Descartes to the twentieth century.[3] Such a view is already familiar in Heidegger, and is perhaps close to becoming the reigning academic orthodoxy. But there is a crucial difference between Barzun and the postmodernist heirs of Nietzsche and Heidegger: the latter celebrate the death of Renaissance culture and assist at the demise of reason, whereas Barzun views these developments with regret, even while conceding them as faits accomplis. Such a view indeed raises a philosophical problem: on what grounds is it possible to criticize historical developments? For if we take for granted the historicist view that history is the fundamental principle of human understanding, then culture and values become historically determined, and transcendent truth disappears. To paraphrase Nietzsche: the logical end of every historical system of thought will be nihilism—and, moreover, the present can derive its legitimacy only from the extent to which it breaks its ties with the past. Thus historicism necessarily ends in what I shall call "presentism," the belief that the present is the only source of values, and is authentic only when it rejects the past in its totality. But then it becomes impossible to criticize the present in its newness. Barzun's critique has no force against the deeply embedded presentism of the twentieth century.

Indeed, the arts have become impervious to criticism in this century. With respect to morality and social institutions, there always remain some minimal standards by which to judge the present, for the barest social utility suffices to preserve the possibility of criticism. With respect to the arts, it is quite otherwise. Following the demand of Kant, reigning aesthetic theories have rejected all notions of social utility: on the side of the artists, self-expression is taken to need no further justification, and on the side of art's reception, the simple apprehension and appreciation of formal properties is taken to be an adequate pleasure in itself. Thus, although one may speak of an unparalleled divorce between the aesthetics of production and the aesthetics of reception in this century, both approaches to conceiving and justifying art are rooted in a notion of individuality from which, in fact, all historicity is excluded, and all grounds for criticism banished. For it is the genius of aesthetic formalism to eliminate form as a critical category: all created things have form, even if they do not have clear structure. And if the actual structure cannot be criticized because it is the artist's sacrosanct expression of himself, then anything may be art, and there certainly can be no distinction drawn between good art and bad art—as long as the art is presentist in style, based on a repudiation of the defunct, mimetic past. Hence, even when a philosopher such as Jerrold Levinson attempts to restore some sense of historical context to the definition of art in terms of a connection to a hypothetical *ur*-art, he is still unable to define that *ur*-art, or to ground a critical discussion of historically competing concepts of art.[4] Thus, presentism is not banished, for there is no normative definition. Historicism and presentism remain two sides of the same coin.

The prevailing presentism and its elimination of criticism in the arts have a substantial part of their origin in the historicism of Hegel. It is true, as Stanley Rosen argues, that Hegel's historicism was not of the postmodern kind: he did not understand the process of history as radically contingent.[5] Nevertheless, Hegel's view of history was historicist in the traditional sense of seeing history as the fundamental epistemological principle for understanding the human world.[6] That Hegel understood human history as the working out of God's self-revelation meant that he elevated history to a position of cardinal importance for the understanding of God or the Absolute. But this heterodox understanding of divine revelation was rooted, as Cryil O'Regan and many others have argued, in a heterodox doctrine of God.[7] As a consequence, the present of Hegel's time was elevated to the position of being the culmination of God's self-revelation: in some sense, therefore, it became the teleological end of history.[8] Thus presentism was a corollary of Hegel's historicism, as it is for today's historicism—but with this difference, that Hegel's presentism did not involve the utter rejection of the past. Since history was understood dialectically, all the stages had some importance, even as they were transcended by the reconciliation of intrinsic contradictions.

The implication of Hegel's heterodox theology of history for his aesthetic theory was that the arts of his day were the culmination of the Spirit's manifestation in humankind. Hence, the arts were strongly marked by subjectivity and inwardness: the individual human spirit was now the locus of the divine Spirit.[9] In this, he prefigured the modern doctrine of subjective artistic self-expression—although it has been left to the twentieth century to eliminate the connection with the divine. Thus, in spite of important differences, the roots of today's historicism, presentism, and aesthetic subjectivism may indeed be found in Hegel.

Given all of this, and especially the view of the present as the culmination of history, one would expect to find that Hegel was as incapable of criticizing the arts of his day as we are unable to justify criticizing the arts today. Yet Hegel unmistakably engages in such criticism in the *Aesthetics*. Having defined art in terms of its vocation "to unveil the truth in the form of sensuous artistic configuration,"[10] Hegel finds that the arts of his day do not fulfill their vocation in every instance. The unity of form and content in which Hegel located the ideal of artistic beauty was now broken, and not by any accidental misfortune: on the contrary, the historical development of art was to free art from the representation of any specific content.[11] But to free art from its content is to break the tie with truth, and so to cease to be art. In spite of clear attempts to put a good face on this development and to see it as historically necessary, it is impossible to miss the tone of lament: "No Homer, Sophocles, etc., no Dante, Ariosto, or Shakespeare can appear in our day; what was so magnificently sung, what so freely expressed, has been expressed; these are materials, ways of looking at them and treating them which have been sung once and for all."[12] It would appear that complete decadence is to be the state of the arts at the moment of the culmination of history.

Indeed, Hegel dwells on the deficiencies of the contemporary arts in a manner that should be instructive for us today. He believes that romantic art in principle allows the artist greater freedom than classical art had done, with two consequences. First, the romantic principle of inwardness allows the external world to be represented as subsisting in its own manner. But second, the same principle allows the subjective world of the heart and spirit its own inherent dignity, so that the specific representation will be equally accidental. In other words, the first consequence for romantic art will be a far greater degree of realism than obtains in classical art: "everything has a place, every sphere of life, all phenomena, the greatest and the least, the supreme and the trivial, the moral, immoral, and evil. . . ."[13] But what he could praise in the plays of Shakespeare had come by Hegel's day to constitute "the collapse of romantic art." For carried to an extreme, the portrayal of the prosaic world ended in stripping ordinary life of its ethical character and its connection with the eternal. The second consequence, however, will be the exaltation of the subjectivity of the artist in his expression of opinions, feelings, and originality.[14] That is, the endpoints of romantic art are either a pure realism with no ethical truth, or a pure subjectivism lacking in both reality and ethical truth.

This is a perceptive observation of trends already evident in literature and the arts in the 1820s, which the future course of the nineteenth century bore out in spite of Hegel's warning in the *Philosophy of Right* that philosophy could not prophesy the future. The rise of realist art and prose literature after 1830 was widely criticized, especially in France, and in terms not essentially different from Hegel's: "Thereby art becomes not only what romantic art is more or less throughout, i.e. portrait-like, but it completely dissolves into the presentation of a portrait . . . ; and it reverts to the imitation of nature, i.e. to an intentional approach to the contingency of immediate existence which, taken by itself, is unbeautiful and prosaic. Therefore, the question soon arises whether such productions in general are still to be called works of art."[15] Indeed so: earlier in the *Aesthetics*, Hegel had decisively rejected any definition of art in terms of the mere imitation of nature, on the grounds that such imitation is always superfluous, inadequate, uncreative, and unbeautiful.[16] Hence purely realist art could not be regarded as a further development of style within the general category of romantic art; it would have to be rejected altogether as not being art. Only if the artist remained "faithful to the manifestations of spirit and also to the inherently substantial life of nature" could his work be seen as art.[17] That is, realism would have to be tempered with faithfulness to human freedom as the essential life of the Spirit, with all its moral and ethical implications.

The second pole of development for romantic art, toward subjectivism, lay in the emergence of humor or irony as an essential ingredient in art. Hegel notes that the intrusion of the artist's own personality risks destroying the unity of form and content that is the essence of artistic beauty, so that art quickly loses its seriousness and dignity. In Hegel's day, the preeminent practitioner of humor in the novel was Jean Paul Richter, and Hegel makes clear that he had little use for his endless "drawing together and concatenating material raked up from the four corners of the earth and every sphere of reality," without development or substantive aim.[18] Thus the development of extreme subjective domination of the material by the writer constituted both "the end of romantic art"—as the pole toward which the artistic spirit was moving—and its nadir. Hegel's criticisms of contemporary artistic trends, therefore, merit attention all the more for being rooted in his historicist view of history.

How this is possible demands our attention, for in the explanation will lie an important clue for how to escape the prison of an historicism that appears to bar critical judgment altogether. Hegel's historicism would seem to commit him to a positivist acceptance of all historical creations as art: especially since Hegel accords each historical era its own dignity in the unfolding of the potentiality of the Spirit, the artworks of each period should share in that dignity. And since his historicism issues in a pronounced presentism, in what sense his own age could be at once the completion of history in the sense of fulfillment and the end of the arts in the sense of their nadir certainly demands an explanation. The latter issue has been a subject of debate among commentators on Hegel's *Aesthetics:* Stephen Bungay sees Hegel as arguing for the necessity of the dissolution of art at the end of history, because of the decline of religious belief in the eighteenth century; he criticizes Hegel's argument on this score.[19] William Desmond, on the other hand, emphasizes the openness of art itself as a model for understanding what the notion of the completion of history might mean in Hegel; hence, he does not see Hegel as arguing for the necessary dissolution of art in the modern era.[20]

Hegel's own words, however, raise an even more disturbing problem for his understanding of history: "In our day, in the case of almost all peoples, criticism, the cultivation of reflection, and, in our German case, freedom of thought have mastered the artists too, and have made them so to say, a *tabula rasa* in respect of the material and the form of their productions. . . . The artist thus stands above specific consecrated forms and configurations and moves freely on his own account, independent of the subject-matter and mode of conception in which the holy and eternal was previously made visible to human apprehension." Hence, the development of artistic subjectivism was indeed the result of the decline of the Christian faith.[21] Yet how could the Christian faith decay at the very moment of the completion of the Spirit's self-revelation in history?

This question takes us to the heart of the problem of Hegel's conception of history. In the *Aesthetics,* the principle of historical development is fundamentally religious: symbolic art is the product of a pantheistic worldview; classical art is the realization of the personality of the divine objectified in polytheism; romantic art is the creation of Christianity, the result of the spirit dwelling in the subjective consciousness of the Christian believer.[22] But this schema is not the same as that given in *The Philosophy of History,* where the principle of historical development is fundamentally political.

Here, it is the idea of freedom which emerges gradually, from the despotism of the East, where only the ruler was free, to the aristocracy and democracy of ancient Greece and Rome, where all citizens were free, to the Germanic world in Christian times, where under a benevolent monarchy all had finally become free.[23] Both views, of course, are reductionist, but Hegel attempts to reconcile their apparent divergence by identifying Reason as the substance of the universe, the eternal essence of both the material and the temporal phenomena of the world.[24] The human attainment of self-conscious knowledge will therefore be an attainment of freedom of the human spirit, since complete, self-conscious knowledge will be unbounded Reason.[25] At the same time, when the human spirit attains such knowledge of eternal Reason, it becomes identical with the divine Spirit for Hegel: what must be counted as a heresy from the perspective of the faith he sought to defend was the key to linking Christianity to the development of the idea of freedom in this manner. The result, therefore, is a more optimistic account in the *Philosophy of History* than the *Aesthetics* seems to provide.

This optimism is further grounded in the three periods Hegel distinguishes in the history of Christendom. The first period extended from the Germanic invasions of the Roman Empire to Charlemagne, the second from Charlemagne to Charles V, and the third from Charles V to Hegel's time.[26] Hegel regards the first period, astonishingly enough, as an undifferentiated unity, of little interest except as the formation of Christendom. The second period was characterized by the emergence of the antithesis of church and state, the former aiming at theocracy, the latter at feudal monarchy. For Hegel, it was the low point of the idea of freedom, for both the religious and secular spheres. Again, this is astonishing as a characterization of the entire period and all Christendom, however much it may fit the Investiture Controversy and Germany specifically. For Hegel, however, the antithesis was resolved only in the third period, which included the Reformation; secularity now came into its own, in the form of ordinary activity and morality. At the same time, the Reformation (in Hegel's view) rescued the Christian faith so that the Free Spirit became not only the rallying point of the world, but the source of the universal axioms of Reason.[27] For Hegel, then, the Reformation realized the specifically Christian notion of freedom and, in making Reason the measure of all things, enabled political—and cultural—life to become rational for the first time.

Hegel's conception of history must appear utterly contestable. Only an ardent Protestant could perhaps sympathize with Hegel's view of the Reformation as the culmination of Christian history, but hardly anyone today would accept the equation of God's Free Spirit with the source of the axioms of Reason in Hegel's sense. Indeed, the Church Fathers identified the Word of God with Truth: they relied on John 1:1, where *logos* could mean both "word" and "rational principle."[28] Thus God, and specifically the Second Person of the Trinity, was the source of the axioms of Reason—but the Spirit, the Third Person of the Trinity was not. Hegel's shift of the locus of

Reason both undermines the significance of Christ by eliminating the divine redemption of human nature through the incarnation and rationalizes the concept of the Spirit by eliminating its association with divine grace and love. But because Hegel understands the tripartite schema of history in analogy to the Trinity—based on Joachim of Flora and Jakob Boehme—the result is the devaluation we have noted in both the first age of the Father, in which Christendom was established, and in the second age of the Son, when the Church vied so strenuously with the feudal monarchy.[29] As a consequence, then, the age of the Spirit—the present age, inaugurated by the Reformation—emerges in Hegel's heretical historicism as the only period of full merit. But presentism in any sense must be counted as a theologically heterodox conception of history.

The tensions within Hegel's conception of the post-Reformation era, however, account for how he could perceive the decay of the Christian faith at the very moment of the completion of the Spirit's self-revelation in history. For the Spirit, according to Hegel's theology, was both the Third Person of the Trinity and the source of the axioms of Reason: its religious dimension was fulfilled in the Reformation, which Hegel understood as realizing the spiritual freedom of the individual, but its intellectual dimension was realized fully in the domain of philosophy, which reached fruition later in the subsequent history. The development of philosophical self-consciousness was only a potential latent within the principles of the Reformation; its full attainment, together with its attendant freedom of thought, was the work of the Enlightenment. Hegel saw the Enlightenment as the completion of the Reformation because it accomplished the recognition of the validity of natural law—that is, Reason—in both science and morality.[30] The final step was establishing the actuality of freedom as the will willing itself alone: Hegel saw this as Kant's achievement in philosophy, and the French Revolution's achievement in political history.[31] But to interpret the Enlightenment as the completion of the Reformation in this way is to render the Christian faith redundant with natural law, eliminating the need for faith altogether: in this Hegel shares in the clear tendency of eighteenth-century thought. The result is the illusion of a paradox—of the simultaneous decay and fulfillment of faith—where none exists: it would be better to regard the entire Enlightenment as marked by the explicit secularization of thought.[32] In perceiving this, Hegel was surely correct. It could be regarded as the completion of the Reformation, however, only by calling either the Reformation or the Christian faith itself into question. He, of course, will not resolve the paradox in these ways.

Instead, Hegel introduces an alternative, theological dialectic in the *Aesthetics,* by which he attempts to account for the observed characteristics of the arts in the entire Christian era. Because in Christianity the salvation of the individual believer is of paramount importance, Hegel understands that "it is the actual individual person in his inner life who acquires infinite worth, since in him alone do the eternal moments of absolute truth, which is actual only as spirit, unfold into existence and collect together again." This way of putting it is yet another demonstration of the heterodoxy of this theology; for him, "the actual individual man is the appearance of God. . . ."[33] But while it would be better to say that "God created man in his own image" (Gen.1:27), the broader point that God's spirit is present in the heart of the individual believer is a recognizable rendition of the teaching of the First Letter of John. Hence the content of romantic art must consist in the representation of either God as an infinite Subject "disclosing his inner being to man's inner being," or of the human struggle for spiritual reconciliation in the face of grief and death, or finally "the finite as such, both on the side of spiritual aims, mundane interests, passions, collisions, sorrows and joys, hopes and satisfaction," and so forth. The last potential content of the finite, in turn, may be treated in two ways, either as possessing a positive character or as being merely contingent and negative.[34] These potentialities, therefore, arise from the dialectical nature of the Christian faith and serve to ground a historical dialectic of romantic art.

Hegel understands the history of romantic art as a working out of the theological dimensions of the Christian faith, so that it, like the course of political history, will exhibit a trinitarian aspect. The first phase of romantic art, therefore, "is formed by religion as such; its centre is supplied by the history of redemption, by the life of Christ, his death and Resurrection." Accordingly, there is little concern for the external world in such art. In the second phase, however, "the emotion which at first is exclusively religious loses its negative attitude to human affairs as such" and seeks to affirm the subjective inwardness of the individual in the chivalric virtues of honor, love, fidelity, and bravery.[35] Such ethical ideals were central to Hegel's concept of the Ideal. They are found in literature from the medieval Arthurian poems to plays such as *King Lear.* But Shakespeare belongs preeminently to the third phase, in which the representation of inner character becomes an end in itself; thus Shakespeare's realism about human character, in which the motives of Macbeth and Othello are explored, for example, possesses the positive quality that Hegel finds as one pole of this phase.[36] The purely negative treatment of contingent reality, on the other hand, was the end at which literature had arrived in Hegel's day, resulting in either pure realism or complete subjectivism without ethical truth, as we have seen. In retrospect, we might designate this a fourth phase of romantic art, since it has informed so much literature and art since Hegel. For him, this marked the "dissolution of romantic art" altogether.

We are now in a position, however, to understand how Hegel was able to criticize contemporary developments in the arts in spite of his historicism and apparent presentism. For his notion of the culmination or end of history was inherently ambiguous. On the one hand, it involved the complete realization of human freedom—and there are passages in *The Philosophy of Right* which celebrate that with even greater complacency than does *The Philosophy of History.*[37] On the other hand, that very culmination entailed a loss of the dialectically related element of the divine. The confusion between the divine and the human spirit, which is central to Hegel's theology of history, conceals a tension that is better expressed in the orthodox doctrine of divine transcendence and the independence of creation. Hegel's theology would rewrite Philippians 2:7 to speak of God the Father, rather than Christ, emptying himself and "being born in the likeness of men." But the fact that Hegel did recognize a pole of the Spirit that was other than the merely human spirit meant that what was a gain for the latter necessarily entailed a loss of the former.[38] Hence, the present was not to be judged by a strictly immanent standard: in spite of all his presentist rhetoric, Hegel did not hold that the present was the embodiment of the whole of the Spirit. As long as the present is only partially related to a transcendent principle, however implicated in historical development that principle may be, there is the possibility of genuine criticism of both the present and the past on the ground of metaphysical truth and moral standards. It is a principle of transcendence which we lack today and yet do not count as a loss.

Hegel, in contrast, was aware of the spiritual poverty of the emerging modern world. He saw evidence of this in the absence of genuine epic poetry; the prosaic organization of modern life militated against the writing of such poetry. In particular, the development of the modern state rendered the writing of epic poetry impossible; what was a gain for political life became a loss for art.[39] Although the novel had arisen, taking the epic's place, the substitution was not an equivalent replacement. For earlier in the *Aesthetics* Hegel had argued that it was precisely because the modern state was thoroughly bureaucratized that people needed the heroes which epic poetry provides; because the public authorities now do not act as individuals, the individual no longer appears to have the personal independence to make moral decisions. "Therefore, for the free configuration of individuality we have required the opposite state of affairs, in which the authority of the ethical order rests on individuals alone, who, in their private will and the outstanding greatness and effectiveness of their character, place themselves at the head of the real world in which they live."[40] Thus the modern world needs heroic literature, yet cannot produce it. All it can hope to do is to retain the great epics of the past as a corrective to the one-sidedness of ethical life in the modern state. But as we realize today, even that will be exceedingly difficult.

It is easy to see why Hegel seemed at times to despair of the condition of the arts in the modern world. Indeed, in an often-cited passage from the introduction to the romantic form of art, he states: "Therefore we acquire as the culmination of the romantic in general the contingency of both outer and inner, and the separation of these two sides, whereby art annuls itself and brings home to our minds that we must acquire higher forms for the apprehension of truth than those which art is in a position to supply."[41] Here there is joined to the theme of the dissolution of art at the end of history the additional implication that art has no more role to play in the representation of truth to humanity; this, at any rate, is what many commentators have taken Hegel to mean.[42] Yet that might be a hasty overreading of the passage, for two reasons. First, although Hegel does regard religion and philosophy as the two higher means of knowing truth, his definition of art as the sensuous representation of truth means that art, in principle, always has a role to play in communicating the truth to people; it cannot cease altogether to be important. Second, if there is a problem with art at a particular moment of history, then other forms of knowledge—such as religion or philosophy—might indeed be better able to discover and to communicate truth. It would be a mistake to take this passage as a funeral oration for art, therefore; if the arts become false to their essence as representations of truth by descending into mere contingency or subjectivism, then we would certainly do well to look elsewhere for inspiration. Hegel's aesthetic has the integrity of not making a religion out of art.

There is another reason, however, for not reading Hegel's analysis of the dissolution of romantic art as a verdict pronouncing the absolute end of art altogether. For Hegel was not without hope, or evidence to support that hope—a point frequently overlooked by his commentators. If the romantic form of art had dissolved into the apparent antithesis of realism and subjectivism, then the antithesis might yet be resolved. Hegel was cautious in envisioning the resolution, but he saw as one possibility "an inner movement of the spirit devoted entirely to its object and retaining it as its content and interest"—that is, by a union of deep feeling with the object.[43] This is indeed the principle underlying what we call popular, rather than ironic, romanticism in poetry, music, and painting; lacking such terminology, Hegel could only point to Goethe and Rückert as the leading poets of the new movement. Their poetry relied on the pathetic fallacy to project moods onto nature, so that human feeling could be specified by natural metaphor, and at the same time nature be revivified through the representation of its sympathy with the human spirit. The result, as Hegel noted, was to rise above the merely subjective feelings of the poet: such poetry possessed "a depth of feeling and a cheerfulness of the inwardly self-moving heart which through the serenity of the outward shape lift the soul high above all painful entanglement in the restrictions of the real world."[44] But this was to accomplish precisely the goal of all true art: it embodied the Ideal.[45] Hence Hegel's aesthetic was able both to ground a criticism of contemporary decadence in the arts and to allow an appreciation of the best fruits of the emerging romantic movement, which was to dominate German literature for the next half-century. For all the faults of Hegel's interpretation of history, his historicism did not prevent a perceptive and nuanced assessment of contemporary artistic developments.

Hegel's aesthetic succeeded, therefore, in doing what every good aesthetic theory must do, that is, in providing a ground for the critical assessment of particular works of art and trends in art. The task of an aesthetic is to supply a universal standard by which to judge particular instances.

Hegel's aesthetic succeeds in this task in spite of its historicism, because its standards are in fact transcendent and not rooted merely in the contingencies of human history. For Hegel, the content of art is the divine and the human spirit, but even he in his heterodoxy cannot subsume the divine completely in the human: as his art criticism shows, when art seeks to do so, it fails miserably to have any human interest. The tension between the divine and the human spirit is vital to both art and life. Moreover, the form of art is a given element for Hegel: it is the sensuous representation of truth. He justified this is the *Aesthetics* by means of dialectical inquiry into the deficiencies of competing definitions of art, but in fact it is consistent in intent with the main tradition of aesthetic inquiry since Plato, with its emphasis on the identity of truth, beauty, and goodness.[46] The great merit of Hegel's historical approach to philosophy ought to be seen as lying in the recognition he accorded to the weight of tradition. For tradition and transcendence are the two things utterly rejected in the twentieth century, the loss of which imprisons us in the present and prevents any criticism of the arts in our day. In the doctrines of formalism and expressionism we have no aesthetic at all.

Thus, in spite of Hegel's historicism, his aesthetic points the way out of our own historicism and presentism. If we can recover a perspective that recognizes the validity of transcendence and tradition, it will become possible once again to construct intelligent criticisms of contemporary art. Such a development would go a long way to deconstructing the postmodernist mythology of Nietzsche, Heidegger, and their followers. We are not obliged to accept everything labeled "art" as being indeed art, for the definition of a word is rooted in its history, and the great weight of tradition identifying art as the representation of truth, beauty, and goodness cannot be ignored. Most pertinent to the twentieth century, a word such as "art" cannot be used to mean the opposite of what it has always meant. But simple traditionalism is not the most important lesson we have to learn from Hegel, for both the tension and the confusion in his thought between the human and the divine point to the necessity of recovering an account of the transcendent in which to ground the transcendentals of truth, beauty, and goodness. Human thought and practice can deny the transcendentals only at the price of denying the deepest needs of the human spirit altogether; in aiming at them, thought and practice aim at the divine. But humanity is not God: recognizing this is the key to avoiding the worship of the present, with its imperviousness to all criticism of the contingent. To restore the possibility of criticism is the one thing needful for the arts today.

Notes

1. Jacques Barzun, *The Use and Abuse of Art* (Princeton: Princeton University Press, 1974), 23.

2. Barzun, *The Use and Abuse of Art,* 146–47.

3. Gianni Vattimo, *The End of Modernity: Nihilism and Hermenuetics in Postmodern Culture,* trans. Jon R. Snyder (Baltimore: Johns Hopkins University Press, 1988).

4. Jerrold Levinson, *Music, Art, and Metaphysics: Essays in Philosophical Aesthetics* (Ithaca: Cornell University Press, 1990), especially 3–21, 38–56.

5. Stanley Rosen, *G. W. F. Hegel: An Introduction to the Science of Wisdom* (New Haven: Yale University Press, 1974), 33.

6. On historicism in modernity, see Charles Bambach, *Heidegger, Dilthey, and the Crisis of Historicism* (Ithaca: Cornell University Press, 1995), 1–19.

7. See Cyril O'Regan, *The Heterodox Hegel* (Albany: State University of New York Press, 1994).

8. On the question of the end of history, see Rosen, *Hegel,* 29ff., and William Desmond, *Art and the Absolute: A Study of Hegel's Aesthetics* (Albany: State University of New York Press, 1986), 57ff.

9. G. W. F. Hegel, *Vorlesungen über die Ästhetik, Werke in zwanzig Bänden,* ed. E. Moldenhauer and K. M. Michel, 20 vols. and Index (Frankfurt am Main: Suhrkamp Verlag, 1969ff.), 14:128–33; English translation, G. W. F. Hegel, *Aesthetics: Lectures on Fine Art,* trans. T. M. Knox, 2 vols., (Oxford: Clarendon Press, 1975), 1:519–21. Further references will be given in the form: *Werke,* 14:128; *A,* 1:519.

10. *Werke,* 13:82; *A,* 1:55.

11. *Werke,* 14:234; *A,* 1:604.

12. *Werke,* 14:238; *A,* 1:608.

13. *Werke,* 14:221; *A,* 1:594.

14. *Werke,* 14:222; *A,* 1:595.

15. *Werke,* 14:223; *A,* 1:596.

16. *Werke,* 13:64–67; *A,* 1:41–44.

17. *Werke,* 14:223–24; *A,*1:596.

18. *Werke,* 14:230–31; *A,* 1:601–2.

19. Stephen Bungay, *Beauty and Truth: A Study of Hegel's Aesthetics* (Oxford: Oxford University Press, 1984), 82–83.

20. Desmond, *Art and the Absolute,* 75.

21. *Werke,* 14:235; *A,* 1:605.

22. *Werke,* 13:107–13; *A,* 1:76–81.

23. G. W. F. Hegel, *Vorlesungen über die Philosophie der Geschichte,* ed. H. Glockner, *Sämtliche Werke in zwanzig Bänden,* (Stuttgart: Frommanns Verlag, 1928), 11:45.

24. *Philosophie der Geschichte, Sämtliche Werke* 11:34–35.

25. *Philosophie der Geschichte, Sämtliche Werke* 11:44.

26. *Philosophie der Geschichte, Sämtliche Werke* 11:440–41.

27. *Philosophie der Geschichte, Sämtliche Werke* 11:441.

28. Cf. St. Athanasius, *De Incarnatione Verbi,* ed. J. P. Migne, *Patrologia Graeca,* 25 (Paris: Migne, 1857), section 3, Col. 102; *On the Incarnation,* trans, A. Robertson, in *Christology of the Later Fathers,* ed. E. R. Hardy and C. C. Richardson (Philadelphia: Westminster Press, 1954), 58. Also St. Augustine, *De Trinitate,* ed. J. P. Migne, *Patrologia Latina,* 42 (Paris: Garnier and Migne, 1841), Book 15, section 19–20, Col. 1083–88; *The Trinity,* trans. Edmund Hill, O.P., ed. J. E. Rotelle, O.S.A. (Brooklyn, N.Y.: New City Press), 409–10.

29. *Philosophie der Geschichte, Sämtliche Werke* 11:441–42; cf. O'Regan, *The Heterodox Hegel,* 265ff.

30. *Philosophie der Geschichte, Sämtliche Werke* 11:551.

31. *Philosophie der Geschichte, Sämtliche Werke* 11:552–54.

32. See G. W. F. Hegel, *Vorlesungen über die Philosophie der Religion,* ed. E. Moldenhauer and K. M. Michel, *Werke in zwanzig Bänden,* 20 vols. and Index (Frankfurt am Main: Suhrkamp Verlag, 1969ff.), 17:333–34; where his understanding of the Enlightenment appears deeper.

33. *Werke,* 14:131; *A,* 1:520.

34. *Werke,* 14:132–36; *A,* 1:521–24.

35. *Werke,* 14:141–42; *A,* 1:528.

36. *Werke,* 14:200; *A,* 1:578.

37. G. W. F. Hegel, *Grundlinien der Philosophie des Rechts,* ed. E. Moldenhauer and K. Michel, *Werke in zwanzig Bänden,* 20 vols. and Index (Frankfurt am Main: Suhrkamp Verlag, 1969ff), 7, sections 358–60; *Philosophy of Right,* trans. T. M. Knox (Oxford: Clarendon Press, 1952), 222–23.

38. *Philosophie der Religion, Werke* 17:298–99, emphasizes the transcendence of the Spirit, while it recognizes its role in creating the Christian community.

39. *Werke,* 15:414; *A,* 2:1109.

40. *Werke,* 13:242; *A,* 1:184.

41. *Werke,* 14:142; *A,* 1:529.

42. Bungay, *Beauty and Truth,* 83–84; Knox, translator's preface to *Aesthetics,* v.

43. *Werke,* 14:240; *A,* 1:609.

44. *Werke,* 14:242; *A,* 1:610.

45. *Werke,* 13:207–8; *A,* 1:157.

46. Plato, *Republic* 507b–9b, in *Dialogues of Plato,* 4 vols., trans. B. Jowett (Oxford: Clarendon Press, 1871), 2:341–44; Plotinus, *The Enneads,* trans. S. McKenna, ed. B. S. Page, 2nd ed. (London: Faber and Faber, 1956), I, 6, 56–64; F. W. J. Schelling, *Die Philosophie der Kunst,* ed. M. Schröter, *Werke* (Munich: C.H. Beck and R. Oldenbourg, 1959), 3:377ff.; *The Philosophy of Art,* trans. D. N. Stott (Minneapolis: University of Minnesota Press, 1989).

IV

Art as a Mode of Thought: Hegel's Aesthetics and the Origins of Modernism

Jere Surber

I. Introduction

If there is one principle that any sympathetic reader of Hegel might be expected to affirm, it is that every end is also a beginning. However, for reasons that would be complicated to explain, the preponderance of interpretations of Hegel's writings have tended to emphasize the senses in which his views represent an end or completion of the historical tradition in which they stand, at the expense of how they may contain the positive seeds of what has followed them. Nowhere has this tendency been more evident than in the case of Hegel's writings on aesthetics and the philosophy of art.

Consider three recent and, I think, representative examples. Stephen Bungay concludes his *Beauty and Truth: A Study of Hegel's Aesthetics* with the claim that Hegel has little to say about art that could be directly relevant to the various later "modernist" or "postmodernist" theories and practices. For Bungay, the real significance of Hegel's aesthetic writings lies in that fact that, "[i]f modern art is a negation of the tradition, we can begin to understand it by understanding what it is not";[1] it is Hegel's philosophy of art which he recommends as a starting-point for such negative understanding. William Desmond, in *Art and the Absolute,* adopts a rather different stance toward the significance of Hegel's aesthetic thought, while nonetheless sharing Bungay's basic interpretive assumption. According to Desmond, while "Hegel is open to the future as the ground of the renewed disclosure of the essential," what is most to be learned from Hegel for the present perspective is how "these monuments [of the "beautiful art" of the past, which Hegel discusses] can still offer back life to the living."[2] In recommending Hegel's philosophy (especially his reflections on art) as a potential source of contemporary renewal, the author points, here and elsewhere in the work, to a radical historical break with Hegel's "constructive effort to ground a new whole," a fissure which creates the current need for such "renewal." Again, Hegel's relation to many subsequent developments in art and aesthetics is seen as primarily oppositional or disjunctive, not as continuous or anticipatory. Finally, and much closer to the specific focus of the present essay, Brian Etter, in "The Sounds of the Ideal: Hegel's Aesthetic of Music," asserts that "[i]t should be Hegel who appears as a challenge to the self-understanding of the twentieth century." Most pointedly, he claims that what he calls the musical "avant-garde" is "nothing less than a rupture with everything that has gone before, the significance of which a proper understanding of traditional aesthetics helps us to comprehend."[3] Once again, Hegel's aesthetic thought is presented as a major compass-point by which to gauge the aesthetic chaos which allegedly followed him.

Before we rush to revive some version of Hegel's philosophical or aesthetic thought as an antidote to the (alleged) modernist abandonment of "philosophical wholeness" or the "aesthetic Ideal," we should also become clear about the degree to which Hegel's own writings laid the groundwork for and perhaps even inspired such developments. My aim here is not to deny that such views as those I have just cited are without merit so far as they go, but just that they present only one side of a question, both historically and philosophically complex, which deserves some counterweighting. In this essay, then, I want to present the other side of this issue: that Hegel's own treatment of aesthetic questions already harbors within it positive anticipations of the sort of later modernist developments that have often been held to represent a radical break with Hegel and the tradition preceding him.

Obviously, this would be a large undertaking if we were to consider the full range of Hegel's aesthetic thought. Here, I will limit myself to Hegel's treatment of musical aesthetics. I should note, however, that music, on the face of it, seems to offer a particularly relevant test case, in that it can, at least in some important ways, be regarded as the most remote among the traditionally recognized art forms from the sort of conceptual discursivity that characterizes Hegel's overall philosophical project. My point is that if, on Hegel's account, discursive or conceptual features turn out to play an essential role in his aesthetics of music, then they will be all the more determining for other art forms whose conceptual content is generally uncontested.

In the most general terms, my thesis can be stated in this way. *The most important historical result of Hegel's own treatment of art was to open the way for art to become regarded as a vehicle for raising what were previously treated as distinctly "philosophical" issues and as providing an important means for expressing specifically "philosophical" viewpoints.* Put in terms of the title of my essay, Hegel's own philosophy of art had the effect of sanctioning artistic production as itself a philosophically viable (if not entirely autonomous) mode of thought.

Within the narrower focus of this essay, the leading question will be, In what sense(s) can music serve as a form of philosophical expression? I will take it as obvious to anyone familiar with the closely intertwined writings and compositions of such modernist composers as Wagner, Debussy, Schoenberg, Messaien, Cage, and Stockhausen, as well as with such theorists as Weber, Bloch, and Adorno, that a good deal of the European classical tradition of music after Hegel has come to function in this way.[4] My question will concern what connection there might be between Hegel's aesthetics (especially of music) and these later avant-garde developments, a connection which most writers on Hegel, such as those cited above, would characterize as purely negative.

In order to develop this connection, I will (1) consider Hegel's systematic placement of art in relation to that of his immediate predecessors Kant and Schelling; (2) highlight the position that music occupies within Hegel's own philosophy of art; and (3) argue, by highlighting the linguistic backdrop of Hegel's aesthetic reflections, that there is a more discursive or conceptualist, hence modernist, strand in his musical aesthetics than is usually recognized by prevailing expressivist interpretations.

Two preliminary notes. The first concerns the way in which I will be using the term "modernism." While the authors I have cited above tend, correctly I think, to associate modernism with the repudiation of traditional forms of artistic creation, it is important to recognize an equally important modernist characteristic: modernism rarely appears as mere iconoclasm without comment. Most of the major modernist figures—Schoenberg, Cage, Mann, Eliot, Joyce, Pound, Proust, Kandinsky, Malevitch, Ernst, Duchamp, Brecht, Artaud—were obsessive theorizers, whether this took place in texts separate from their artworks or within the works themselves (indeed, usually both). To be iconoclastic in a modernist sense presupposed both a theoretical characterization of the tradition to be overturned, as well as a theoretical account of exactly how that was to be accomplished within a particular creative praxis.[5] I want, therefore, to suggest that the alleged iconoclasm of modernism is, to a great extent, the result of the erasure of the traditional distinction between art and philosophy, which was already well under way in Hegel's aesthetic writings. Second, while I grant to those who read Hegel as an antimodernist that Hegel's own artistic preferences, as revealed in the discussions of specific works of art scattered through his aesthetic writings, are usually staunchly traditionalist, I want to claim that, despite this, his general philosophical approach to aesthetics, together with many of its basic operating assumptions, point clearly in modernist directions. Indeed, that Hegel the systematic philosopher could adopt the stance of practical art critic as part of his systematic project was itself a modernist gesture and one unprecedented within the scope of modern philosophy before Hegel. To see that this is so, let us now turn to his immediate predecessors.

II. The Systematic Place of Aesthetics: Kant, Schelling, Hegel

It is well documented that, whatever uncertainties Kant may have had specifying the relation of the *Critique of Judgement* to the other two *Critiques,* he remained firm on one point: that neither aesthetics nor the teleological consideration of nature had a rightful place in his final vision of a "critical metaphysics." Since, on his view, both were based upon "subjective grounds," the former on "reflective judgments of taste," the latter upon regulative ideas, they had no place in a "system of metaphysics," the exclusive concern of which was elaborating the "objective principles" of the essentially "rational" realms of nature and morals. Indeed, Kant's entire approach to art and teleology was based upon the analysis of their distinctive sorts of judgment, and dealt with concrete artworks or organic configurations only as ancillary to or illustrative for this project.[6]

In so proceeding with regard to the realm of art, Kant was reflecting the prevalent ideas of his Enlightenment milieu. While the realm of art did offer to the philosopher a challenging and not insignificant set of problems, neither Kant nor most of his contemporaries (with a few important exceptions of such "proto-romantic" thinkers as Rousseau, Diderot, Herder, and Goethe) would have suggested either that the philosopher had anything significant to learn from the artist that she or he could not discover by philosophy's own rational devices, or that the creative artist would somehow benefit from any detailed acquaintance with the doctrines of the philosopher. I do not want to claim, of course, that, from a practical perspective, there were no points of contact or contiguity between philosophical reflection and artistic activity, only that the two were regarded as concerned with different spheres of activity which had no *essential* relation to one another.

With the "Earliest System Fragment" of 1796/7 (?), in which both Schelling and Hegel, along with Hölderlin, probably had some hand, the elevation of art and aesthetic reflection within the sphere of systematic philosophical concerns dramatically emerged.[7] By 1800, the year of the appearance of Schelling's *System of Transcendental Idealism,* not only the ideal realm of art, but the real or concrete artwork itself, had come to be posited, not just at the apex of philosophical systematics but as *transcending* it and, in important ways, autonomous of it. Already in this work, the central principle of philosophy was "*identity,*" the unity of the ideal and the real or of consciousness and nature, but it was precisely (and paradoxically) this which could not be attained within philosophical reflection itself, which always proceeded by a construction which necessarily presupposed a positing of its object as nonidentical to the reflective process directed toward it. As Schelling clearly stated the point, "What the philosopher has thus separated already in the first act of consciousness is reflected back through the miracle of art out of its own products, even though this is inaccessible to any (philosophical) intuition."[8] A few lines later, Schelling concludes, "Art is therefore that which is ultimate for philosophy" (my translations).

We should note, however, that Schelling does not mean to claim either that philosophy is capable of articulating the truth of art (since its very truth lies in its identity which is in principle inaccessible to philosophical reflection) nor that the truth of art is in any way enhanced or completed by philosophical reflection (since he equates the identity presented in the work of art as absolute and hence autonomous). For Schelling, the essential feature of art is its identity, rendering it essentially nondiscursive, just as that of philosophy is separation or objectification, which provides precisely the opening for its own characteristic discourse. Of course, Schelling does want to claim that philosophy (especially the philosophy of nature as he develops it) and art are complementary within the ambit of a systematic perspective, but this complementarity never amounts to a blurring of the essential differences between the two realms. As a concrete presentation of the absolute identity inaccessible to philosophy, the work of art stands as the ultimate limit of philosophical discourse. It can, as well, instruct the philosopher about her or his own starting-point in intellectual intuition, but this is a general point which has nothing to do with any concrete content which the work of art might otherwise have to offer. Such, for Schelling, would be mere *Erscheinung* or appearance, which, while not inaccessible to philosophical articulation, would be irrelevant to the genuine significance of the artwork itself as the *Darstellung* or presentation of the absolute identity.[9] One hardly needs to mention that such a view resonated widely, if not entirely uncritically, among the first generation of the German romantics, who shared an idealized notion of art together with a distrust of language when used in any exclusively discursive manner.

Hegel, for his part, soon introduced three crucial transformations of Schelling's systematic treatment of art. First, in the various versions of the *Jenaer Realphilosophie* (dating from around 1804–6), Hegel comes to include art, together with religion and philosophy, as a more or less distinct element in an expanded notion of the ultimate level of systematic thought.[10] Second, about the same time he relegates art to a place systematically preceding the spheres of religion and philosophy (though he sometimes tended to blur art and religion together in regarding Greek religion as itself aesthetic.) Finally, in the *Phenomenology of Spirit* (1807), he came to refer to this entire moment, including art, religion, and philosophy, as Absolute Spirit, and continued to do so throughout his later writings.[11]

These transformations of Schelling's systematic treatment of art naturally had the most far-ranging consequences for understanding the relation between art and philosophy. My argument is that we can locate, at this very point, the continuous strand of Hegel's thought which ultimately leads in the direction of post-Hegelian modernist and postmodernist stances. First, Hegel's transformations here, long before the refinements of the Berlin system and the many examples introduced in the closely related *Lectures on Aesthetics,* entailed that the spheres of art and philosophy would henceforth be connected in significant and essential ways. Art, viewed as a necessary systematic presupposition of philosophy, could and, in principle, must have immediate significance for philosophy, not just ideally and formally but historically and materially. Second, however, there could be nothing essential in art which, in principle, defied philosophical, that is, discursive articulation (this, of course, *contra* the romantics). Rather than appearing as the philosophically inaccessible locus of an absolute identity, Hegel came to view art as *sharing* with philosophy and religion an identical absolute content. It was the forms in which this content was expressed that constituted the *differentiae* of these three realms. In particular, since art and philosophy were expressing the same truth or absolute content in different ways, there was no reason in principle why any philosophical view could not have some (even if not entirely formally adequate) corresponding artistic representation, nor why any artwork could not be interpreted as having philosophical import (even if other of its nonessential elements might be disregarded in the process). Finally, in nonetheless maintaining the ultimate precedence of the philosophical/discursive over the aesthetic form of expression, Hegel ultimately endorsed the ascendancy of philosophical over aesthetic concerns: henceforth, art could no longer be viewed as an autonomous sphere, but as necessarily and essentially philosophical (and therefore, one might also add, potentially political) in import.

I would also observe that these features of the relation between art and philosophy would later become operative assumptions and even hallmarks of modernist and even postmodernist aesthetics, as it attempted to eradicate the boundaries between artistic practice and philosophical (or political) theory. The point, then, is that, whoever else one might want to invoke here, Hegel, at least in his overall approach to art, would not appear to be a very congenial sponsor of countermovements to modernist or postmodernist stances.

III. The Place of Music in Hegel's Aesthetic Thought

Hegel's transformation of the place of art within the context of systematic philosophy was accompanied by a dramatic reassessment of the role of music among the other recognized art forms, a revision that, on its face, would seem to be directly contrary to his systematic convictions. Indeed, the de facto elevation of the status of music in Hegel's aesthetics was the single most conspicuous and dramatic alteration in the schema of art forms which one finds in Kant and Schelling.

In his *Critique of Judgment,* Kant was straightforward in claiming that music was a "mere play of sensations," possessing only a minimal degree of rational content, and hence relegating it to the very lowest place among the arts.[12] Schelling's view of music was somewhat ambiguous. On the systematic grounds we have already considered, he naturally viewed music, as a form of art, as superordinate to philosophy, at least with respect to its ability to present absolute identity. However, on the one hand, he, like Kant, continued to regard music as the lowest or least developed of the art forms, while, on the other, he argued that all the other art forms are developed out of the basic features first and most purely presented in music.[13]

Hegel followed the lead of neither Kant nor Schelling on this, and the underlying reasons for the dramatic shift in his assessment of the place of music among the art forms proves to be very instructive. In his Jena lectures of 1805/6, Hegel, like Schelling, is more concerned with the systematic place of art in a general sense and resists any hierarchization of the various art forms. It suffices for him to note that the art forms fall on a sort of continuum, where music forms one extreme, which he calls "formless movement" (*gestaltlose Bewegung*), while the plastic arts constitute the other, which he refers to as "the abiding presentation of the divine" (*die ruhende Darstellung des Göttlichen*).[14] However, by the time of the Berlin system and the associated *Lectures on Aesthetics,* Hegel had developed a definite schema of systematic ordering among the various art forms.

His intervening discovery (beginning with his work on the *Phenomenology of Spirit*) of the importance of historical concerns for his later system-construction clearly played a decisive role in his thinking about such issues, and this in itself is significant in the present context. Whereas Kant and Schelling (at least in his Jena writings) had considered the various art forms almost entirely ahistorically, concentrating solely on their essential forms or ontological presuppositions, Hegel's later approach to aesthetics unfolded as an interplay among historical developments, art forms taken to be characteristic of given historical or cultural epochs, and formal considerations of the art forms themselves. This mixed mode of aesthetic discourse, involving an indissoluble interplay of historical, cultural, and formal concerns in the consideration of art, is at least as much anticipatory of typical modernist views as it is continuous with more traditional stances.[15]

All readers of Hegel's lectures on aesthetics will be aware that, on his schema for the art forms, architecture turns out to be the least developed among them and is associated, at least in a general way, with the oriental or pre-Greek world; sculpture, as the principal form of representation of the "Classical Ideal," comes next; and painting, music, and poetry (broadly conceived), in that order, are grouped together as the art forms most characteristic of the Christian, but more specifically modern "Romantic world." (In his lectures on aesthetics, Hegel uses the term "romantic" in a sense much broader than it is normally employed today.)

First, we should observe that, for Hegel, what most sets modern art forms apart from preclassical architecture and classical sculpture is the fact that the former's fundamental principle is *subjectivity*. By way of clarification, Hegel writes

> What we understand here by subjectivity is the notion of an intelligence which ideally exists in free independence, withdrawing itself from objective reality into its own more intimate domain, a conscious

> life which no longer concentrates itself with its corporeal attachment in a unity which is without division.[16]

His characterization of the relations of painting, music, and poetry to subjectivity can be summarized in this way. Painting, while remaining a spatial and external medium, though one reduced to two dimensions, begins the process of the detachment from the "tranquillity and all-inclusive rondure" of sculpture by deemphasizing the objectivity of the artwork in favor of the perceptual interpretation and choice of material of the artist. A painting, that is, is clearly a representation of something subjective in a way in which sculpture (at least in its self-sufficient classical manifestation) is not. Music, viewed as tone in Hegel's synoptic account, represents a complete withdrawal from spatiality into the inner temporal realm of subjectivity. Finally, poetry, or the art of speech as Hegel refers to it, signals the reemergence from the inner subjectivity of music into the objective realm of human communication, expressing the innermost recesses of subjectivity in a lingustically accessible, fully intersubjective form. Thus, in the same passage where he refers to poetry as "the universal art," Hegel writes

> It is at this point that *poetry,* or the art of speech, confronts us, which now incorporates its art-productions in the medium of a speech elaborated to an instrument of artistic service, precisely as intelligence already in ordinary speech makes intelligible to spiritual life all that it carries in itself.[17]

Clearly, if one wanted to make a case for Hegel's "logocentrism," as Bungay does, this reference to the relation of ordinary language, poetry as the universal art, and (implicitly) its kinship with the "discursive medium" of philosophy would make a good beginning.

Given Hegel's general characterization of the modern arts, the question now arises concerning the degree to which Hegel regarded music as sharing in the discursivity which is so essential to his notion of subjectivity. Certainly the fact that he sees the essential character of music to lie in its temporality would not, of itself, exclude a conceptual element from it, since he often refers to even logical or philosophical thought as essentially a *Bewegung* and, in the section on language in the *Encyclopedia,* presents the temporal aspect of language as a crucial element in the process of its development toward a fully conceptual medium.[18] What evidence, then, can be found for Hegel attributing to music a similar unity of the inner temporality of subjectivity and conceptual discursivity? We must, of course, tread carefully, since Hegel does say that the content of music lacks "the objectivity of intellectual ideas and images,"[19] but we will later see some important qualifications under which this statement must be taken.

Several points here are worth considering.

1. First, and very unlike Kant, Hegel claims, in his comparison of music and architecture, that "we find operative in music not merely the profoundest ideality and soul, but the most rigorous rationality."[20] Music, on Hegel's view, cannot be adequately viewed as some "mere play of sensations"; rather, its determining feature is precisely the rational rigor of the laws of tone, only under which conditions it is then able to serve as "the direct expression of soul-life."[21]

2. Hegel's treatment of the relation between "purely musical value" or "tone" (as he usually expresses this) and texts set to music is complicated and not always consistent. Relevant passages to support any one of (at least) three seemingly inconsistent views can be cited.[22] On the first view, the pure experience of tone, regarded as the determining and essential constituent of music, can be undermined or spoiled by an accompanying text: "[A]s a general rule in this association of music and poetry the preponderance of one art is injurious to the other."[23] Second, there are those often remarked passages where Hegel manifests a distinct dislike for "purely instrumental music." For example, he writes, "In recent times, especially, the art of music, by its wresting itself from all content that is independently lucid, has withdrawn into the depths of its own medium. But on this very account and to this extent it has lost its compelling power over the soul."[24] Finally, he often points to the possibility of an "ideal balance" between the "language of music" and the "language of the text."

> Music in short is not primarily concerned with the bare form of the inward soul, but with that innermost life as replenished, the specific content of which is most closely related to the particular character of the emotion roused, so that the mode of the expression will, or should, inevitably assert itself with essential differences according to the varied nature of the content. . . . Now what we mean by the detail of the content is just that which is supplied by the *libretto* or words.[25]

What, then, are we to make of this? I would suggest that, in his uncertain and ultimately unresolved, though very extensive, treatment of the relation between "tone" and "text," Hegel is opening a question that comes to occupy a central place in virtually all modernist musical aesthetics: the problematic nature of the connection between music and thought, where music has already become assimilated to a linguistic model. Examples are abundant, from Mahler's extraction of symphonic material out of previously composed song-cycles, to Wagner's paralleling of prewritten text with elaborate accompaniment involving complexly interrelated *Leitmotiven,* to Schoenberg's experiments with *Sprechstimme* techniques (to cite only several of the best-known examples.)

3. That even the most formal aspects of music have philosophical import can be seen in a little-cited passage where Hegel, in discussing some

technical points of harmony (a technical field if ever there was one!), refers to his own *Logic* as the basis for his elucidations. In a very suggestive passage indeed he writes

> For the true Concept is indeed unity in itself (like the musical triadic chord); but [it is] unity which is not only immediate, but also essentially split apart in itself and collapsed into oppositions (such as the case of the diminished and augmented seventh tone when added to a triad). Accordingly I have, for example in my Logic, developed the concept as subjectivity, but this subjectivity, as ideal transparent unity, is sublated [*hebt sich auf*] into that which is opposed to it, that is, objectivity.[26]

What such a passage should remind us, of course, is that Hegel's entire discussion of music not only rests upon foundations drawn from the realm of logic and philosophy, but that music's own resources provide the means for conveying, even without being joined to explicit texts, his most profound philosophical convictions. Again, I would argue that this is a distinctly modernist notion and one that is entirely absent from the traditions of both musical practice and musical aesthetics prior to Hegel.

IV. Hegel's Aesthetics of Music: "Emotive Expressionism" or a "Linguistic Model"?

The first generation of German romantics, in a way closely paralleling Schelling's approach, developed a view of music which might be called "emotive expressionism." Wilhelm Heinrich Wackenroder, in a series of essays appended to his *Fantasies Concerning Art for Friends of Art* (1799) and attributed to the fictional musician Joseph Berglinger, presents a classic statement of this widely-held view, which, if indeed shared by Hegel, would challenge my interpretation of Hegel's musical aesthetics.[27] Its basic attitude is well expressed in the words of Berglinger

> But why do I, foolish one, strive to melt words into tones? It is never as I feel it. Come, Thou musical strains, draw near and rescue me from this painful earthly striving for words, envelop me in Thy shining clouds with Thy thousandfold beams, and raise me up into the old embrace of all-loving heaven.

Underlying this radical dissociation of tones and words, music and discourse, are the typically romantic convictions that the most fundamental stratum of human experience is that of feeling and emotion and that this sphere resists any adequate expression or description in discursive terms. Berglinger writes

> Whoever wants to discover with the divining-rod of the investigating intellect that which can only be felt from within will perpetually discover only thoughts about emotion and not emotion itself. An eternally hostile chasm is entrenched between the feeling heart and the investigations of research, and the former is an independent, tightly sealed, divine entity, which cannot be unlocked and opened up by the reason.

For Berglinger, music is privileged among the arts as that mode of expression most adequate to expressing and communicating all those shades, nuances, and movements of emotion that defy rational discourse. It is also instructive to note that, quite unlike Hegel, Berglinger is enthusiastic about "the latest, highest triumph of musical instruments: I mean those divine, magnificent symphonic pieces . . . in which not one individual emotion is portrayed, but an entire world, an entire drama of human emotions, is poured forth."

While Hegel is by no means insensitive to some of the important connections between music and emotion, these constitute only one aspect of his musical aesthetics and certainly not one which he chooses to dwell upon. The fundamental reason for this is that Hegel no longer shares the fundamental assumption of the early romantics that the subjective sphere of the emotions constitutes some unmediated, nondiscursive stratum of experience. For Hegel, the modern notion of subjectivity is already fully mediated by language, so that whatever "emotive content" it is that music might express nonetheless falls within the ambit of discursive articulation or intelligibility.

> To make this essentially veiled life and inweaved motion ring forth through the independent texture of tones, or attach itself to expressed words and ideas, and to steep such ideas in this very medium, in order to re-emphasize anew the same for feeling and sympathy, such is the difficult task assigned to music.[28]

In particular, rather than emphasizing some unique way in which music gives expression to a stratum of experience which must otherwise remain internal, mute, and inaccessible, Hegel stresses that the sphere of subjectivity—which *already* exists in the realm of *der Begriff* or *Geist* become self-conscious—is also *temporal* and that music is preeminently suited to highlight precisely this *aspect* of subjectivity rather than some more determinate yet inarticulable ensemble of feelings.

The basic model upon which Hegel relies in his musical aesthetics (as well, I would argue, as elsewhere) is to be found in his theory of the crucial role of language in the formation of consciousness. Already in his Jena system, Hegel devoted an extended discussion to language, in which he noted, "Imagination is only empty, form-giving, signifying, positing form as something inward, but language is that which is inward as existing, as a positing power. This then is the true being of Spirit as Spirit in general."[29]

He goes on to point out that *das Ich* or an integrated self is first possible only through the development of the linguistic resources in which it can be articulated and that, consequently, there can be no *Geist* (absolute or otherwise) without the mediation of language. In the Berlin *Encyclopedia,* Hegel refines this analysis by arguing, in the section entitled Psychology (again well prior to his discussion of art in the section on Absolute Spirit), that it is "the vocal note [*Ton*] where the inward idea manifests itself in adequate utterance." He continues

> The vocal note which receives further articulation to express specific ideas—speech and, its system, language—gives to sensations, intuitions, conceptions, a second and higher existence than they naturally possess—invests them with the right of existence in the ideational realm.[30]

In the same section, he also credits language with first mediating the spatial existence of "exteriority" and the temporal existence of "interiority," thus making possible thinking and its more "concrete" concepts.

What is crucial to bear in mind in considering Hegel's aesthetics, and more specifically that of music, is that, systematically viewed, the realm of fine art appears only within a context already fully mediated by language. For example, to apprehend a sequence of sounds as purely musical already implies a distinction with a fullness of linguistic expression already available and in place. A similar point could be made with respect to the other art forms that Hegel discusses. Put more generally, then, the various art forms exist only as abstracted moments of a totality of experience which is already linguistically mediated, fully discursive, and amenable to conceptual analysis. Thus, when Hegel considers music from a linguistic viewpoint, he should not be taken to imply that music somehow constitutes a mode of expression alternative to and autonomous of ordinary discourse or its philosophical development, as many early romantics did; rather, he means, I think, that it is appropriate to view music linguistically because it shares in, while highlighting one more abstract moment of, the intrinsic linguisticality of Absolute Spirit itself.

V. Conclusion

Against those more prevalent interpretations of Hegel's aesthetics, which have tried to discover there a *summa* of the tradition, especially in its expressionist guises, and thus a bulwark against later modernist and postmodernist tendencies which have allegedly severed the intimate connection between art and human experience, I want to oppose another way of regarding Hegel's philosophy of art. If read within its systematic context, one must conclude, I think, that Hegel's aesthetics provided the first fully developed modernist theory of art, particularly in the sense of blurring the boundary between artistic practice and philosophical theory. After Hegel, as the history of the various art forms clearly testifies, not only is it possible for art to begin to function as a medium in which decidedly philosophical views can be articulated, but reflection upon both the formal issues as well as the determinate content provided by the arts begins to be a major and often decisive concern of the philosopher. Whether one looks for examples of modernist attitudes to the tone rows of Schoenberg, the cubist experiments of Picasso and Braque, the found objects of Duchamp, or the stream of consciousness techniques of Joyce or Proust, one sees artistic practices that are inseparable from their philosophical import. True, they may not strike us as expressive of human emotion or as relevant to the sort of truth assumed by the tradition, but they are nonetheless children, if not very beautiful ones, of Hegel's aesthetics, which taught us to approach art always as a complex interplay of formal, historical, and conceptual dimensions, not as some pristine, privileged, or autonomous realm of its own. To give Hegel the final, as well as the first, word, "For this reason the work of art, in which thought divests itself of itself, belongs to the realm of comprehending thought; and mind, by subjecting it to scientific contemplation, thereby simply satisfies its most essential nature.[31]

Notes

1. Stephen Bungay, *Beauty and Truth: A Study of Hegel's Aesthetics* (Oxford: Clarendon Press, 1984), 192.

2. William Desmond, *Art and the Absolute: A Study of Hegel's Aesthetics* (Albany: SUNY Press, 1986), 164.

3. Brian K. Etter, "The Sounds of the Ideal: Hegel's Aesthetic of Music," *The Owl of Minerva* 26 (Fall 1994). See, especially, 58.

4. For illuminating discussions of these various theorizing tendencies connected with the development of modern music, see Edward Lippman, *A History of Western Musical Aesthetics* (Lincoln: University of Nebraska Press, 1992). Sections 4 and 5 are especially relevant to my argument.

5. Michael Phillipson presents an extremely interesting and trenchant statement of this view of modernism in his *Painting, Language, and Modernity* (London: Routledge and Kegan Paul, 1985). Cf. 45 for an especially pointed formulation of this issue.

6. The Introduction to Kant's *Critique of Judgement* presents his full account of this matter. Cf. I. Kant, *Kritik der Urteilskraft,* 5 (Königlich Preussische Akademie der Wissenschaften, Berlin: De Gruyter, 1902–), 171–99.

7. A readily available translation of this much-discussed document can be found in H. S. Harris, *Hegel's Development: Toward the Sunlight, 1770–1801* (Oxford: The

Clarendon Press, 1972), 510–12. On 249ff., Harris discusses its *Entstehungsgeschichte,* reviews the various positions taken with regard to it, and offers his own conclusions as to its authorship.

8. F. W. J. Schelling, *System des tranzendentalen Idealismus* (Hamburg: Felix Meiner Verlag, 1957), 295, my translation. The section in which this occurs presents the full argument which I have summarized here.

9. Cf. Schelling, *System,* "Sechster Hauptabschnitt" (281–303), for his discussion of the relations among nature, art, and systematic philosophy.

10. Cf. G. W. F. Hegel, *Jenaer Realphilosophie* (Hamburg: Felix Meiner Verlag, 1969), 263ff.

11. G. W. F. Hegel, *Phänomenologie des Geistes, Werke in zwanzig Bänden,* ed. E. Moldenhauer and K. M. Michel, 20 vols. and index, (Frankfurt am Main: Suhrkamp Verlag, 1969ff), 3:512ff. Cf. also, in the same edition, *Enzyklopädie der philosophischen Wissenschaften im Grundrisse,* III, (1830), 10, section 553ff.

12. For Kant's "division" and "ranking" of the arts, see *Kritik der Urteilskraft,* section 51. Kant's treatment of music can be found at 324–25.

13. Schelling's early discussion of the particular art forms exists in the form of handwritten manuscripts which served as the basis for lectures given at Jena in the winter of 1802/3 and repeated at Würzburg in 1804/5. Cf. *Schellings Werke,* ed. Manfred Schroeter, Supp. 3 (München: C. H. Beck Verlag, 1968), 139–56.

14. Hegel, *Jenaer Realphilosophie,* 264

15. Hegel provides the rationale for and an overview of his manner of approaching aesthetic issues in the introduction to his *Lectures on Aesthetics.* G. W. F. Hegel, *Vorlesungen über die Ästhetik, Werke in zwanzig Bänden,* ed. E Moldenhauer and K. M. Michel, 20 vols. and index (Frankfurt am Main: Suhrkamp Verlag 1969ff), 13:13ff. English translation, G. W. F. Hegel, *Aesthetics: Lectures on Fine Art,* trans., T. M. Knox, 2 vols. (Oxford: Clarendon Press, 1975), as well as by F. B. Osmaston, *The Philosophy of Fine Art* (London: G. Bell and Sons, 1920). In general, I have preferred the latter since it seems to me a bit more "elegant" (if not always as accurate), reflecting Hegel's own style in his lectures (as opposed to his strictly written texts). Further references will be given in the form: *Werke,* 15:11; Osmaston, 3:217.

16. *Werke,* 15:11; Osmaston, 3:217. This passage occurs in the opening paragraph of Hegel's introduction to the "Romantic Arts," which forms the basis for the ensuing discussion in the present essay.

17. *Werke,* 15:16; Osmaston, 3:222.

18. *Enzyklopädie der philosophischen Wissenschaften,* III, *Werke,* 10, section 458ff.

19. *Werke,* 15:136; Osmaston, 3:344.

20. *Werke,* 15:139; Osmaston, 3:346.

21. *Werke,* 15:139; Osmaston, 3:347.

22. Hegel tends to return to the question of the relation between tone and language throughout his discussion of music. The lengthy section entitled "Music as Accompaniment" is specifically dedicated to this issue. See *Werke,* 15:195ff.; Osmaston, 3:403 ff.

23. *Werke,* 15:147; Osmaston, 3:355.

24. *Werke,* 15:145; Osmaston, 3:353–54.

25. *Werke,* 15:200; Osmaston, 3:408–9.

26. My translation. This very suggestive discussion, deserving of further attention, occurs at *Werke,* 15:183.

27. A detailed discussion, together with the passages cited below, of Wackenroder's romantic, "expressivist" musical aesthetics can be found in Lippman, *A History of Western Musical Aesthetics,* 203ff. Lippman quotes the translation of the texts by M. H. Schubert in *W. H. Wackenroder: "Confessions" and "Fantasies"* (University Park, Pa.: Pennsylvania State University Press, 1971).

28. *Werke,* 15:149; Osmaston, 3:358.

29. *Jenaer Realphilosophie,* 183, my translation.

30. *Enzyzklopädie der philosophischen Wissenschaften* III, *Werke* 10, section 459. The translation cited is that of William Wallace in *Hegel's Philosophy of Mind: Part Three of the Encyclopedia of the Philosophical Sciences* (1830) (Oxford: Clarendon Press, 1971), 214.

31. *Werke,* 1:28; Osmaston, 1:16.

V

Presidential Address: Hegel and the Art of Painting

Stephen Houlgate

I. Introduction

Svetlana Alpers makes one approving reference to Hegel's account of Dutch painting in *The Art of Describing*, but there is nothing whatsoever on Hegel in Kenneth Clark's *The Nude*, Ernst Gombrich's *The Story of Art*, or Marcia Hall's *Color and Meaning*, even though Hegel has significant things to say on the depiction of the human body, the history of art, and the use of color in painting.[1] It appears that, with rare exceptions, art historians and art theorists do not regard Hegel anything like as highly as do theorists of tragedy, and that most indeed feel quite justified in ignoring him altogether.

I would like to suggest, however, that Hegel in fact offers one of the most profound philosophical meditations on the nature of painting we have. It is true that, with the possible exception of his astute analysis of Raphael's *Transfiguration* (which he never actually saw at first hand), Hegel does not offer an interpretation of any individual painting to compare with the influential readings he gives of *Antigone, Oedipus Rex,* or *Hamlet.*[2] Yet, what he does provide is a subtle account of the nature of painting *as such.* It is this philosophical account—not just historically contingent prejudice—that leads Hegel to esteem so highly the paintings of the Italian Renaissance and of the Dutch seventeenth century. Furthermore, Hegel's account seems to me to provide an important way of understanding—and of criticizing—certain developments that have taken place in painting since his death. For it suggests that during the last one hundred and fifty years painting has increasingly lost sight of its distinctive nature and function.

Before we look at Hegel's account of painting, however, a few words need to be said regarding the various sources on which he drew and his direct personal experience of works of art. Hegel was clearly very knowledgeable about the theory, practice, and history of painting. In Jena he engaged closely with Schelling's philosophy of art, and his attention was drawn by A. W. Schlegel's lectures to Goethe's translation of, and commentary on, Diderot's

Essais sur la peinture.[3] He also knew well the aesthetic writings of Winckelmann and Lessing, as well as Karl Friedrich von Rumohr's *Italienische Forschungen.*[4]

Hegel also counted painters, collectors, and art historians amongst his personal friends. Among his students at Heidelberg, for example, was Gustav Friedrich Waagen who went on to publish a book on the brothers van Eyck in 1822 which Hegel had in his library; and one of his closest colleagues in Berlin was the art historian Aloys Hirt, whom Hegel describes as "one of the greatest genuine connoisseurs in our time."[5] Hegel played whist with the painter Johann Rösel in Berlin and enjoyed the company of other painters, such as Christian Xeller and Johann Jakob Schlesinger.[6] Schlesinger's former employer in Heidelberg, Sulpiz Boisserée, was also a friend of Hegel—even if their relationship was at times strained—and Hegel knew Boisserée's collection of Old German and Old Netherlandish masters well.[7]

We should thus remember that Hegel did not develop his understanding of painting in a vacuum. For much of his working life Hegel was in contact with people who knew about the practice of painting and restoring, about collecting paintings, and about the history of painting. He readily admitted that he was by no means a specialized *Kunstkenner;* but, unlike Kant, he clearly brought to the study of art an eye that was both schooled in, and sensitive to, the subtleties of painting.

Also in marked contrast to Kant, Hegel traveled widely to see as many paintings firsthand as he could—usually in great discomfort and without the company of his dear wife. He never visited Greece or Italy, and so had to rely solely on reproductions (and reports) for his knowledge of Greek and Roman paintings and of such works as Leonardo's *Last Supper* and Raphael's *School of Athens.*[8] But he was able to visit Munich, Dresden, Cologne, Paris, Vienna, and the Low Countries, and to experience a great many of the finest paintings in the world "in the flesh," including (in Dresden) Raphael's *Sistine Madonna* and Correggio's *Holy Night,* (in Cologne) Stephan Lochner's *Dombild,* (in Ghent) the central panel of the van Eyck altarpiece, (in Amsterdam) Rembrandt's *Night Watch,* and (in Paris) "famous items by the noblest masters one has seen a hundred times in copper engravings: Raphael, Correggio, Leonardo da Vinci, Titian."[9]

Hegel also had access to major paintings in Berlin itself. The new museum was not formally opened until August 3, 1830, but for a long time prior to that Hegel was able to visit the Royal collections, as well as the Solly collection.[10] It is clear, therefore, that his philosophical account of painting is thoroughly mediated by extensive and informed experience of individual works of art.

II. Hegel's Theory of Painting

It needs to be noted at the outset that what Hegel provides is not a philosophical account of the simple, material activity of applying paint to a surface, but a philosophical account of the *art* of painting.

Handicraft, for Hegel, is simply the activity of making something, of fashioning a new object out of materials supplied by nature. Artistic activity, on the other hand, is the specific kind of making that produces not just an object of utility or decoration, but an object in and through which we become *conscious* of what we truly are—both as human beings as such and as members of particular historical societies. "The universal need for art," Hegel says, is "man's rational need to raise the inner and outer world to spiritual consciousness as an object in which he recognizes again his own self."[11] For Hegel, therefore, the purpose of the artwork is to bring before us what it is to be a truly *human* being, that is to say, what it is to exhibit freedom, reason, spirit, and vitality in different historical ways.

In art the true nature of human life is disclosed not by means of pure concepts (as in philosophy), nor within the inwardness of feeling and faith (as in religion), but by means of sensuously intuited materials and phenomena, such as stone, wood, sound, and colored pigment. When such natural materials and phenomena are worked by the artist into the presentation of human freedom and vitality, what results is *beauty*. Beauty is thus not something ethereal or other-worldly; it is actual stone, wood, colored pigment, or sound worked in such a way that we can see our own life, freedom, and spirit expressed in it. As Hegel puts it in his 1820–21 lectures, "the connection between the beautiful and ourselves is that we catch sight of our own essence in the beautiful."[12]

Architecture, for Hegel, is the art in which we are least able to see our own spirit expressed, since the material it employs is too massive and the forms with which it endows its material—symmetry and regularity—are too abstract and formal.[13] Nevertheless, in the balance and harmony of the Greek temple or in the soaring pillars and intricate tracery of the Gothic cathedral, we can clearly see human spirituality *symbolized*. In sculpture we can much more obviously find our own spirit expressed, because in the sculpted figures of idealized men and women we can see human freedom and spirituality given recognizable *bodily* form. The sculptor is thus able to imbue stone and wood with much more living humanity than is the architect. However, there are limits, in Hegel's view, to the degree of humanity the sculptor can invest in his works. This is precisely because the sculptor gives three-dimensional *shape* to human freedom and so only lets us encounter human freedom as a material, *bodily* presence.[14] Sculpture thus does not let us encounter human freedom as that which has withdrawn *out of* the sphere of material embodiment into its own inwardness. "A person's own subjective inwardness," Hegel says, is "not revealed in the sightless figure [of the sculpture], nor can such a figure convey a concentrated expression of the inner life." Sculpture thus cannot bring into view all that it means to be truly human; it is "not anthropomorphic enough." This, Hegel notes, "is the reason why the sculptures of antiquity leave us somewhat cold."[15]

But human beings, especially in the modern, Christian world, need to find their subjective inwardness fully expressed in art. "Reflection into self, this subjectivity for itself, is the higher principle," Hegel says, "and must be presented." Only thus can art achieve "completed anthropomorphism" and so allow us truly to "catch sight of our own essence in the beautiful."[16] The art in which such inner subjectivity first finds adequate expression, for Hegel, is the art of painting. Painting is necessary, therefore, because, rather than submerging human subjectivity in material corporeality, it is able to render subjectivity sensuously intuitable in a way that lets our immaterial inwardness as such shine through.

If painting is to give concrete sensuous expression to subjectivity, it must not fall back into the abstract forms that characterize architecture, but must build on the achievement of sculpture and give subjectivity visible *human* form. Furthermore, it must set the human figures and faces it presents in a recognizable space in which concrete human beings could indeed be seen. Yet such human figures must not have the material solidity of a statue, and the space they occupy must not be the real, three-dimensional space of nature, because, as we have seen, material embodiment in real space fails to let inner subjectivity as such come into view. Painting must thus present human subjectivity in a space that is concretely visible, but that has been deliberately and artificially produced or "posited" by subjectivity itself for the purpose of its own self-expression. Such space, which is concretely visible, yet which is not the real space of nature but rather one created by the free activity of Spirit itself, can thus only be the space that is made to *appear* three-dimensional on a two-dimensional surface: the space of visual *illusion* or *Schein*.[17]

A sculpture always confronts us with the presence of a material body, however beautiful, idealized, and spiritualized that body might be. A painting, on the other hand, replaces the solidity and materiality of sculpture with the *Schein* of natural space, and so explicitly dissolves the idea that what we behold is irreducibly material. A painting thus opens the way for us to regard what we see not just as material presence, but as the manifestation of what is immaterial and inward, as the "shining forth" (*herausscheinen*) of the human spirit.[18] Indeed, painting does not just allow us to interpret what we see as the manifestation of Spirit, it actually encourages us to do so: because it presents a space that has not just been remodeled by human activity, but that has been wholly created by human activity and only exists through and for human consciousness. For Hegel, therefore, it is precisely because the space presented in a painting is not real, natural space itself, but the mere *Schein* of natural space, produced by human activity, that it can be interpreted as nothing but the *Widerschein* or "reflection" of the human spirit.[19]

The fact that painting works with a two-dimensional surface, rather than three-dimensional space, is thus not a defect of painting, but its very virtue: because it is what allows the painter to create the visual illusion of space, and it is only by creating the illusion of three-dimensions on a two-dimensional surface that the painter produces a space that can be interpreted as explicitly *manifesting* human spiritual freedom. The surface, in Hegel's view, thus ranks higher than solid matter as a medium of artistic expression. It is the sign of spirit's radical freedom to break with three-dimensional matter and to create a new illusory space of its own. "The reduction of the three dimensions to a level surface," Hegel claims, "lies in the principle of interiorization, which is only able to assert itself as inwardness in space by not allowing the totality of externality to stand, but limiting it."[20]

What needs to be emphasized here is that Hegel's commitment to the view that painting is meant to create visual illusion on a two-dimensional surface stems from his distinctive approach to painting. If one begins from the idea that painting is merely the application of paint to given surfaces, then there is nothing about painting that requires it to create the illusion of space, as many modern artists have recognized. Hegel does not, however, start from the simple activity of applying paint to a given surface; he begins from the human need to create *art* in which we can come to see our own freedom and spirituality given concrete sensuous expression. Starting from this conception of art, Hegel maintains that human freedom can only be rendered concretely visible by means of the created image of the human face and body. But he also shows that inner freedom can only be made manifest as such when the human forms in which it is expressed are created not in real space, but in an illusory space produced by human freedom itself. Hegel thus shows that the painter as artist does not just paint surfaces because they are there, but deliberately seeks out surfaces so that he can create the visual illusion of space in which concrete human freedom and subjectivity can shine forth. He thus shows that, at least in so far as it is an art, painting must be "representational," because its very raison d'être is to produce the "*deliberate appearance* [*den absichtlichen Schein*] of what sculpture . . . shape[s] in reality."[21]

The element in which painting creates this appearance is one that has been deprived of its material solidity and, in this sense, "spiritualized" (*vergeistigt*). "This element," Hegel says, "is the element of *visibility* [*Sichtbarkeit*]."[22] What painting has to do, therefore, is simply render visible figures through which human inwardness and freedom become manifest. Painting achieves this through applying color to a two-dimensional surface. Hegel appears to accept that ancient sculptures were in fact colored, but he argues that color is not intrinsic to sculptural presentation because the purpose of sculpture is to embody spirit in material shape.[23] Color is intrinsic to painting, however, because it is only through color that painting can create, in two dimensions, a credible visible world. In the absence of a third spatial dimension, Hegel says, "shape, distance, boundaries, contours, in short all the spatial relations and differences of objects appearing in space, are produced in painting only by color."[24]

This is not to say that Hegel altogether ignores the role played by drawing, undermodeling, and linear perspective in the constitution of the painted image. Bernadette Collenberg maintains that the sections in the Hotho edition of Hegel's lectures on aesthetics that deal specifically with drawing and linear perspective have no parallel in the existing transcripts of the lectures, and that Hotho added those sections himself in order to give a veneer of classical academicism to Hegel's account.[25] But it is clear even from the transcript of Hegel's 1820–21 lectures that he placed considerable value on drawing, in particular in portraiture, and indeed that he thought drawing provided a framework and outline from which all painting could begin. In fact, Ernst Gombrich's claim that artists could not create a credible illusion of reality "without a schema which can be moulded and modified" is anticipated by Hegel's remark that drawing makes the shapes of the human body, mountains, and rivers available to the painter "in their principal forms" (*in Hauptformen*).[26]

Nevertheless, it is equally clear that Hegel considers drawing to be secondary in importance to color. It is the use of color, he says, that actually makes the painter into a painter, because it is through color that the painter creates his characteristically concrete visual illusion of three-dimensional space. Many people regard sketching more highly, Hegel notes, because they think it suggests genius; "but color is what first makes the whole thing complete, what enables the painting on the canvas to completely stand out."[27]

The idea that the use of color is what distinguishes painting as painting is also to be found in Schelling's 1802–3 lectures on the philosophy of art.[28] Schelling insists, however, that drawing, rather than the use of color, is what ultimately makes painting an *art*. This is because, like Kant, he believes that "form is . . . the primary element in all things whereby they also are adapted for art," and, like Kant, he believes, that "all form . . . depends on drawing." Drawing thus does not just supply the figures and outlines from which the painter begins; rather, it constitutes the very core of the painter's work as an artist, for it is what creates beautiful form. The painter has certainly to delight the eye with color; but "without the deeper foundation of his excellent drawing," Schelling states, "even the greatest beauty of colors would be unable to charm the connoisseur."[29]

For Hegel, in contrast to Schelling, color is what makes painting painting *and* what makes it art. This is because Hegel believes that the purpose of painting as art is not simply the creation of beautiful form, but the creation of a credible and beautiful illusion of natural objects through which human spirituality can become manifest, and because he believes that color is the means through which that illusion is fully generated. The move away from Kant—the move from the primacy of drawing to the primacy of color—is thus completed by Hegel, not by Schelling.[30]

It is the use of color, in Hegel's view, that enables painting to surpass sculpture in the expression of human subjectivity: for by subtly blending and overlaying colors the painter can create visual nuances in a face or in a gesture which express the most delicate nuances of inner feeling and character which the sculptor can never capture. The material consequence Hegel draws from the importance of such blending and overlaying of color is that painting is ideally to be done in oils. It is much easier to glaze with oil than egg tempera and so it is much easier to achieve the "translucency of different layers of color" that Hegel believes is needed, for example, for the most subtle flesh-tone. Due to the fact that oil dries much more slowly than tempera, "oil color . . . [also] permits the most delicate and soft fusion and shading of colors, with the result that the transitions are so unnoticeable that we cannot say where a color begins and ends." Oil thus allows of much subtler modeling than egg tempera, such as Hegel admires in the work of the two "masters of *chiaroscuro,*" Leonardo da Vinci and Correggio, whose paintings Hegel knew from Paris and Dresden. Needless to say, the color effects that Hegel prizes most in painting, such as translucency and delicacy of transition, can be achieved least well by mosaic. This, ultimately, is why the art that creates the visual illusion of three-dimensions on a two-dimensional surface is understood by Hegel to be the art of painting, not the art of mosaic or collage, and why Hegel would probably not have approved of the pointillist work of Georges Seurat.[31]

As we have seen, Hegel understands the art of painting to be the art of creating, by means of color on a surface, concrete three-dimensional visual images that manifest the human spirit. The visual images created by painting—the bodily gestures and facial expressions it depicts—are thus to be understood as the "shining forth of inwardness concentrated in itself."[32] The subjectivity that finds visual expression in painting is not, however, just one that expresses itself, but one that has withdrawn into itself out of the materiality of sculpture. It is "spiritual inwardness that can only come to appearance in the external as retiring into itself out of it [*als aus demselben in sich hineingehend*]."[33] Hegel argues that in withdrawing into itself out of the sphere of externality in this way, subjectivity necessarily pushes the sphere of the external itself outside of subjectivity and "lets it go free": "free subjectivity [thus] allows independent existence to the entire range of things in nature and all spheres of human activity."[34] If painting is the visual expression of inner subjectivity, it must give visual expression to the fact that subjectivity releases the sphere of the external as independent of itself. It is for this reason that Hegel claims that painting has to depict natural objects, buildings and the landscape next to, indeed at times independently of, human figures. In giving expression to subjectivity that has withdrawn into itself and let nature go free, therefore, painting is required by its very nature to portray human beings as *situated* in an architectural or natural context. Indeed, "only in this involvement with concrete reality does [subjectivity] prove itself to be concrete and living."[35] Thus, whereas sculpture tends primarily, though not exclusively, to present individual figures standing alone, "painting . . . only begins on its proper task when it departs from the relationless independence of its figures, from lack of definiteness in the situation, in order to be able to enter the living movement of human circumstances, passions, conflicts and actions, in steady relation to their environment."[36]

By its very nature, therefore, painting tends primarily, though not exclusively, to present characters in situation, in relation to one another and to the surrounding buildings and landscape, indeed often in relations of explicit dependence. Even portraits require a background, according to Hegel, if only one of light or dark color, which is why he says that we find painted figures cut out of a picture and placed by themselves to be "repulsive" (*widrig*).[37]

The appropriate objects for painting, in Hegel's view, are thus "the objects of self-particularizing subjectivity" *and* "the objects of self-particularizing externality."[38] It is crucial to understand, however, that painting depicts human beings and natural objects in order to manifest inner subjectivity, not in order to *imitate* what exists in nature or to deceive the viewer into mistaking what is depicted for something real.[39]

As far as portraiture is concerned, the goal of painting for Hegel is liveliness of characterization (*Lebendigkeit*), not the "deceptive imitation of tiny hairs and wrinkles," such as are to be found in the work of the German painter, Balthazar Denner.[40] The point of a portrait is not simply to provide an accurate likeness of a face, but to reveal, through the depicted face and posture, the character and spirit within, which we often fail to see in the person's actual physiognomy. If the portrait is well executed, Hegel says (following Schelling), we can thus say that it is in fact "more like the individual than the actual individual himself";[41] and he adds that a person's character can often be captured very effectively through a few "individual strokes" (*einzelne Striche*)—though the picture must also be modeled enough and real enough to provide us with a concrete intuition of the actual person.[42]

In landscape painting and still life, the aim is not to capture every detail of a scene either, but to imbue nature and the objects in it with "new life."[43] Indeed, Hegel claims (once again following Schelling) that the point of landscape is ultimately to give expression to a human, spiritual mood (*Stimmung*). "The different features of the natural landscape in their calm serenity, their fragrant peace, their freshness in spring and deadness in winter, their morning wakening and their evening repose, etc., correspond to specific states of the soul," Hegel says, and it is this "characteristic sympathy" between nature and the human soul that landscape painting is to intimate.[44] Subjectivity is thus to let nature go free, but at the same time is to present nature as "mirroring"—as the *Abspiegelung* of—the human soul.[45]

Ordinary, prosaic reflection judges the merit of a painting by comparing it with the real person or object depicted and noting whether or not the copy matches the original. In Hegel's view, however, the point of painting is not to copy nature's original, but to create a new, autonomous visual space, with its own harmony and integrity, in which human character, spirit, and mood find expression. Painting fulfills its task as art, therefore, not when it accurately reproduces what is given in nature, but when it creates a new reality that is itself "ensouled" (*für sich beseelt*).[46] The space created for the observer has to look like the real space of nature, because it has to render human character and subjectivity concretely visible. But in creating that space, the true painter is not endeavoring to match the work of nature in every detail. On the contrary, he is overcoming nature by taking three-dimensional natural space and transforming it into a new, "spiritualized" space, that is, into an illusory space which exists solely for the sake of spirit's self-expression.[47]

The form of spiritual inwardness that can best find expression in painting, according to Hegel, is that which can most easily manifest itself in visible gestures and facial expressions, that is, feeling (*Empfindung*), the highest form of which is the feeling of love.[48] Since love lies at the heart of the Christian religion—indeed, the Christian God *is* love—painting is best able to fulfill its aesthetic role in Christian civilization, that is, in the period of what Hegel calls romantic art (though Hegel acknowledges that painting has long been practiced by the ancient Egyptians, Greeks, Romans, and other, non-Western, civilizations).[49] The highest calling of the art of painting, for Hegel, is thus to render visible "that religious love without desire which gives to the human spirit reconciliation, peace and bliss" and which is found in the love of the Virgin Mary for the Christ child, the love of the Magi and the Apostles, and the repentant love of Mary Magdalene.[50] In the contemplation of the greatest religious paintings, by Jan van Eyck, Raphael, or Correggio, our heart is raised, as in true prayer, into the presence of the highest truth, the presence of that "love that has nothing for itself alone" (*die nichts für sich allein hat*) and that finds its fulfillment and satisfaction in the purest devotion to another.[51] Even though Sophocles' *Antigone* may be "the most excellent and most satisfying work of art," therefore, the "immortal" religious paintings of the late Middle Ages and of the Renaissance are the most soulful and most *inward* works that art is able to produce.[52]

Painting's task is not just to give expression to religious love and devotion, however; it must also give expression to other, more worldly and prosaic features of our inner life. Indeed, "it must proceed to anything and everything in which a human being as an individual subject can take an interest or find satisfaction."[53] Painters should thus explore human character through portraiture and present the wide array of feelings and moods that are to be encountered in the diverse situations of everyday life. For Hegel, the masters of what he calls "this prose of painting" are the Dutch painters of the sixteenth and seventeenth centuries, who are able to imbue the most insignificant scenes of domestic life with an irresistible "spiritual cheerfulness," and who are able to triumph over transitoriness by seizing the most fleeting phenomena—"a smile, the expression of a swiftly passing emotion, ludicrous movements, postures, facial expressions"—and render them permanent for intuition in the fullness of their life.[54]

Schelling dismissed the products of Dutch painting as "uncouth" (*derb*); but Hegel delights in the "joy and exuberance" of spirit he sees manifesting itself in the work of the Dutch, just as he delights in the carefree love of life suffusing Murillo's beggar-boys in Munich.[55] Hegel also points out that in many cases what interests us in Dutch painting is not only—indeed not primarily—the people or objects presented, but the *way* in which they have been made to appear and brought to life. That is to say, what often captures our attention in such cases is less what appears, and more the means whereby it appears. By such means Hegel understands above all the combination of colors and light effects through which the visual illusion of a child's smile or a glint of light is created.[56]

Hegel calls the effects produced by such colors and light effects "magical" because through the simple juxtaposition of colors and of light and shade the visible appearance of objects is miraculously conjured up. What gives paintings their natural look is thus the "magic of appearance," or the "magic of shining" (*die Magie des Scheinens*)—a magic worked by nothing but color and light. Such magic is, of course, at work in all painting that creates the visual illusion of the natural world, but Hegel thinks that it captures our attention most of all in the works of Dutch painters, who have been explicitly concerned with exploring the effects produced by color and the reflection of light since the time of Jan van Eyck.[57]

Hegel notes that in conjuring up recognizable forms through simply being juxtaposed, colors work much like musical notes:

> Just as in music the single note is nothing by itself but produces its effect only in its relation to another, in its counterpoint, concord, modulation, and harmony, so here it is just the same with colour. If we look closely at the play of colour, which glints like gold and glitters like braid under the light, we see perhaps only white or yellow strokes, points of colour, coloured surfaces; the single colour as such does not have this gleam which it produces; it is the juxtaposition *alone* which makes this glistening and gleaming.

The play of colors through which such glistening and gleaming—indeed, the whole visual illusion—is produced, is thus, "as it were, an objective music, a peal in colour [*ein Tönen in Farben*]."[58] (Schelling, by the way, saw drawing, rather than color, as the musical element in painting, calling drawing "the rhythm of painting.")[59]

The parallel drawn by Hegel between painting and music (which of course is a nonrepresentational art) suggests that part of the pleasure we derive from painting stems from the purely formal play and harmony of colors as such, in abstraction from the constitution of visual illusion. Hegel reinforces this suggestion when he refers in the Hotho edition to the "wonderful, delicate, transparent nuances of color in a rose," as if those nuances themselves, irrespective of the role they play in enabling us to see a rose, are what cause us delight. Shortly after this, Hegel then states explicitly that the magic in painting consists

> in so handling all the colors that what is produced is an inherently objectless play of pure appearance [*ein für sich objektloses Spiel des Scheines*] which forms the extreme soaring pinnacle of colouring, a fusion of

> colours, a shining of reflections upon one another which become so fine, so fleeting, so soulful, that they begin to pass into the realm of music.[60]

Hegel thus clearly does recognize the legitimacy of delighting in the formal play and harmony of colors in abstraction from the object presented. It is also clear, however, that he believes such delight in purely formal, abstract play must itself be part of the delight we take in the way colors create the appearance of objects and human beings. The "objective music" of painting, for Hegel, is thus inseparable from the "subjective recreation of externality in the sensuous element of colors and lighting."[61] This is because it is only in the creation of the appearance of objects that the painter proves his freedom over the world into which he is cast—his freedom to transform that world into one that has been deprived of material solidity and so "spiritualized," one that only exists through the spirit which produces it and for the spirit who sees it.[62] Although painting is indeed to delight us through colored and formal abstraction, therefore, it is not to do so through such abstraction alone. Painting is not to delight us through abstraction *in the abstract,* but only through abstraction as a moment in the constitution of concrete visual illusion that manifests the human spirit.

III. Hegel and Abstract Painting

As I—and others—have pointed out elsewhere, Hegel does not maintain that art dies in the modern world. Art has ceased to be the highest form of self-consciousness for humanity, but we can justifiably hope that "art will always rise higher and perfect itself."[63] Painting in particular has two main functions to perform in the modern world. On the one hand, like poetry, it has to explore the realm of Goethe's *Humanus*—"the depths and heights of the human heart as such, . . . everything in which the human being as such is capable of being at home."[64] On the other hand, it has to depict natural objects as reflecting states of mind and as resonating with vitality in themselves and to explore the ways in which color and light can magically conjure such objects into appearance—what Hegel calls *die Kunst des Machens.*[65]

It is clear, however, that many artists since Hegel's death have turned their back on the idea that we should feel "at home" in the encounter with a painting, in favor of the idea that painting should exercise a more critical, political role, or that it should arouse in us a sense of anxious unease. There are certainly few painters after the Impressionists whose work could be said to express anything of the "cheerfulness" that so enchanted Hegel in Dutch art. In some cases, of course, this may well be due to changed historical circumstances—to the corrosive effects of industrialization and the horrors of two world wars which painters have felt they had to reflect. But there has also been a cultural turn away from what Hegel calls "healthy serenity" and "healthy beauty" towards a certain "enervation" (*Nervengereiztheit*) which dates back at least to the romantics and which Hegel finds, for example, in the paintings of the Düsseldorf school.[66]

I propose to conclude, however, not with a discussion of the relative presence or absence of healthy serenity and wholeness in modern painting, but with a discussion of what is surely the most central characteristic of modern art, namely, the move towards abstraction, or at least towards diminished naturalism, and the consequent abandonment of the idea that it is painting's task to produce a convincing visual illusion of human beings or nature. Such a move is often justified in the name of the artist's freedom to experiment with different visual effects. From Hegel's point of view, however, by abandoning the concern to create illusion, painting is no longer able to fulfill its role as art, because it is no longer able to give expression to concrete human freedom in a distinctively painterly way.

In the twentieth century the move from representational to abstract art has been justified from two quite contrasting points of view. Wassily Kandinsky—perhaps the outstanding pioneer of abstract art—held that the purpose of painting is to give expression to the artist's inner feelings and to arouse corresponding "spiritual vibrations" within the viewer.[67] Inspired by Mme. Blatavsky's theosophical doctrines, he argued that the portrayal of physical objects in a painting prevents the viewer from focusing properly on the inner feelings that the painting is meant to evoke, by directing attention out towards the external, natural world. Kandinsky thus advocated a form of painting that would avoid association with the natural world and instead allow the viewer to concentrate wholly on the inner feelings that are aroused by color and form as such. This does not mean that the painter has to reject anything that looks remotely like a natural form; but it does mean that such forms—for example, the three mountainlike forms in Kandinsky's own *Black Lines No 189*—have to be so *reduced* that they no longer appear to represent anything in the visible, material world as such, but can be thought of as giving expression to purely spiritual feelings and meanings. "The more obvious is the separation from nature," Kandinsky writes, "the more likely is the inner meaning to be pure and unhampered."[68]

It should be noted that Kandinsky does not turn toward abstraction in order to eliminate all visual depth and to reduce painting to the art of producing flat, colored surfaces. He well recognizes that one can create the visual impression of depth in abstract painting through varying the thinness or thickness of a line or through "the overlaying of one form on another"—just as Jackson Pollock would later recognize that one can generate an interplay of surface and depth through the overlaying of dripped paint.[69] Kandinsky turned toward abstraction, not out of any devotion to flatness, but out of a desire, as he saw it, to "emancipate" color and form from their role in the representation of natural objects and to allow them to arouse inner feelings directly by themselves in the manner of musical notes. Kandinsky turns toward abstraction, therefore, in order to break the hold of material nature over art and to show that art's role is to give expression purely to our inner life.[70]

An alternative—indeed diametrically opposed—justification of abstract art is provided by Clement Greenberg. Greenberg contends that modernism is the process whereby each art tries to determine "the effects peculiar and exclusive to itself" and to eliminate from itself "every effect that might conceivably be borrowed from . . . any other art."[71] The way modernist painting has determined its own effects, he argues, is by progressively emancipating itself from literature (through getting rid of imitation) and from sculpture (through abandoning modeling) and by bringing more and more to the fore the material aspects of painting itself: the texture of paint, the shape of the support and, above all else, the flatness of the surface. Beginning with Courbet and Manet, Greenberg writes, "Modernist painting oriented itself to flatness as it did to nothing else" and gradually collapsed the plane of the picture into "the real and material plane which is the actual surface of the canvas."[72] Abstract art, for Greenberg, is simply the logical conclusion of this process: the pure exploration of the material medium of painting and the endeavor to affect the spectator directly through the simple application of colored paint to flat surface. With abstraction, therefore, the painting no longer seeks to represent anything or to express anything, but "exhausts itself in the visual sensation it produces."[73]

If modernist painting draws our explicit attention to the medium of painting, especially to the flatness of the canvas, "realist, illusionist art," according to Greenberg, "dissembled the medium" by creating the illusion of three-dimensional space. Illusionist painting thus obscured what is distinctive about a painting—that it is a flat colored surface—and failed to focus specifically on producing effects that are uniquely painterly. Indeed, Greenberg argues that, in creating the illusion of relief through shading and modeling, traditional painting was actually applying techniques learned originally from sculpture. If it is to retain its purity as painting, therefore, modernist painting has to abandon "the representation of the kind of space that recognizable, three-dimensional objects can inhabit." For Greenberg, as for Kandinsky, but for quite different reasons, true painting must thus turn its back on the creation of naturalistic visual illusion.[74]

Hegel would have had very little sympathy for twentieth-century abstract art. By comparing Hegel's account of painting with the accounts given by Kandinsky and Greenberg, however, we can see that he would not simply have rejected abstract art out of personal conservatism, but would have criticized it for clear philosophical reasons.

The philosophical problem with Kandinsky's justification of abstract art is that he assumes that naturalistic forms draw the viewer's attention away from the inner feelings expressed in a painting, rather than rendering such inner feelings concretely visible. Kandinsky thus fails to see that in the visual arts human subjectivity actually manifests itself most clearly in recognizable facial expressions and visible gestures, and that by making painting abstract he is in fact depriving painting of its most effective means of giving expression to our inner life. Hegel does not object in principle to Kandinsky's idea that painting can express inner feelings directly through sheer color and abstract form: he well recognizes, for example, that the form of the pyramid can calm the eye, just as he agrees with Kandinsky that blue by itself is restful.[75] However, Hegel holds that a painter who wishes to give proper expression to the human spirit should integrate color and abstract form into a picture that renders the spirit concretely visible. Hegel thus does not object to the *abstract* expression of inner feelings; he objects to abstracting such abstract expression from the concrete expression of inner feelings. For, from a Hegelian point of view, by abstracting color and form from visible nature, the painter necessarily retreats into a abstract—indeed, sublime—inner life, withdrawn from nature, that is inappropriate for the modern world.[76]

The philosophical problem with Greenberg's justification of abstract art is that he assumes that what is distinctive about painting is the material process of creating visual effects on an openly two-dimensional surface, rather than the process of rendering human subjectivity concretely visible through the *illusion* of three-dimensional space. Greenberg thus overlooks the very thing that Hegel thinks makes painting art. Hegel would agree with Greenberg that traditional painting subordinates the material qualities of the painting—the texture of the pigment and the flatness of the canvas—to the painting's expressive purpose. But then, for Hegel, that is the whole point of painting: for painting's role is precisely to draw our attention, by means of its material qualities, to what is ultimately immaterial—to spirit, to life, and to the sheer look of things. "Inwardness and the subjective side of life," Hegel says, "should not appear on a surface as laid on [*aufgetragen*], as material color in strokes and points, etc., but as itself a living whole." What we see in the painting thus "should not be in our eyes a resistant surface, but something in which we must be able to immerse ourselves."[77] If Greenberg is right that abstract art reduces painting to an overtly material practice, then abstract art goes against what Hegel sees as the very purpose of art.

Hegel's position is closer to that of Kandinsky than to that of Greenberg. But, from Hegel's point of view, both Kandinsky and Greenberg fail to see that painting fulfills its distinctive function by creating credible images of human beings and natural objects in order to give expression to our spirit and life. Both thus fail to recognize the real importance in painting of creating the purely visual *illusion* of natural forms. For Kandinsky, naturalistic illusion in painting orients the viewer too much towards the physical, material world. For Greenberg, by contrast, such illusion directs our attention away from the physical, material world by concealing the materiality of the painting itself. For Hegel, however, naturalistic illusion neither reinforces nor occludes the physical, material world; rather, it bears witness to our freedom to transfigure and spiritualize the material world by recreating it, deprived of its material weight, in the element of sheer visibility. The painter thus not only gives concrete expression to subjectivity and life through the specific naturalistic illusions he creates, he also manifests his freedom in the very creating of naturalistic illusion as such, in the very lightening of matter.

In Hegel's view, sculpture remains too external, spatial and solidly material to express adequately the concentrated inwardness of spirit, whereas music withdraws from the external and the spatial altogether into the sphere of time and sound. Painting avoids both extremes of sculptural materiality and musical inwardness and links the external *and* the internal together: "in the external it can express complete inwardness," Hegel says.[78] That, indeed, is what specifically distinguishes painting as an art. Painting can only fulfill its distinctive role, however, by transforming external nature into something that exists through and for human inner subjectivity alone, that is, by transforming it into sheer visible illusion. To reject illusion, as Kandinsky does, in the name of freeing painting from external nature, is thus to push painting too much in the direction of music; and to reject illusion, as Greenberg does, in the name of emancipating the materiality of painting itself, is to push painting too much in the direction of sculpture (sculpture being characterized, not as Greenberg thinks, by modeling and relief, but by free-standing material presence).[79] In either case, to reject illusion is to reject precisely what Hegel sees as unique to, and definitive of, the art of painting, because it is to reject painting's unique way of turning nature itself into a merely visual, virtual, and immaterial presence.

Hegel, the alleged traditionalist, says that the essence—spirit—must appear (*erscheinen*), and must appear in the very seeming (*Schein*) of nature, and he sees painting as the art of seeming, of *Scheinen, par excellence.*[80] It appears, however, that the avant-garde painters of the twentieth century have lost the taste for seeming and illusion and prefer instead to hold to the abstract *realities* of the "purely" inward spirit or the "purely" material character of painting. Indeed, from Hegel's point of view, there is something oddly old-fashioned and metaphysical about those painters who turn their backs on illusion—as if they have never read the beginning of Hegel's logic of essence. In my view, however, Hegelians should no more endorse pictorial abstraction—and the metaphysical abstraction that underpins it—than they should endorse the abstraction of the state or of civil society, but, like Nietzsche, they should insist on the irreducible importance of *Schein.*

This does not mean that Hegelians cannot like modern abstract art, or appreciate its expressive, decorative, or deconstructive qualities. But it does mean that they have to reject Greenberg's claim that modern painting "continues to provide the experience of art *in all its essentials.*"[81] For to the extent that modern painting no longer seeks to recreate nature as sheer visibility and, through that created visual illusion, to explore the richness of human vitality and freedom, painting has ceased to exercise the specific role that falls to it as *art.*

Notes

1. S. Alpers, *The Art of Describing: Dutch Art in the Seventeenth Century* (Chicago: University of Chicago Press, 1983), 249. See also K. Clark, *The Nude: A Study of Ideal Art* (Harmondsworth: Penguin Books, 1960); E. Gombrich, *The Story of Art,* 14th ed. (Oxford: Phaidon Press, 1984); and M. Hall, *Color and Meaning: Practice and Theory in Renaissance Painting* (Cambridge: Cambridge University Press, 1992).

2. For Hegel's remarks on Raphael's *Transfiguration* (from 1797 to 1815 in France, but now in the Vatican Museum, Rome), see G. W. F. Hegel, *Vorlesungen über die Ästhetik: Berlin 1820/21, Eine Nachschrift, I Textband,* ed. H. Schneider (Frankfurt am Main: Peter Lang, 1995), 271 (hereafter *Ästhetik 1820/21*), and Hegel, *Vorlesungen über die Ästhetik,* ed. E. Moldenhauer and K. M. Michel, *Werke in zwanzig Bänden,* 20 vols., and Index (Frankfurt am Main: Suhrkamp Verlag, 1969ff), 15:96; English translation, G. W. F. Hegel, *Aesthetics: Lectures on Fine Art,* trans. T. M. Knox, 2 vols. (Oxford: Clarendon Press, 1975), 2:860. Further references will be given in the form: *Werke,* 15:96; *A,* 2:860. When quoting from Knox's text, I have occasionally emended his translation. For a comparison of Hegel's interpretation of the *Transfiguration* with those given by Ludwig Tieck and Wilhelm Heinse, see S. Bungay, *Beauty and Truth: A Study of Hegel's Aesthetics* (Oxford: Oxford University Press, 1984), 128–30.

3. See G. Stemmrich/A. Gethmann-Siefert, "Hegels Kügelgen-Rezension und die Auseinandersetzung um den 'eigentlichen historischen Stil' in der Malerei," in *Welt und Wirkung von Hegels Ästhetik,* ed. A. Gethmann-Siefert and O. Pöggeler, *Hegel-Studien,* Beiheft 27 (Bonn: Bouvier, 1986), 139–40, and B. Collenberg, "Hegels Konzeption des Kolorits in den Berliner Vorlesungen über die Philosophie der Kunst," in *Phänomen versus System: Zum Verhältnis von philosophischer Systematik und Kunsturteil in Hegels Berliner Vorlesungen über Ästhetik oder Philosophie der Kunst,* ed. A. Gethmann-Siefert, *Hegel-Studien,* Beiheft 34 (Bonn: Bouvier, 1992), 91–192.

4. See Hegel, *Werke,* 15:111; *A,* 2:872.

5. On Waagen, see *Hegel in Berlin: Preussische Kulturpolitik und idealistische Ästhetik, Zum 150 Todestag des Philosophen,* ed. O. Pöggeler et al. (Berlin: Staatsbibliothek Preussischer Kulturbesitz, 1981), 150, 209; and O. Pöggeler, "Der Philosoph und der Maler: Hegel und Christian Xeller," in *Kunsterfahrung und Kulturpolitik im Berlin Hegels,* ed. O. Pöggeler and A. Gethmann-Siefert, *Hegel-Studien,* Beiheft 22 (Bonn: Bouvier, 1983), 374. On Hirt, see Pöggeler, "Der Philosoph und der Maler," 359; *Hegel: The Letters,* trans. C. Butler and C. Seiler (Bloomington: Indiana University Press, 1984), 612; and Hegel, *Werke,* 13:33; *A,* 1:17.

6. On Rösel, see *Hegel: The Letters,* 184, 644; Pöggeler, "Der Philosoph und der Maler," 353. On Xeller and Schlesinger, see Pöggeler, "Der Philosoph und der Maler," 352; and *Hegel in Berichten seiner Zeitgenossen,* ed. G. Nicolin (Hamburg: Felix Meiner, 1970), 452. Xeller and Schlesinger had worked as picture restorers in the gallery of the brothers Boisserée in Heidelberg and had come to Berlin to continue their trade there. Schlesinger went on to restore the damaged head of Leda in Correggio's *Leda and the Swan* when it was brought to the new Berlin museum in 1830 (Pöggeler, "Der Philosoph und der Maler," 375; *Hegel in Berlin,* 232), and he is also responsible for the rather fearsome looking painting of Hegel's head that now

adorns the covers of both Stanley Rosen's and Raymond Plant's Hegel books (see F. Wiedmann, *G. W. F. Hegel in Selbstzeugnissen und Bilddokumenten* [Reinbek bei Hamburg: Rowohlt, 1965], 111).

7. See F. Strack, "Hegels Persönlichkeit im Spiegel der Tagebücher Sulpiz Boisserées und der Lebenserinnerungen C. H. A. Pagenstechers," *Hegel-Studien* 17 (1982):25–31, *Hegel in Berlin,* 97; and *Hegel: The Letters,* 335–336. For a detailed and indispensable study of the Boisserée collection, see *Kunst als Kulturgut: Die Bildersammlung der Brüder Boisserée—ein Schritt in der Begründung des Museums,* ed. A. Gethmann-Siefert and O. Pöggeler (Bonn: Bouvier, 1995). The book contains black and white reproductions of almost all the paintings in the Boisserée collection. I am very grateful to Dr. Gisela Goldberg at the Bayerische Staatsgemäldesammlungen for drawing my attention to this book.

Among the paintings Hegel specifically discusses from the Boisserée collection are the *Three Kings Altar* which at the time was thought to be by Jan van Eyck but today is attributed to Rogier van der Weyden (Hegel, *Ästhetik 1820/21,* 262; *Werke,* 15:55; *A,* 2:828; *Hegel in Berlin,* 233–35; E. Steingräber, *The Alte Pinakothek Munich,* trans. E. Callander [London: Philip Wilson/Summerfield, 1985], 38; *Kunst als Kulturgut,* 247), and two pictures which were thought to be by Hans Memling (or Hemling as he was then called), one depicting the head of Christ (actually a copy of a painting by van Eyck), the other depicting the Jews gathering manna in the desert (actually a work by Dieric Bouts) (*Ästhetik 1820/21,* 257, 272; *Werke,* 15:47; *A,* 2:821; *Hegel: The Letters,* 595; *Kunst als Kulturgut,* 251, 249). Hegel also picks out for special praise a picture of the dying Virgin Mary, which was attributed by Sulpiz Boisserée (and Hegel) to Jan van Scorel, but is actually by Joos van Cleve (*Ästhetik 1820/21,* 261; *Werke,* 15:53; *A,* 2:826; *Hegel: The Letters,* 594; *Kunst als Kulturgut,* 286). In a letter to his wife written from Brussels in October, 1822 Hegel writes that he has seen a similar, but slightly smaller painting in the collection of Ferdinand Wallraf in Cologne in which the position of the Virgin's bed in the central panel is slightly different from that in the Boisserée picture, but in which the figures in the wing-panels are exactly the same, and on this basis he attributes Wallraf's picture to Jan van Scorel, too (*Hegel: The Letters,* 594, 586). The Wallraf painting Hegel saw is in fact also by Joos van Cleve (see M. Friedländer, *From Van Eyck to Breugel,* trans. M. Kay [London: Phaidon Press, 1956], 87). Hegel was thus correct in his judgment that both paintings were by the same artist, but he attributed them to the wrong man. (I am grateful to Dr. Roland Krischel of the Wallraf-Richartz-Museum in Cologne for supplying me with very helpful information about the Wallraf "Dying Virgin Mary.")

8. See Hegel, *Ästhetik 1820/21,* 252, 264.

9. The first journey on which Hegel was able to visit a major collection was that undertaken in 1815 from Nuremberg to Munich (*Hegel: The Letters,* 317–18, 331). Hegel had gone to Munich primarily to speak to Niethammer about his future, but whilst there he took time to visit the city's Central Gallery as well as the nearby gallery at Schleissheim. The only paintings he later mentions having seen in Munich are Guido Reni's *Assumption of the Virgin Mary* (Hegel, *Ästhetik 1820/21,* 263; *Werke,* 15:57; *A,* 2:829–30) and Murillo's pictures of beggar boys (*Werke,* 13:224; *A,* 1:170), and the only painting he mentions having seen at Schleissheim is the picture of a head which

he believes is by Guido Reni (*Werke,* 15:50; *A,* 2:824). However, it is possible that the unidentified portraits by Sir Anthony van Dyck, which he says in his 1820/21 lectures "seem as it were to step out of the frame" (p. 246), were also seen by Hegel in Munich (see *The Alte Pinakothek Munich,* 84).

In 1820 Hegel traveled from Berlin to Dresden, this time in the company of his wife, and returned there alone in 1821 and 1824, on each occasion visiting Ludwig Tieck and, of course, spending time in the art gallery (*Hegel in Berlin,* 134, 138, 141; *Hegel: The Letters,* 608ff). Among the paintings he mentions having seen there are Raphael's *Sistine Madonna* (*Ästhetik 1820/21,* 258, 262) and four paintings by Correggio: the *Madonna of St. Francis* and the *Madonna of St. George* (*Ästhetik 1820/21,* 259, 262), *Holy Night* (*Hegel: The Letters,* 595; *Hegel in Berlin,* 142; *Hegel in Berichten seiner Zeitgenossen,* 213–14), and *Maria Magdalena,* which was later destroyed in the Second World War (*Ästhetik 1820/21,* 267; *Werke,* 15:106; *A,* 2:868; *Hegel in Berlin,* 143; Bungay, 126). Hegel also studied four paintings by the contemporary German painter Gerhard von Kügelgen (*Ästhetik 1820/21,* 268; *Werke,* 15:86, 107; *A,* 2:852, 869; *Hegel in Berlin,* 144; see also Hegel, *Berliner Schriften 1818–1831,* ed. E. Moldenhauer and K. M. Michel, *Werke in zwanzig Bänden,* 11 [Frankfurt am Main: Suhrkamp Verlag, 1970], 562–4).

1822 took Hegel on a trip via Brunswick and Kassel through the Rhineland to Flanders and Holland. He saw the altarpiece in Linz-am-Rhein by the Master of the Life of the Virgin (*Hegel in Berlin,* 147; *Hegel: The Letters,* 578, 585), before stopping in Cologne where he toured the Wallraf collection, with its picture of the Death of the Virgin Mary mentioned in note 7, the Lyversberg collection, and Cologne Cathedral with its magnificent *Dombild* by Stephan Lochner (*Werke,* 15:55; *A,* 2:828; *Hegel in Berlin,* 148; *Hegel: The Letters,* 585–86, 594, 663). In Aachen Hegel visited the Bettendorf collection, with work by Dieric Bouts attributed by Hegel to Memling (*Hegel in Berlin,* 148; *Hegel: The Letters,* 594–95; *Kunst als Kulturgut,* 201), and in Holland he saw paintings by Rembrandt (in particular the *Night Watch*), Wouwermann, van Dyck, and many others (*Werke,* 13:223; *A,* 1:169; *Hegel: The Letters,* 599; *Hegel in Berlin,* 151–52). On his return to Flanders in 1827, he was finally able to see the central section of the van Eyck Altarpiece in Ghent and "the most noteworthy, splendid, and magnificent original works by van Eyck and Memling" in Bruges (*Hegel: The Letters,* 661–62; *Hegel in Berlin,* 150; *Werke,* 15:46; *A,* 2:820).

In 1824 Hegel traveled to Dresden and then on to Prague, where he was delighted by the Old German paintings in the Cathedral and the Estates Gallery, but decidedly unimpressed by the frescoes at nearby Karlstein that had so excited Hirt (*Hegel: The Letters,* 612–13; *Hegel in Berlin,* 157). In Vienna Hegel visited several collections and galleries, as well as the Imperial Library, but does not mention any particular paintings that impressed him (though he does mention a series of sketches by Michelangelo which he saw in Archduke Karl's collection of sketches and copper engravings) (*Hegel: The Letters,* 616–26; *Hegel in Berlin,* 97, 160).

In 1827 he was finally able to visit Paris, where he saw in the Louvre paintings by Raphael, Correggio, Leonardo da Vinci, and Titian (*Hegel: The Letters,* 654; *Hegel in Berlin,* 168). The only individual painting he specifically mentions having seen in Paris, however, is Raphael's *Portrait of a Young Boy* which he finds similar in mood to the paintings of beggar boys by Murillo he saw in Munich in 1815. The boy's "head lies at rest, leaning on an arm," Hegel says, "and he gazes out into the wide and open distance with such bliss of carefree satisfaction that one can scarcely tear oneself away from gazing at this picture of spiritual and joyous well-being" (*Werke,* 13:224; *A,* 1:170).

10. See Bungay, 124, and *Hegel in Berlin,* 96, 98. Hegel mentions in particular seeing the wing-panels from the Ghent altarpiece which were at the time in the Solly collection (*Hegel: The Letters,* 661; Pöggeler, "Der Philosoph und der Maler," 374). On other paintings Hegel saw in Berlin, see *Hegel in Berlin,* 236–37. The exhibition of 1828 afforded Hegel the opportunity to see paintings by Dusseldorf artists, such as Carl Ferdinand Sohn and Wilhelm von Schadow (*Werke,* 15:91–92; *A,* 2:856–57; Bungay, 124–26).

11. *Werke,* 13:52; *A,* 1:31.

12. Hegel, *Ästhetik 1820/21,* 57.

13. *Werke,* 14:258–59; *A,* 2:624.

14. *Werke,* 14:369; 15:11, 16–17; *A,* 2:716, 792, 797.

15. *Werke,* 15:17; *A,* 2:797; Hegel, *Ästhetik 1820/21,* 240.

16. Hegel, *Ästhetik 1820/21,* 241, 57.

17. Although Hegel usually talks of *Schein* in his lectures, in the 1820–21 lectures he also uses the word *Illusion;* see *Ästhetik 1820/21,* 274.

18. *Werke,* 15:14; *A,* 2:794.

19. *Werke,* 15:27; *A,* 2:805.

20. *Werke,* 15:26; *A,* 2:805.

21. *Werke,* 15:32; *A,* 2:809.

22. Hegel, *Ästhetik 1820/21,* 243.

23. Hegel, *Ästhetik 1820/21,* 209; *Werke,* 14:388–89; *A,* 2:731–32.

24. *Werke,* 15:33–34; *A,* 2:810.

25. Collenberg, "Hegels Konzeption des Kolorits," 139–40.

26. See Hegel, *Ästhetik 1820/21,* 266, 300, and E. Gombrich, *Art and Illusion: A Study in the Psychology of Pictorial Representation,* 5th ed. (Oxford: Phaidon Press, 1977), 126.

27. Hegel, *Ästhetik 1820/21,* 272.

28. F. W. J. Schelling, *Ausgewählte Schriften,* ed. M. Frank, 6 vols. (Frankfurt-am-Main: Suhrkamp Verlag, 1985), 2:348 (hereafter *Schriften*); Schelling, *The Philosophy of Art,* ed. and trans. D. W. Stott, foreword by D. Simpson (Minneapolis: University of Minnesota Press, 1989), 129 (hereafter Stott).

29. Schelling, *Schriften,* 2:348–49 ; Stott, 129. See also I. Kant, *Kritik der Urteilskraft, Kants Gesammelte Schriften,* 5 (Königlich Preussische [now Deutsche] Akademie der Wissenschaften, Berlin: G. Reimer [now de Gruyter], 1902ff), section 14.

30. See Collenberg, "Hegels Konzeption des Kolorits," 95.

31. Hegel, *Werke,* 15:79–81; *A,* 2:847–48. On the relative merits of painting and mosaic, see also *Ästhetik 1820/21,* 274. On the differences between oil and egg tempera with respect to glazing, see M. Hall, *Color and Meaning,* 52–53.

32. *Werke,* 15:15; *A,* 2:795.

33. *Werke,* 15:27; *A,* 2:805.

34. *Werke,* 15:24; *A,* 2:803.

35. *Werke,* 15:25; *A,* 2:803.

36. *Werke,* 15:88–89; *A,* 2:854.

37. Hegel, *Ästhetik 1820/21,* 245.

38. Hegel, *Ästhetik 1820/21,* 245.

39. Hegel, *Ästhetik 1820/21,* 249; *Werke,* 13:66; *A,* 1:42–43. See also Schelling, *Schriften,* 2:348; Stott, 129.

40. Hegel, *Ästhetik 1820/21,* 249; *Werke,* 15:63; *A,* 2:834. See also Schelling, *Schriften,* 2:355; Stott, 133.

41. Hegel, *Ästhetik,* 265–66; *Werke,* 15:104–5; *A,* 2:866–67. See also Schelling, *Schriften,* 2:375; Stott, 146.

42. Hegel, *Ästhetik 1820/21,* 249; *Werke,* 15:103–4; *A,* 2:866–67.

43. *Werke,* 15:67; *A,* 2:837.

44. Hegel, *Ästhetik 1820/21,* 268; *Werke,* 15:60; *A,* 2:831–32. See also Schelling, *Schriften,* 2:373–74; Stott, 145.

45. *Werke,* 15:18; *A,* 2:798.

46. Hegel, *Ästhetik 1820/21,* 248–49; *Werke,* 15:63; *A,* 2:834.

47. See Hegel, *Ästhetik 1820/21,* 244: "Die Kunst soll aber nicht Naturwerke produziren . . . ," and J. Kaminsky, *Hegel on Art: An Interpretation of Hegel's Aesthetics* (Albany: SUNY Press, 1962), 111: "when the artist seems to be imitating nature he is really using nature in order to express some fundamental feeling."

48. Hegel, *Ästhetik 1820/21,* 241–42, 252–53; *Werke,* 15:25, 41–45; *A,* 2:803–4, 816–19.

49. Hegel, *Ästhetik 1820/21,* 244–45, 252; *Werke,* 15:19–23, 110; *A,* 2:799–802, 871–72.

50. *Werke,* 15:42, 51–58, 106; *A,* 2:816–17, 824–30, 868; *Ästhetik 1820/21,* 267–68.

51. Hegel, *Ästhetik 1820/21,* 262; *Werke,* 15:41–42, 54; *A,* 2:816–17, 827.

52. *Werke,* 15:550, 59; *A,* 2:1218, 831.

53. *Werke,* 15:61; *A,* 2:832.

54. Hegel, *Ästhetik 1820/21,* 247; *Werke,* 13:223; 14:227; *A,* 1:170, 599.

55. Schelling, *Schriften,* 2:349; Stott, 129; *Werke,* 13:223–24; *A,* 1:169.

56. Hegel, *Ästhetik 1820/21,* 251; *Werke,* 14:227–28; *A,* 1:599.

57. Hegel, *Ästhetik 1820/21,* 251; *Werke,* 15:74–75; *A,* 2:843, especially: "with what skill have the Dutch painted the lustre of satin gowns with all the manifold reflections and degrees of shadow in the folds, etc., and the sheen of silver, gold, copper, glass vessels, velvet, etc., and, by van Eyck, the lighting of precious stones, jewels, and gold-braid." The manifold ways in which Dutch art explores reflections and surfaces are also examined in detail by Svetlana Alpers in *The Art of Describing* (see, for example, 90–91), though Alpers does not appear to place as much emphasis as Hegel does on the Dutch use of color.

58. *Werke,* 14:228; *A,* 1:599–600.

59. Schelling, *Schriften,* 2:348; Stott, 128. See also Collenberg, "Hegels Konzeption des Kolorits," 160.

60. *Werke,* 15:79–81; *A,* 2:847–48.

61. *Werke,* 14:227–28; *A,* 1:599–600.

62. *Werke,* 15:22, 28; *A,* 2:801–2, 805–6.

63. *Werke,* 13:142; *A,* 1:103. See also S. Houlgate, *Freedom, Truth and History: An Introduction to Hegel's Philosophy* (London: Routledge, 1991), 168.

64. *Werke,* 14:238; 15:130–31; *A,* 1:607, 2:886–87. See also M. Donougho, "Remarks on 'Humanus heisst der Heilige,'" *Hegel-Studien* 17 (1982):214–25.

65. *Werke,* 15:35; *A,* 2:811.

66. *Werke,* 15:92–93; *A,* 2:856–58. Hegel is not blind to the absence of "healthy beauty" in older paintings, either. He detects more than a hint of sentimentalism, for example, in Guido Reni's *Assumption of the Virgin Mary* in Munich; see *Ästhetik 1820/21,* 263; *Werke,* 15:57–58; *A,* 2:829–30.

67. W. Kandinsky, *Concerning the Spiritual in Art,* trans. with an introduction by M. T. H. Sadler (New York: Dover Publications, 1977), 24. See also R. Hughes, *The Shock of the New: Art and the Century of Change* (London: BBC Publications, 1980), 299.

68. Kandinsky, *Concerning the Spiritual in Art,* 50, 32. On Kandinsky's *Black Lines No 189,* see Hughes, *The Shock of the New,* 301–3.

69. See Kandinsky, *Concerning the Spiritual in Art,* 44. In interpreting Pollock's work in terms of the interplay of surface and depth, I am indebted to Andrew Benjamin's immensely illuminating account of Pollock's *Lavender Mist* in his *Object: Painting* (London: Academy Editions, 1994), especially 104–5. Robert Hughes, by contrast, sees in Pollock's painting "no in-and-out movement of the eye in depth, only the weaving, serpentine, darting movement of particles across the surface" (*The Shock of the New,* 314).

70. See Kandinsky, *Concerning the Spiritual in Art,* 19 ("that modern desire for rhythm in painting"), 46 ("The revolt from dependence on nature is only just beginning"), 32–33 (on "inner need").

71. C. Greenberg, "Modernist Painting," in *Reflecting on Art,* ed. J. A. Fisher (Mountain View, Calif.: Mayfield Publishing, 1993), 155–56.

72. Greenberg, "Modernist Painting", 156, and "Towards a Newer Laocoon," in *Abstract Expressionism: A Critical Record,* ed. D. Shapiro and C. Shapiro (Cambridge: Cambridge University Press, 1990), 71.

73. Greenberg, "Towards a Newer Laocoon," 70.

74. Greenberg, "Modernist Painting," 156–57.

75. On blue, see *Werke,* 15:73; *A,* 2:842, and Kandinsky, *Concerning the Spiritual in Art,* 38. On Hegel's view of the pyramid as "calming for the eye," see *Werke,* 15:98; *A,* 2:862.

76. Hegel's criticism of the Düsseldorf school is perhaps relevant here: "If therefore, the poetic element in painting is supposed to lie in its expressing inner feeling in posture and facial expression directly without any precise motif and action, this only means thrusting painting back into an *abstraction* [*eine Abstraktion*] *which is exactly what it must be rid of.*" (*Werke,* 15:91; *A,* 2:856, my emphasis).

77. *Werke,* 15:79; *A,* 2:847. Greenberg, by contrast, claims that "the history of avant-garde painting is that of a progressive surrender to the resistance of its medium; which resistance consists chiefly in the flat picture plane's denial of efforts to 'hole through' it for realistic perspectival space" ("Towards a Newer Laocoon," 71).

78. *Werke,* 15:40; *A,* 2:815.
79. See Greenberg, "Modernist Painting," 157.
80. Hegel, *Ästhetik 1820/21,* 243.
81. Greenberg, "Modernist Painting," 159, my emphasis.

VI

The Spirit of Gravity: Architecture and Externality

David Kolb

Hegel wrote that "*Die Architektur . . . ist die Kunst am Äusserlichen.*" We might translate this as "Architecture is art in the external."[1] But since all art is sensuous externalization, perhaps we should translate Hegel as saying "Architecture is the art of the external." Architecture is art at its most external. What is this "externality" that is so important to architecture? There are many dimensions to the answer.

We might say that architecture is "external" because it constructs in physical space "out there" and uses external material such as wood and stone and steel. But other arts, for instance sculpture and painting, work with external materials. There are further kinds of externality more specific to architecture. I will discuss first architecture's special relation to gravity, then the unorganic externality of architectural purpose, the outward architectonic act, and the externality of meaning in symbolic art. My conclusion will suggest going beyond Hegel on this topic by following his directions.

I. Gravity

First, then, to gravity: Hegel states that architecture "becomes an inorganic surrounding, a whole built and ordered according to the laws of gravity."[2] That is, architecture produces works posited as explicitly subject to the external law of gravity.

Though Hegel's phrase *Gesetz der Schwere* is the normal German for "law of gravity," it could also be read as "the law of weight." It is appropriate that Hegel mentions "the law of weight," since in what he considers the most authentic architecture the expression of weight and bearing and support gives conceptual necessity to the built forms.

In his philosophy of nature Hegel distinguishes gravity as weight (*Schwere*) which is expressed in falling as bodies seek a center outside themselves,[3] from the conceptually more complex and concrete notion of the system of gravity (*Gravitation*) which is expressed in the free motion of the planets of the solar system.[4] Both of these are distinguished from that conceptually more primitive attraction (*Attraktion*) which is the negative unity of the being-for-self of matter in its being outside itself.[5] Weight is the unity of that attraction and the equally primitive repulsion (*Repulsion*) that expresses the being-for-self of matter.

Hegel is here reworking and arguing with Kant's construction of matter out of the two forces of attraction and repulsion, and he is refusing to separate the forces or to identify gravity or weight with the one force of attraction. Hegel is also working towards one of his polemics against Newton.[6] He also shows a curious hesitation about dealing with gravity in terms of the attraction of many different bodies for one another; later I will discuss this lingering Aristotelianism in Hegel's notion of gravity. For our architectural purposes we do not need to emphasize these distinctions because though they are on different levels what they all express is a togetherness of matter in its very separateness. Externality is both posited and overcome. Gravity through its very externality denies the seemingly immediate separation and next-to-each-other-ness of material objects. This external linkage is conceptually necessary in order for bodies to be spread out at all.

Likewise, on all the levels of discussion, gravity and weight offer relation and attraction that ignore internal differentiation. Gravity disregards the details of a body's inner composition or inner structure. Gravity is the premier external relationship, dealing with items characterized by weight as one abstract totalizing characteristic. Such undifferentiated heaviness opposes Spirit's inner self-differentiation, but also shows how Spirit's motion of self-return has already begun in the pure external side-by-side-ness of matter.

Heaviness is an external prefiguring of Spirit's turning to itself: "The concept of heaviness . . . contains both the moment of being-for-itself and the continuity that sublates that [isolated] being-for-itself."[7] Gravity provides a unity within external relations and forces. This is already a first overcoming of externality.

In the realm of art, architecture does much the same; it provides a first (external) overcoming of externality. It is the art of the external because it posits and proclaims its own externality as a (external) way of transcending that externality. The architect creates a structure that speaks its subservience to gravity. But the building's functional unity goes beyond what the physical law can demand or notice. In architecture gravity is shown as transcended within Spirit's self-construction. Architecture displays the external as external in relation to other more inner unities.

II. External Nature

Hegel says that it is "the special vocation of architecture, to be a pure enclosure . . . to show an unorganic nature built by human hands."[8] What does it mean to say that this built surrounding is *unorganic*? It means more than that we build with non-living material. The architect builds within unorganic nature and produces unities that are unorganic. Introducing architecture, Hegel says that "The first task of art consists in giving shape to . . . the external environment of spirit, and so to build into what has no interiority a meaning and form which remain external to it because this meaning and form are not immanent in the objective world itself."[9] The external environment has no inner life of its own, and the meaning and form we build remain external to that external nature.

The nature within which architecture builds does not itself have any organic principle that determines its form. Of course unorganic nature has its own structures that are studied by science and discussed in the first two divisions of Hegel's philosophy of nature, but such structures have no inner self-directed teleology. They have neither the self-contained purposiveness of the organism nor the external purposiveness of the tool. This lack of purpose is exactly unorganic nature's place in the system. We might say that the purpose and meaning of the unorganic is to lack purpose and meaning, to be the other, the surrounding for Spirit's world. As part of the overall vocation of Spirit to come to itself, this unorganic moment of Spirit's self-othering needs to be shown as itself, but this showing can only be to Spirit, not to unorganic nature it-*self*, since unorganic nature has no self.

This positing of external nature as external means that in the overall career of Spirit we need something like architecture. Architecture is the art that works in the outer world, with material things, and produces products whose purpose remains external to the objects produced. A piece of music or a poem, for Hegel the most spiritual of the arts, will transcend such externality. But then we might ask, why still have architecture as an art; why not leave art's vocation to the higher arts, and just treat buildings as functional tools?

The answer is that architecture does something artistic that a poem cannot do. It does not merely function; it symbolizes and shows forth its own functioning.[10] It artistically enacts our relation to outer unorganic reality, to gravity, to bearing and covering and enclosing, and, in romantic architecture, it spatializes our movement beyond the spatially external. Poetry can talk about these but not enact them in this (albeit external but unique precisely because external) way. Architecture makes art—a self-showing of Spirit—out of something that has only externality and lack of purpose to offer, and architecture shows that externality forth in its imposition of (external) purpose and internality.[11]

III. External Purposes

Architecture deals with external unorganic nature as Other. It makes of that nature purposive structures. Their purpose, however, remains "outside" the material structure. We may speak metaphorically of this or that function as "the soul of the building" but in fact architectural structure as such has no true inner governing and limiting principle. This lack of immanent form and meaning is the key to architecture's vocation as an art.

> [Architecture's] vocation lies precisely in fashioning external nature as an enclosure shaped into beauty by art out of the resources of the spirit itself, and fashioning it for the spirit already present, for man, or for the divine images which he has framed and set up as objects. This enclosure does not carry its meaning in itself but finds it in something else, in man and his needs and aims in family life, the state, or religion, etc., and therefore the independence of the buildings is sacrificed.[12]

> When architecture acquires the place belonging to it in accordance with its own essential nature, its productions are subservient to an end and a meaning not immanent in itself. It becomes an inorganic surrounding, a whole built and ordered according to the laws of gravity. . . . Architecture at this stage . . . corresponds with its authentic concept, because it cannot entirely endow the spiritual with an adequate existence and therefore can only frame the external and spiritless into a reflection of the spiritual.[13]

> The fundamental character of architecture proper consists in the fact that the spiritual meaning does not reside exclusively in the building . . . but in the fact that this meaning has already attained its existence in freedom outside architecture.[14]

In order to pursue these ideas further we need to know more precisely what it means to say that the purpose of architecture remains external to the building.

Hegel develops several concepts of purpose. The least inward is the purpose of tools, which have the shape they do because that shape serves some end held by another being.

> A house, a clock, may appear as ends in relation to the tools employed for their production; but the stones and beams, or wheels and axles, and so on, which constitute the actuality of the end fulfil that end only through the pressure that they suffer, through the chemical processes with air, light, and water to which they are exposed and that deprive man of them by their friction and so forth. Accordingly, they fulfil their destiny only by being used and worn away and they correspond to what they are supposed to be only through their negation. They are not positively united with the end, because they possess self-determination only externally and are only relative ends, or essentially nothing but means.[15]

Deeper than such external purpose is the inner teleology of an organism, which is "the ideal unity which has found itself and is for itself."[16] The organism contains a unity that "as its own goal, possesses its means in its objectivity and posits the latter as its means, yet is immanent in this means and is therein the realized end that is identical with itself."[17] In an organism

> objectivity is . . . taken up into the subjective unity. . . . Since the concept is immanent in it, the purposiveness of the living being is to be grasped as inner; the concept is in it as determinate concept, distinct from its externality, and in its distinguishing, pervading the externality and remaining identical with itself. . . . the concept constitutes its substance; but for that very reason this means and instrument is itself the realized end. . . . In respect of its externality the organism is a manifold, not of parts but of members.[18]

This is the kind of realized unity that architecture can never achieve. Buildings are at least tools, and their purpose is to be found in the activities of some other being. Hegel says that

> Organic products, as they are portrayed by sculpture in the shape of animals and men, have their beginning and end in their own free outlines, because it is the rational organism itself which settles the boundaries of its shape from within outwards. For the [architectural] column and its shape, however, architecture has nothing but the mechanical determinant of load-bearing and the spatial distance from the ground to the point where the load to be carried terminates the column.

However, buildings are also works of art, self-showings of Spirit, so they are more than tools. Their externally derived purposes result in shapes that should be given an appearance of inner inevitability. Hegel continues the previous passage:

> But the particular moments implicit in this determining [of their proportions] belong to the column, and art must bring them out and give shape to them. Consequently the column's specific length, its two boundaries above and below, and its carrying power should not appear to be only accidental and introduced into it by something else but must be displayed as also immanent in itself.[19]

Architecture must perform its art and bring the external as external into an appearance of indwelling unity, even as the purpose of the building remains external rather than a true organic form.

Such externality is most extreme in the stage Hegel calls symbolic architecture. Although no architectural work can have organic unity in the strong sense in which an animal body possesses such unity, symbolic architecture is particularly unorganic. Symbolic architecture is more paratactic than syntactic. According to Hegel, Egyptian temples combine sculptures, columns, rooms, and other elements, but their mode of combination is an uncontrolled one-thing-next-to-another not guided by the more complex internal relations typical of classical architecture.

This adjoined-ness or next-to-ness is not only characteristic of symbolic art; it is what is specifically architectural. Hegel argues that the use of sculpture in Egyptian temples remains "more . . . architectonic than sculptural."[20] What is it that distinguishes the architectonic from the sculptural? The Egyptian sculptures are ordered in rows, and "in this ordering in rows acquire their architectural character."[21]

It is in classical architecture that the external putting things next to other things becomes permeated by an inner logic (deriving from the structural actions of the building parts) that supplements their external purpose and gives the building a sense of inevitability. Hegel speaks of classical architecture as "organic." But even in classical architecture externality wins the day. Concerning the parts of classical columns, Hegel says

> the differences . . . must come into appearance as differences; on the other hand it is equally necessary for them to be united into a whole . . . this unification, which in architecture cannot be more than a juxtaposition, and an association, and a thorough-going eurhythmy of proportion.[22]

Even in classical architecture, then, the architectonic deals in next-to-each-other-ness and stuck-together-ness rather than true inner development.

IV. External Meanings

There is a further dimension of externality. The mode of signification found in all architecture is the symbolic, where there are no inner bonds between form and meaning, nor among the various meanings found in the artwork.

Hegel says that in symbolic art we find an abstract mode of thought where general representations, concepts, and philosophical categories are adjoined, treated (by the understanding, not reason) as separable and permutable without necessary orders or connections.

> The meanings taken as content here, as in symbolic art generally, are as it were vague and general representations, elemental, variously confused and sundered abstractions of the life of nature, intermingled with thoughts of the actuality of spirit, without being ideally collected together as moments within a single subjectivity.[23]

These many meanings are not united in an inner articulated unity; they remain external to one another. Symbolic thought does with ideas and images what architecture does with blocks and beams: puts one next to another.

Architecture remains low in the hierarchy of the arts because of the mutual externality of purpose and parts, and of meanings to one another and to their symbols. On the other hand, this low position is a necessary aspect of Spirit's articulation of itself. Spirit could not make everything purely inner, or there would be no inner. Spirit's being and activity demand that externality be both real and expressed.

V. Positing Externality as Such

In discussing symbolic art in general, Hegel says that the externality of its meaning relations should itself be expressed within the art. "Since this externality is present in itself in the symbolic, it must also be posited".[24]

If Spirit is to be, that is, if Spirit is to come to itself, then all the dimensions and presuppositions of its being must be explicitly posited and incorporated as such. Art is a mode in which Spirit presents its reality to itself. So the externality characteristic of symbolic art should be itself expressed in an artwork where the externality of the relation between the meanings becomes itself the action performed by the artwork.

Can this happen within symbolic art itself? It does, for Hegel, in those forms of symbolic literary art that make explicit external comparisons relating diverse areas of meaning while maintaining their externality to one another. These include fables, parables, riddles, allegories, explicit metaphors and similes, and other verbal forms whose action is to bring about explicit comparisons between diverse areas of meaning.[25]

However, there is no stage in Hegel's treatment of architecture that functions as do those types of literary art. There is no self-conscious positing of architectural externality as such. Architecture is called to bring externality under at least the appearance of inner necessity. The externality of its material and purpose is never completely mastered by that inner necessity, for the inner necessity is itself an external imposition of loosely associated meanings. But there is no stage of architecture that itself posits, performs, or comments on these dimensions of specifically architectural externality. The externality of symbolic art as such is shown within the stronger interiorization of literary art. Nowhere is architectural externality made the explicit theme or action of an artwork.

There is one seeming exception. During his general discussion of symbolic art Hegel discusses the Egyptian pyramid as a metasymbol of the enigmatic quality of symbols in general. Hegel discusses the pyramid's closed shape and hidden content to itself symbolize the more general relation of symbols to meaning.[26] However, Hegel does not discuss the pyramid as showing forth a specifically architectural externality.

I said earlier that architecture "is the art of the external because it posits and proclaims its own externality as an external way of transcending that externality." Now we can see that that is not entirely true. Architecture does not make art that explicitly takes up all the dimensions of its own externality.

Need this be so? Might there be an architecture whose action was to present and thematize the dimensions of architectural externality in the self-performance of the building? Could or should there be an architecture that explicitly posited its symbolic, external, unorganic meaning and relation to meaning? That "did" its architectonic unity as external next-to-ness, or that presented its purpose as external to its form? Could there be an architecture that explicitly showed forth the externality of adjoined forms or elements or meanings to one another? Or, recalling our first dimension of externality, a building that presented itself as a presentation of the lack of intrinsic meaning in material objects?

Such buildings would not be traditional, if traditional means to sit neatly within a received set of meanings presented as organically united with one another. The meanings borne by the building would be shown as adjoined and uneasy in their relation. Such buildings would be not modern, if modern means to be permeated by function and rationality. Rather their forms would refuse to be controlled by function and rational unity. Such buildings would not be postmodern, if postmodern means to be infused with historical quotation or ironic sensibility, for that too manifests a form of interiorizing subjectivity, though one that finds its inwardness in its distance from the material it treats.[27]

One thinks for example of some of Zaha Hadid's designs, or of Frank Gehry's own house and others of his early buildings where materials and functions and forms were separated and adjoined to one another. Some of the work of architects like Peter Eisenman and Bernard Tschumi may also attempt such moves, though unlike Gehry's works their buildings often stand more as illustrations to theories. Their buildings ask to be "understood" by reading certain texts, so their demonstrations of externality are compromised. Buildings that really "did" externality would have to resist being footnotes to theories—even Hegel's theories.

How might such resistance come about? Like brute matter, the building would be held together by a law of gravity that kept its adjoined forms and functions and meanings together without inquiring into their inner structures or producing internal semiotic relations. Such gravitational attraction would refuse the transparency of the building's parts to one another or to any overarching purpose or meaning or essence. Togetherness in exteriority.

The points raised in these last several paragraphs offer challenging suggestions. However, we should remember that Frank Gehry's externalism was recouped as a style, "the Santa Monica School," and the architects I mentioned were lumped together as "deconstructive architects" and so made a stage in an interiorizing narrative. In fact we should realize that it is impossible for any building to purely "do" pure externality. Pure externality and otherness cannot be presented as such, since any presentation involves semiosis.

Nor, in fact, is gravity itself totally indifferent to internal structure. There are tides. In physics it is not strictly true that an object is affected by gravity independently of its internal structure. While for many calculations gravitational forces can be summed up as if they acted at the single center of gravity, in fact each mass point in the one object is affected by each point in the others. This means that if an object is sufficiently large it can feel tidal forces when its different parts are closer and farther away from an attracting object. The near part of the first object is attracted more than its farther away part, so the object is subject to tidal forces. Depending on the internal structure of the object, tidal forces can move its parts (as with our oceans), warp its form and change its motion (as with our moon), or disrupt or prevent its unity or even tear it apart (as with Roche's Limit and the rings of Saturn).[28]

So our building that is trying to posit the externality of its parts and meanings to one another will find that its juxtaposed parts and functions and meanings do influence one another even while and because they stand apart. This influence is not a general attraction to a center, but rather a tidal influence that distorts and bends each shape and space effect, each meaning and function in relation to the particular others surrounding it. There is no purely external juxtaposition.

But if this is so, then how could a building ever posit its externality as such? It could not do so completely. But perhaps the building could return, as it were, to that silent nature of that first dimension of exteriority. It would foreground its external, physical presence in a way that emphasized both its put-together-ness and the physical muteness and singular otherness that everywhere underlie and resist transparency. A building might be designed in such a way as to show itself as resisting domination by functions and narratives and meanings and centers, even as those functions and meanings could not be fully kept away.

Frank Gehry's house plays with standard dualities in an unresolvable way as materials assert themselves outside their normal places and roles. The pure cement of Tadao Ando's highly ordered works offers a mute but shining presence beyond narrative.[29] These and other ways of building can emphasize architecture's resistance to meanings and centers, but it happens to some degree with any building, in any style. We and our products are inevitably complicit in such schemes and narratives, yet our life is more than what those narratives comprehend, though such a "more" and such resistance can only be shown as slipping aside, as it were, from the conceptual or narrative thrust. Art can enact this better than philosophy. Architecture can enact it better than poetry.

VI. Conclusion

So we have arrived back where we began, with the need for the art of architecture, as in Hegel's story. But we have also put pressure on that story. For if we consider Hegel's notions about art showing the moments of Spirit's becoming as such, and if we take Hegel's treatment of architectural externality even more seriously than he does, then architecture can play the role he assigns it even better than he realizes. But in doing so architecture will resist Hegel's attempt to keep it on the first level of a hierarchical story that presents externalization self-consciously only in more interiorized literary art and philosophy.

Following the prescription in Hegel's modern narrative to self-consciously posit every condition of Spirit's possibility, we end up positing externalities that put the building somewhat outside the prescriptive power of his narrative. But not simply outside. Nor simply a dialectical relation, either. The tension between the externality Hegel attributes to architecture and the interiorizing narrative drive of his philosophy of art is something like a dialectical tension, because it is precisely the attempt to fulfill the demands of Hegel's narrative that reveals in buildings something in their being that refuses to be incorporated into Hegel's narrative, and therefore refuses to be subject to those demands. In fulfilling the role Hegel assigns to it architecture resists its location in his story of the arts. This dialectic does not lead to a full enfolding, but to the positing of an externality even to the dialectical story.

VII. Gravitic Coda

The spiritual aspect of physical gravity is its positing of a necessary external togetherness that links things while keeping them external to one another. It is the physical analogue of every being's sharing in the overall motion of what it means to be.

But there is a lingering Aristotelianism in Hegel's discussion of gravity. It shows in his curious reluctance to discuss gravity in terms of the mutual attraction of every body for every other. This shows when he makes falling the first concept of concrete motion, where he emphasizes the movement of bodies towards an ideal center rather than shared motion of mutually attracting bodies.[30] It can be seen when he claims that thrust and attractions apply to an existence of matter other than the free godlike motion of the celestial bodies.[31] His discussion of the solar system speaks of a free motion proper to each body; it keeps Aristotle's idea of natural motion particular to these bodies, and avoids the externality of a Newtonian motion that results from many outside forces acting on each body. In his insistence that Kepler is superior to Newton, Hegel emphasizes mathematical pattern and conceptual divisions rather than motion as resulting from a composition of empirical forces.

Hegel's discussion of gravity thus gives a privileged place to ideal and real centers, expressed finally by the sun as the posited embodiment of the unity of the gravitational system. What if that central sun were multiplied in the mutual tidal attraction of bodies for one another?

We might think of different buildings and art works (or social unities, discourses and practices) as being external to one another in ways that cannot be totally interiorized, but also as all affecting one another, not by a uniform central attraction but by multiple tidal attractions that affect each differentially, reshaping and pulling each away from its self-enclosed roundness. These would not quite be dialectical relationships, for tidal effects take hold not directly on the central concept but on the extended bodies of moons, discourses, and art objects. Tidal influences move across conceptual borders, warping conceptual skeletons, bringing the outside in and denying neat separation of levels.

What would come of rethinking the externality of buildings and social practices and discourses in tidal terms? We might find ourselves within such a polycentric system of mutual attractions. Yet this lack of a center would not result in a dramatic explosion of disunity, but in a complex skein of relations and tidal influences. Could we think the influences of architectural context that way? Would dialectic be mimicked by a version of Roche's Limit for the approach to one another of buildings, or discourses or practices? Would close approach put enough pressure on one another to force them into new shapes?

In closing we should recall that our title phrase, "the spirit of gravity," has other more famous connotations. Nietzsche vigorously opposes a "spirit of gravity" that denies our Dionysian freedom to create our own values and dance with masks. There is no doubt that anything Hegelian, even if polycentric, will maintain the seriousness that Nietzsche attacks. Hegel's dance of relations and transitions includes the work of the concept and the negative, and both of these require more constitutive connections than do Nietzsche's contending wills to power. For the spirit of gravity, in Hegel's sense, insists on mutual attractions and tensions precisely in externality.

Notes

1. G. W. F. Hegel, *Vorlesungen über die Ästhetik, Werke in zwanzig Bänden,* ed. Eva Moldenhauer and K. Michel, 20 vols. and Index, (Frankfurt am Main: Suhrkamp Verlag, 1969ff), 14:271, ". . . is an art whose medium is purely external." English translation, G. W. F. Hegel, *Aesthetics: Lectures on Fine Art,* 2 vols., trans. T. M. Knox (Oxford, Clarendon Press, 1975), 2:634. Further references will be given in the form: *Werke,* 14:271; *A,* 2:634. As here, I have occasionally modified the translations given in the text.

2. *Werke*, 14:302; *A*, 2:660. Hegel is here speaking of classical architecture.

3. See the discussion in G. W. F. Hegel, *Enzyklopädie der philosophischen Wissenschaften im Grundrisse* (1830), *Werke in zwanzig Bänden*, ed. E. Moldenhauer and K. Michel, vol. 9 (Frankfurt am Main: Suhrkamp Verlag, 1969ff), Sections 262–68. English translation by A. V. Miller, *Hegel's Philosophy of Nature* (Oxford: Oxford University Press, 1970).

4. *Enz.* (1830), sections 269–270.

5. *Enz.* (1830), section 262.

6. *Enz.* (1830), section 266 and 270.

7. *Enz.* (1830), section 269, Zus.

8. *Werke*, 14:294; *A*, 2:653.

9. *Werke*, 14:267; *A*, 2:631.

10. I have discussed the relation of Hegel's three stages of architecture to the expression of function, and the several different kinds of function involved, especially in Hegel's ideas about classical architecture, together with some possible changes in Hegel's scheme, in "Before Beyond Function" (available on the Web at http://abacus.bates.edu/~dkolb/bbfunction.html).

11. The survival of older forms of art raises similar issues for Hegel as the survival of previous social forms within a modern society. Those may be changed (slavery, duelling, feudal loyalty) or they may survive as a moment (family and clan), but in either case they are no longer able to make ultimate claims. Hegel says that given their logical forms certain stages of Spirit expressed themselves in symbolic art, and architecture was the form most appropriate for symbolic art. It expressed Spirit's self-conception when that was unmediated enough to be adequately expressed through symbolic art. Our self-conception is more complexly interiorized. Architecture survives as a part of the modern self-presentation of Spirit but not as a dominant part. It is qualified and reduced, but it is not replaced. Nothing replaces anything else in Hegel, though things lose their absoluteness.

12. *Werke*, 14:270; *A*, 2:633. For a sensitive and thoughtful discussion of the theme of enclosure in Hegel's treatment of architecture, and its relation to Heidegger's theme of dwelling, see John Sallis, *Stone* (Bloomington: University of Indiana Press, 1994), especially ch. 3.

13. *Werke*, 14:303; *A*, 2:660.

14. *Werke*, 14:303; *A*, 2:661.

15. G. W. F. Hegel, *Wissenschaft der Logik*, ed. F. Hogemann and W. Jaeschke, *Gesammelte Werke*, vol. 12 (Hamburg: Felix Meiner), 167. English translation by A. V. Miller, *Hegel's Science of Logic* (London: Allen and Unwin, 1969), 750.

16. *Enz.* (1830), section 252.

17. *Logik*, 177; Miller, p. 760.

18. *Logik*, 184; Miller, p. 766.

19. *Werke*, 14:311; *A*, 2:668.

20. *Werke*, 14:282; *A*, 2:643.

21. *Werke*, 14:284; *A*, 2:644.

22. *Werke*, 14:318; *A*, 2:674.

23. *Werke*, 14:274; *A*, 2:637.

24. *Werke,* 13:486; *A,* 1:378.

25. *Werke,* 13:485–539; *A,* 1:378–420.

26. *Werke,* 13:458ff; *A,* 1:354ff. The relation of symbolic meaning to its external expression remains distant and approximate. Elsewhere Hegel asserts that "the symbol, strictly so called, is inherently enigmatical because the external existent by means of which a universal meaning is to be brought to our contemplation still remains different from the meaning that it has to represent, and it is therefore open to doubt in what sense the shape has to be taken." (*Werke,* 13:509; *A,* 1:397)

27. See my *Postmodern Sophistications* (Chicago: University of Chicago Press, 1992) for a discussion of the relation of modern subjectivity and postmodern irony.

28. Roche's Limit is that distance from a planet at which a moon will be pulled apart by tidal forces. Closer than the limit, the resultant force due to the difference between the attractive force felt by the near side and that felt by the far side will be greater than the strength of rock to resist being torn apart. The rings around the outer planets may have been caused by older moons being destroyed in this way, or by the inability of a stable moon to accrete from material located inside the limit.

29. The building beyond narrative, as for example in Tadao Ando's use of plain concrete, reveals the withdrawn Heideggerian "earth" that is not captured by the duality interior/exterior. See John Sallis's discussion of "shining stone" in *Stone* (Bloomington: University of Indiana Press, 1994).

30. M. J. Petry equates this falling movement towards an ideal center with movement about their common center of gravity, and so as a mutual attraction. But this seems to ignore how Hegel discusses falling in terms of each body singly, and it seems to confuse Hegel's discussion of weight with his later discussion of gravity. (See M. Petry, *Hegel's Philosophy of Nature* (London: Allen and Unwin, 1970), 1:322.)

31. *Enz.* (1830), section 269, Zus.

VII

The Challenge of Architecture to Hegel's Aesthetics

Richard Dien Winfield

I. Architecture as an Aesthetic Enigma

More than any of the traditional fine arts, architecture presents a puzzle to aesthetics. On the one hand, architecture ordinarily does not denote anything at all. Like music and dance devoid of program and abstract visual art, architecture seems to require that beauty shed the last remnants of mimesis and every other form of representation, yet still provide whatever meaning art should possess. On the other hand, architecture departs from other nonrepresentational arts by ordinarily serving a prosaic purpose, essentially housing some activity or artifact, instead of standing sheltered from use as something whose sheer appearance can independently command attention. How then can architecture be accommodated by the philosophy of fine art, without subverting the significance and autonomy of beauty?

This problem takes an acute form for Hegel, even though he repudiates mimesis and any notion of art for art's sake that detaches aesthetic form from content. More than any other past aesthetician, Hegel recognizes that aesthetic phenomena are pervaded by an individuality tying shape and meaning inextricably together. This ubiquitous individuality is exhibited, first, in how the beauty of an artwork is dependent upon the concrete details of its execution, rather than merely upon its embodiment of some universal form, second, in how artistic production subordinates the universal routines of technique to the unique originality of artistic genius, and finally, in how art criticism loses the aesthetic dimension as soon as it judges its object against independently given standards.[1] Despite the aesthetic centrality of beauty's individuality, it escapes the conceptual resources of mimetic theory, pioneered by Plato and Aristotle, and the transcendental aesthetics of reception, inaugurated by Hume and Kant. Both aesthetics fall short of their prey by conceiving beauty to be determined by antecedent factors that inform it with a characteristic universal identity whose particular embodiment becomes incidental to its aesthetic worth. Just as mimetic art is defined by giving expression to the antecedently given form it represents, so transcendental aesthetics derives beauty from the structure of aesthetic reception that underlies each and every aesthetic appearance. In each case, form and content fall asunder, for what individuates the object of beauty from other bearers of the same form or other products of an analogous transcendental constitution drops out of aesthetic consideration.[2]

Because Hegel makes the individuality of beauty central to aesthetics, he realizes that art cannot simply *re-present* given contents, but must *transfigure* whatever it presents so that the form of its appearance is uniquely tied to its content. Consequently, Hegel's departure from mimesis does not entail an exclusion of meaning from beauty; rather it requires locating those meanings susceptible of artistic construal, a construal whose sensuous individuality needs an equally concrete significance to enable form and content to fit. Moreover, because the unity of form and content signifies that beauty be independent of external factors, the meaning of art must inherently deserve display. Instead of depending upon contingent interests and perspectives, artistic meaning must be of universal significance to any possible audience. Hence, the concrete meaning of art must involve what is of fundamental importance to rational agents per se. Although, besides art itself, ethics, religion, and philosophy each have an unconditioned significance, only ethics and religion have concrete dimensions susceptible of sensuous presentation. Accordingly, when beauty unites form and content, the content will express fundamental truths of ethics or religion, providing rational agents with a self-understanding no matter what their personal experiences or cultural community. Moreover, to the degree that ethics and religion have conceptually determinate alternative configurations, beauty will divide into fundamental artistic styles, each comprising the particular mode of artistic construal by which a particular ethical and religious worldview obtains a congruent aesthetic form.

These cardinal desiderata of Hegel's aesthetics magnify the problem of architecture. For not only must architecture somehow retain significance without mimesis, but it must express a meaning fit for art, that is, a fundamental self-understanding of humanity in a unique sensuous configuration. Consequently, the problem is hardly solved by Nelson Goodman's observation that architecture can refer without denotation by literally or metaphorically expressing contents that may have their own mediated references.[3] The identification of these alternative types of reference still leaves unexplained how architecture can signify a worthy content in a distinctively aesthetic way. Moreover, architecture must retain its aesthetic individuality even while serving a function, whose instrumentality fits the very categories of artisan production that otherwise condemn art to the embodiment of antecedent forms, where the individuality of the artifact is incidental to its functionality. Can architecture be nonrepresentational and functional, yet sensuously convey fundamental human truths with aesthetic individuality? Meeting this challenge is difficult enough, but Hegel's account adds one further complication. Because ethical and religious worldviews have conceptually determinate varieties entailing particular modes of artistic configuration, an account of architecture must show how these a priori art forms are architecturally realizable.

Hegel does not flinch from meeting these challenges and few would dispute that his treatment of architecture is without parallel for its conceptual scope and ambition.[4] Yet has Hegel succeeded in deciphering the riddle of architecture? The answer to this question dovetails with whether Hegel has succeeded in bringing aesthetics to its third and final level of determination: the theory of the individual arts, which incorporates, and thereby presupposes, the concepts of art in general and of the particular art forms.

Hegel himself identifies architecture as the keystone of the individual arts, preceding all others both in historical origin and in conceptual ordering. If this claim is taken seriously, Hegel's conception of architecture will make or break the entire edifice that is built upon it.

II. The Principle Suspect Features of Hegel's Concept of Architecture

Almost immediately, Hegel's account of architecture exhibits salient suspect features that persist throughout his treatment of the other arts, calling into question the whole enterprise of his theory of the individual arts.

First, Hegel connects the historical and conceptual primacy of architecture with the symbolic art form, suggesting that architecture is preeminently a symbolic art, limited by its arrangement of heavy masses to relate meaning and shape in the allusive manner defining the discrepancy at the heart of the symbolic art form.[5] Admittedly, if architecture is essentially restricted to erecting immobile, solid masses in conformity with laws of gravity, it cannot present configurations that have a subjectivity of their own. Nevertheless, this limitation hardly prevents architecture from creating environments for sacred and profane conduct expressing markedly different worldviews, each standing in a different relation to the shape that makes it manifest. These possibilities are symptomatic of a basic conceptual confusion lingering in Hegel's subsequent characterization of sculpture as a classical art and of painting, music, and literature as romantic arts. In each case, Hegel seems to conflate two distinct levels of aesthetic determination: that of the particular art forms and that of the individual arts. Instead of treating the art forms as particular modes of relating meaning and shape that are determinable in their own right, independently of the individual arts, Hegel here seems to commit the category mistake of attaching particular art forms to different individual arts, blurring the distinction between the two dimensions of aesthetic reality.

Yet, at the very same time, Hegel cuts off his nose to spite his face, developing architecture into a succession of symbolic, classical, and romantic developments, demonstrating that architecture can exhibit every art form, just as sculpture, painting, music, and literature will prove to do in his own subsequent treatment.[6] Indeed, he even emphasizes that the three art forms play a greater determining role in architecture than in the other arts, whose stylistic differentiations are comparatively limited due to a more encompassing penetration by one art form.[7] At most, Hegel's linkage of architecture to the symbolic art form might support the prescriptive judgment that symbolic architecture will enjoy an artistic success outstripping classical and romantic constructions. Hegel's own analyses of the Greek temple and the Gothic cathedral, however, give the lie to any such verdict, testifying to how artworks of any medium and of any style can rise to aesthetic greatness or sink into banality. For as Hegel's own account of symbolic and romantic art already established, even when meaning and shape are bound to be incongruent, beauty can be attained by making that incongruence as much a part of artistic form as an aspect of artistic content. Similarly, an art form may have greater or lesser privilege as a vehicle for expressing human self-understanding, but so long as it qualifies as art, it gives expression to an essential worldview in a sensuous image linked to the meaning it conveys. Accordingly, the very categories of Hegel's aesthetics provide ample reason to minimize the linkage of architecture with symbolic art and to concentrate instead upon investigating the success with which his own development of symbolic, classical, and romantic architecture brings to a first concrete realization how the universal and particular categories of aesthetics inform an individual art.

It is here, in the actual working out of Hegel's concept of architecture, that a second set of perplexities arise, revolving around how the instrumentality of buildings enters into the development of architectural style. Hegel claims that architectural style begins, both historically and conceptually, with a symbolic construal where architecture does *not* serve any external use, but constitutes a building to be independently beheld like a mammoth, inchoate, inorganic sculpture.[8] Then, by way of transitional constructions like the Pyramids, where a purpose becomes the hidden core of a monument,[9] a classical architecture arises in which form and function are united, producing buildings that serve as means to an end lying outside them. Finally, architecture assumes a third, romantic form, uniting the defining aspects of its forerunners, exhibiting an independence of form from function while still serving a purpose.[10] Admittedly, this threefold differentiation of architecture possesses a logical closure by exhausting the basic ways in which building can relate to external purpose: an edifice can either be independent, purposive, or both. What is less evident is how these three relationships of architectural form and function have anything to do with how symbolic, classical, and romantic styles achieve architectural realization. Why should an independent architecture be mandated by the symbolic construal of a human self-understanding too abstract to have any adequate sensuous embodiment? How can a union of architectural form and function serve the classical ideal of a human spirit whose substance is as it appears? And why should a unification of architectural function and independence be required for the romantic expression of a subjectivity whose essential inward autonomy can never be fully captured in any external manifestation? Has Hegel here inadvertently testified to how the categories of art in general and the particular art forms cannot lay hold of an individual artistic medium, handing over analysis of the individual arts to art historians and art critics? Or does he pave the way for conceiving a priori forms of architectural style?

III. The Puzzle of Independent, Symbolic Architecture

Hegel's first candidate in the division of architecture is most puzzling, since the very independence by which it is distinguished seems to transgress the bounds of architecture. As Hegel himself observes, an architecture that builds structures devoid of use verges on monumental, inorganic sculpture.[11] For if a construction shapes heavy masses without regard for some external purpose, how can it be distinguished from a work of sculpture that equally shapes matter purely in regard to its three-dimensional form? Hegel might appear to have an easy escape from this problem, given his limitation of genuine sculpture to the plastic shaping of the human form. Granted this restriction, independent architecture and abstract statuary would both fall outside sculpture proper into the domain of architectural design, provided independent architecture divested itself of any representations of the human form.[12] Hegel, however, himself refers to works of independent, symbolic architecture, such as the Egyptian Sphinxes and Memnons, that represent human figures. In these cases, what allows otherwise human shapes to fall within architecture is the monumentality of scale and placement in arrangements whose nonrepresentational plan is the real focal point of architectural interest.[13] For these reasons, Hegel is content to distinguish independent architecture from sculpture, despite the absence of an external function.

The question remains, nonetheless, how the independence of such architecture fits its symbolic style. A plausible answer that seems to fit Hegel's treatment of classical and romantic architecture, runs as follows: the restriction of architecture to the arrangement of heavy masses prevents buildings from adequately conveying the subjectivity and autonomy of rational agency. Hence, when that subjectivity and autonomy is understood to be of fundamental significance, architecture can serve the ends of art only by being a means for housing either artworks in other media more capable of presenting the truth of independent agency (such as sculpture and painting) or for housing activity in which rational agency is properly realized. When, by contrast, the self-understanding of humanity rejects the affirmative significance of human finitude and its independent subjectivity, and instead places ultimate value in divine powers into which individuality is absorbed and extinguished as an illusory epiphenomenon, the truth of existence can be directly conveyed with the abstract resources of architecture. In the former case, which fits the worldviews of classical and romantic styles, architecture retains its functionality. In the latter case, which fits the self-understanding expressed by symbolic art, architecture can be independent, simply making manifest the truth to which its static, inorganic forms can so suitably allude.

Such an explanation may account for the linkage between independence and symbolic architecture and between functionality and classical and romantic architecture, but these connections still leave undetermined how the respective independence and dependence of symbolic and nonsymbolic building has ramifications for the specific appearance of these architectural styles. After all, whether a building is constructed for its own sake or for an external use need not automatically affect its design in any fashion whatsoever. The same plan could conceivably fit either option.

Hegel himself seems to admit the indeterminacy of the connection between the independence of symbolic architecture and architectural design when he observes that the variety of both form and content in symbolic architecture can be neither exhausted nor systematically presented.[14] He attributes this to the absence of any set content or mode of design, an absence reflecting how the meanings in symbolic art are abstract universal representations, whose unformed generality fits no sensuous image, but gains expression only by drawing in an arbitrary, haphazard fashion from elementary physical processes, animal and plant life, and aspects of spiritual reality, never achieving unity in an individual subjectivity.[15] Nevertheless, Hegel proceeds to distinguish three forms of independent architecture in an attempt to bring a rational division to the most important options of symbolic construction.[16] These three forms consist first of buildings that unify a nation,[17] both in the task of construction and, upon completion, by providing a focal point of gathering; second, of buildings in which symbolic meanings differentiate themselves in inorganic and organic shapes; and finally, in transitional buildings in which sculptural configuration is excluded from the edifice that now provides enclosure for meanings not directly expressed in its architecture.

The first and third forms offer little towards exemplifying how the meaning tied to the independence of symbolic architecture has any ramifications for architectural design. Buildings identified by their role in unifying a nation seem all too burdened by an external purpose and all too undetermined in respect to shape. If it is the construction of an edifice that unifies a people, as Hegel alleges was the case with the tower of Babylon,[18] the appearance of the completed work is merely a superfluous outcome. If, alternately, the finished work unifies the nation by being a place in which people gather in confirmation of national unity, the achievement of this function seems unrelated to any specific architectural configuration, for as

Hegel himself observes, the form and shape of such a building can only express its unifying function in an external way.[19] By contrast, the third, transitional form of "independent" architecture may well entail the sort of design features Hegel finds exemplified in the Pyramids, whose geometric severity excludes sculptural detail and whose hidden burial chambers serve a significance not manifest on the exterior. Nonetheless, the reference to an end external to the architectural design risks transgressing the independence of independent architecture, even if the concealing and sealing of the interior passages prevents the living from making any use of what lies within.

The second form of independent architecture more squarely offers the sought connection between symbolic meaning and specific building designs. Here, the abstract natural forces in which symbolic meaning invests absolute worth gain architectural expression in such independent monuments as obelisks and lingams, whose concrete forms allude to those powers. Alternately, symbolic architecture erects monuments in the mold of organic forms whose transgression of natural shape and dimensions and whose combination of human and animal features express the sublimity of a divine in which independent subjectivity is overcome. As Hegel admits, symbolic architecture here veers closest to figurative sculpture. Nonetheless, it remains an art of building by, on the one hand, enlarging its figures to colossal proportions that render them lifeless masses, and, on the other hand, placing them in arrangements that make them elements of an inorganic architectural scheme.[20] Although Hegel cites historical examples for each option, these figure as instances of a type of construction that can be conceptually determined: phallus columns and obelisks are representative of nonfigurative, inorganically shaped constructions that have no use other than symbolizing abstract natural powers just as Memnons, and Sphinxes are free standing organic monuments, whose mixture of animal and human features, reduction of the individuality of the figure, and monumentality and schematic placement serve only to allude to divinities for whom individual subjectivity has no independent stature.[21]

If these stylistic options provide a connection between architectural independence and symbolic meaning, the question still arises as to whether a symbolic architecture can construct temples, palaces, and other useful buildings without transgressing its own self-understanding and passing beyond into a classical or romantic mold, where, if Hegel is to be followed, the instrumentality of architecture reflects recognition of the centrality of human individuality. Such possibilities need not be denied, for buildings serving human needs can equally express symbolic art's abstract notions of divinity and self provided they possess the same modalities of design whose independent embodiment has just been described. Indeed, the very examples of symbolic architecture to which Hegel refers combine their obelisks, lingams, Memnons and Sphinxes in architectural complexes in which use is not ignored, but in which form and function are not yet united.

IV. The Unity of Form and Function in Classical Architecture

Symbolic architecture may thus retain an independence in keeping with the worldview it architecturally expresses, but can architecture embody the classical ideal by uniting form and function? Hegel's prescription for an architecture that employs rectilinear geometric form to enclose a form of life sure of its own independent humanity almost seems to converge with slogans of Bauhaus functionality, Le Corbusier's manifesto for a new architecture in the instrumental spirit of modern technology,[22] and Frank Lloyd Wright's call for a natural house fitting human dimensions by excluding superfluous ornament and shape.[23] Can these brands of architectural modernism avoid conflation with classicism and somehow retain a place within romantic architecture, where functionality and independence go hand in hand? Or is the identity of classical architecture too ill defined to save architectural development from wholesale confusion? To resolve these questions, the unity of form and function must be further specified in regard to both the function at issue and the form that fits.

Whether Hegel succeeds in identifying a conceptually distinctive unity of meaning and configuration for classical architecture must be judged from his analysis of the Greek temple, which forms the crux of his treatment. As a realization of the classical style, the Greek temple cannot serve simply as an enclosure for worship. That function is too broad, since any religious building could share that purpose, no matter what architectural style it possessed. Instead, the temple's function must be more narrowly identified in respect to both the anthropomorphic polytheism characterizing the religious self-understanding of classicism and the affirmation of a naturally defined, but independent agency, for whom everything of worth lies in the outer activity of individuals, whose sensuous appearance is sufficient to convey their essential significance. Classical religious representation, unlike its symbolic counterpart, can find a perfect expression of what is divine in the figure of finite rational agency (in our terrestrial terms, the human body), just as the public life of individuals can be a sufficient arena for revealing everything essential in human existence. If classical architecture expresses a worldview with these features, and classical form follows function, the design of the classical temple must distinctively serve them.

Since the classical divine can be adequately represented in the figure of finite rational agents, figurative arts can be relied upon to convey the presence of divinity within the temple precincts. To the degree that sculpture presents only the surface of its figures, without supplying the idealization that two-dimensional figurative art adds, statues of the anthropomorphic gods would readily fit the demands of representing a form of agency that exhausts its fundamental significance in its outer deeds. Moreover, since such divinities have freed themselves from subordination to natural powers, they find their own suitable element only in an inorganic environment produced by rational artifice.[24] Accordingly, the classical temple can serve the function of enclosing statues of such divinities, together with the activity by which classical worshipers are distinguished. Since the classical worldview invests ultimate significance in the worldly, sensuously manifest, public display of autonomous individuals, the classical temple will not shut off the religious community from the secular public world. Instead of enclosing the place of worship in an ethereal chamber, secluded from profane life, the classical temple will be open to the outside, permitting worship to coexist with the conduct of public life.

When architectural form follows these specific functional considerations, salient features of the Greek temple readily result. To begin with, if building is to restrict itself to housing a type of divinity and rational agency that is adequately represented by idealized human statues and by the public conduct of the members of a naturally defined ethical community, the stylistic signatures of symbolic architecture must be shed.[25] Independent inorganic shapes, alluding to abstract divinities in which individuality is absorbed, have no more a role to play than plant, animal, and spiritual figures and motifs that symbolize sublime forces transcending any given sensuous, let alone human, embodiment. Instead, the edifice must reduce itself to a purely instrumental enclosure for what transparently makes manifest its own significance.[26] In this way, form and function are united, with architectural design governed by the demands of supporting an enclosure that will at once contain statuary of human figures and enable worshipers to view the representation of their anthropomorphic deities without leaving the public world behind.[27] As Hegel painstakingly argues, the classical column provides precisely the architectural element for achieving this dual aim. With its cylindrical base, the column offers support while remaining a free standing element that provides a space for worship without cutting off the outside scenery, as a continuous wall would do.[28] By progressively narrowing as it ascends, the column incorporates in its profile the progressively diminishing burden of support, just as the spacing and thickness of columns precisely reflects their function by being no more frequent and wide than necessary to support the load above.[29] Similarly, the addition of base and capital brings functional closure to the column, giving it a height determined by the needs of support, in contrast to the indefinite reach of a post, whose subterranean depths cannot be fathomed from what juts above the surface.[30] Finally, the roof supported by the rows of columns fits its purely sheltering role by coming to a point, upon which nothing more can find support, unlike a horizontal roof, whose capacity to bear further stories renders it an arbitrary summit to a building that might as well continue to ascend.[31] Here the needs of enclosing anthropomorphic statuary and of coming and going between worship and public life precludes any upward striving; instead, the facade extends primarily in width, allowing the eye to take in the design without having to gaze upwards.[32] In these ways, the rows of columns get connected by horizontal beams, bearing friezes and cornices underlying a peaked roof, creating a unified structure whose design neatly fits the functional demands of the classical ideal. Although the resulting temple may approach the geometric severity of modernist fashion, the open rows of tapering columns and the peaked roof have little in common with the reflecting glass facades and barren plazas of our unadorned Bauhaus boxes. The fit of form and function in classical architecture is predicated upon a very particular purpose that only the self-understanding of a substantial subjectivity can provide: the housing of a rational agency whose outward appearance is at one with its essence.

VI. The Unity of Independence and Functionality in Romantic Architecture

If the anatomy of the Greek temple testifies to how unity of form and function gives architectural expression to the classical ideal, can any example of romantic architecture confirm Hegel's claim that a unity of independence and function architecturally expresses the self-understanding of romanticism? Hegel's own treatment of romantic architecture offers only one candidate for vindication: the Gothic cathedral. Although Hegel's general concept of the romantic style divides into three principal developments (one configuring the religious self-understanding generic to Christianity, another portraying the adventures of chivalry, and the last expressing a formally independent character), his analysis of romantic architecture focuses almost solely upon the architectural equivalent of the first option.[33]

In contrast to classical temple construction, romantic architecture must somehow give shape to a religious self-understanding that upholds the infinite worth of a free agency whose independent subjective life cannot find adequate expression in any given appearance, including the exterior of the human body and the purely public face of conduct. The inwardness of each self must here finally find due recognition precisely by transcending each and every particular sensuous embodiment. Consequently, romantic architecture cannot simply be an enclosure for statuary whose bodily surface independently expresses everything of spiritual importance, nor can a romantic place of worship remain open to the scenes of secular life, as if the public appearance of individuals exhausted their integrity.

Hegel maintains that the Gothic cathedral provides the positive architectural answer to these injunctions in several salient ways.

First, the Gothic cathedral provides a fully enclosed space, explicitly severed from the activities of mundane secular life.[34] Whereas the classical temple can join exterior and interior through rows of supporting columns and open cells, the Gothic cathedral blocks out the outer world by all-encompassing walls,[35] punctuated by curtains of stained glass admitting a light distinctly different from prosaic illumination.[36] Moreover, the exterior of the building expressly reflects the totally enclosing design of the interior, emphasizing the architectural priority of what lies sequestered within over external nature and the finite involvements of secular life outside.[37]

Second, instead of employing free-standing columns that support a roof just high enough to serve the needs of displaying anthropomorphic sculpture, the Gothic cathedral encloses its interior space so as to mask the supporting role of its walls, transforming them instead into vehicles of an immense elevation above and beyond any merely rectilinear functional requirement.[38] This transfiguration is achieved in two ways. On the one hand, in place of columns limited by base, capital and cross beam, the Gothic cathedral employs immense pillars, divided into ascending tendrils that meet at the apex of a soaring ceiling.[39] The resulting pointed vaults and arches overcome the perpendicular architectural transition from supporting walls to supported roof, seamlessly joining pillar and peak,[40] while forcing the eyes of all visitors to turn upwards in order to take in the whole view.[41] On the other hand, the soaring walls are pierced and punctuated by vast tapestries of stained glass and ornament that dissolve their load-bearing solidity, suggesting a lightness in keeping with their elevating role.[42]

Through these signature design innovations, the Gothic cathedral provides an environment that fits a spirituality that looks beyond the external sensuous realizations of humanity to an interiority available to all, who literally have space to fit within an inner sanctum sufficiently immense to accommodate all walks of life of the local populace.[43]

Yet if Hegel here succeeds in matching Gothic style with the religious self-understanding of romanticism, has he confirmed the unification of independence and functionality by which romantic architecture was to have exhausted the logical options of architectural design? Functionality is certainly at hand insofar as the Gothic cathedral serves to house the worship of a religious community, instead of standing alone as an independent monument, to be appreciated merely for its allusive appearance. Yet independence is equally present insofar as the design does not simply merge form and function, restricting itself to the geometric simplicities mandated by support and enclosure. The soaring height, the vaults and arches of merging pillars, and the curtains of colored glass and ornament all take on a meaning of their own, congruent with the religious practice they surround, but transcending the practical requirements of worship.[44]

Can the same be said of modernist and "postmodern" architecture, which Hegel never addressed, but which his stylistic scheme would have to place within the orbit of romantic architecture?

The modernist call to liberate architecture of sclerotic ornament and traditional design might appear to be a reversion to the fit of form and function characterizing classical architecture. Whereas, however, classicism could treat architecture as a stage for a humanity fully manifest in its bodily, public appearance, modernism seeks to provide an environment for a humanity to whom no given order can be the final measure of its autonomy.[45] The modernist turn to spare geometric forms is not intended as a backdrop for human meanings requiring a figurative expression, but rather as an independent manifestation of the transcendence of given tradition, where Bauhaus minimalism architecturally configures the same self-understanding as abstract art and atonal music, a self-understanding that confers ultimate significance to a rational agency that avoids reproducing what is already given in nature or tradition by attending to what is merely the product of its own creativity.

"Postmodern" architecture offers a variation on this modernist agenda by ironically quoting past styles as if to show how all stylistic traditions are relegated by their historicity to be mere playthings of the artistic self, for whom no external embodiment can be definitively adequate.[46] Although postmodernism rejects the purified abstractions of modernism as but another stipulated "essentialism" of one more vain tradition, the postmodern quotational distancing from every determinate style only reaffirms, albeit in a perilously formal way, the modern overcoming of foundations and embrace of self-determination as the unique foundation-free alternative to tradition.[47] Once more, building composition transcends the practical use to which construction is put, since here every design can just as well be cast aside and replaced by some other quotation. Whether repudiating all traditional conventions by advancing abstract schemes or acknowledging traditions' relativity by arbitrarily recycling their elements, the architecture of our day readily embodies the shapes of romanticism that Hegel identifies with the independent formal character possessed by the modern self. By recognizing the universal validity of free agency, modern humanity can no longer invest any particular sensuous configuration with ultimate meaning. For architecture, this signifies that building design must create novel works that break free of each particular mold, housing the activities of a free community in structures whose architectural form is liberated from both total subordination to function and slavish reworking of established modes. Whether the Wrights and Le Corbusiers of tomorrow can ever overcome the restlessness of their vocation will depend upon the durability of the institutions and culture of freedom. In providing for this undecided prospect, Hegel's aesthetics proves to have met the challenge of architecture.

Notes

1. Michael B. Foster succinctly makes these points in *The Political Philosophies of Plato and Hegel* (New York: Oxford University Press, 1967), 185–87, 201.

2. For a detailed exposure of these limitations of mimetic, e.g., metaphysical, and transcendental aesthetics, see Richard Dien Winfield, *Systematic Aesthetics* (Gainesville: University Press of Florida, 1995), Part 1, 15–57.

3. Nelson Goodman, "How Buildings Mean," in *Aesthetics: A Critical Anthology*, ed. George Dickie, Richard Sclafani, and Ronald Roblin (New York: St. Martin's Press, 1989), 544–55.

4. The contrast between Hegel's account of architecture and Vitruvius's celebrated *The Ten Books of Architecture* is indicative of the gap between Hegel and the competition. Vitruvius totally ignores the connection between meaning and configuration in architecture, offering only vague notions of harmony and proportion that provide little insight into the distinctive significance and beauty of the Greek temple on which he focuses his attention. See Vitruvius, *The Ten Books of Architecture,* trans. Morris Hicky Morgan (New York: Dover Publications, 1960).

5. G. W. F. Hegel, *Vorlesungen über die Ästhetik, Werke in zwanzig Bänden,* ed. E. Moldenhauer and K. Michel, 20 vols. and Index (Frankfurt am Main: Suhrkamp Verlag, 1969ff), 14:269. Further references will be in the form: *Werke,* 14:269.

6. This is true even though Hegel maintains that literature is divided into epic, lyric, and dramatic forms, instead of into embodiments of the three art forms (*Werke,* 14:271). As Georg Lukács, Peter Szondi, and others have shown, such literary genres either fit a particular art form or undergo developments in which all art forms are represented. Thus, for example, Lukács argues in his *The Theory of the Novel,* (trans. Anna Bostock [Cambridge: MIT Press, 1971]), that the epic is a preeminently classical form of literature whereas the novel is a preeminently romantic literary genre, whereas Peter Szondi argues, in his *The Theory of the Modern Drama,* (trans. Michael Hays [Minneapolis: University of Minnesota Press, 1987]), that drama undergoes a development in which romantic experiments supplant classical models.

7. *Werke,* 14:271.

8. *Werke,* 14:270.

9. The Pyramids are *only* transitional constructions because of key limitations in their unity of form and function: although pyramids serve as enclosures of the dead, using inorganic shapes that are expressly artificial forms, built by and for humanity, the failure to use right angles as a ruling principle gives the structure a tapering closure that is not useful to the living. See *Werke,* 14:296.

10. *Werke,* 14:270.

11. *Werke,* 14:270.

12. In this vein, Hegel observes that although buildings without any distinction in the aim of enclosure and the building as fulfillment of this aim would be like works of sculpture, such independent architecture remains differentiated from sculpture by not producing images that are themselves spiritual and subjective. See *Werke,* 14:269.

13. *Werke,* 14:279, 282–83.

14. *Werke,* 14:274–75.

15. *Werke,* 14:274.

16. *Werke,* 14:275–76.

17. Hegel here anticipates something of Wittfogel's notion of oriental hydraulic civilizations, where national unity centers around vast construction projects (in Wittfogel's case, of irrigation systems and the like). See Karl August Wittfogel, *Oriental Despotism: A Comparative Study of Power* (New Haven: Yale University Press, 1957).

18. *Werke,* 14:276.

19. *Werke,* 14:277.

20. *Werke,* 14:275, 279.

21. *Werke,* 14:280–873.

22. For Le Corbusier's classic statement of this injunction, see his *Towards a New Architecture,* trans. by Frederick Etchells (New York: Dover Publications, 1986).

23. See Frank Lloyd Wright's *The Natural House* in Frank Lloyd Wright, *Collected Writings, Volume 5:1949–1959,* ed. Bruce Brooks Pfeiffer (New York: Rizzoli International, 1995), 77–127.

24. *Werke,* 14:297.

25. *Werke,* 14:302–3.

26. *Werke,* 14:304. As Le Corbusier analogously expresses it, describing the Parthenon, "no symbolical description, no naturalistic representation; there is nothing but pure forms in precise relationships." See Le Corbusier, *Towards a New Architecture,* 220.

27. Le Corbusier expresses an analogous appreciation of this classical departure from symbolic architecture, by observing, in regard to the Parthenon, how "We are in the inexorable realm of the mechanical. There are no symbols attached to these forms." See Le Corbusier, *Towards a New Architecture,* 211.

28. *Werke,* 14:299, 310.

29. *Werke,* 14:299, 306, 310, 312.

30. *Werke,* 14:310–11.

31. *Werke,* 14:314–5.

32. *Werke,* 14:318–19.

33. Although Hegel briefly mentions medieval secular architecture, he brushes it aside, noting that the walls, towers, and bridges of its castle-like fortifications were so governed by utilitarian demands that artistic considerations only entered in as incidental decoration. See *Werke,* 14:348.

34. *Werke,* 14:332.

35. Hegel thus identifies the wall as the prime element in romantic construction. See *Werke,* 14:310.

36. *Werke,* 14:333.

37. *Werke,* 14:334, 340, 342.

38. *Werke,* 14:335.

39. *Werke,* 14:336–37.

40. *Werke,* 14:333–34.

41. *Werke,* 14:337.

42. *Werke,* 14:338, 345.

43. *Werke,* 14:339–40.

44. Le Corbusier acknowledges this independence when he describes the Gothic cathedral as "A fight against the force of gravity, which is a sensation of a sentimental nature". See Le Corbusier, *Towards A New Architecture,* 30.

45. Le Corbusier's "house-machine" is thus hardly congruent with the instrumentality of the Greek temple. See Le Corbusier, *Towards A New Architecture,* 7.

46. David Kolb persuasively argues how the "ironic historicism" of postmodern architecture, despite its own claims to the contrary, is merely an extension of the same modern self-understanding that motivates modernism's search for pure form.

See David Kolb, *Postmodern Sophistications: Philosophy, Architecture, and Tradition* (Chicago: University of Chicago Press, 1990), 87ff.

47. Postmodernism flirts with danger when its ironic play with every tradition turns into a repudiation of the universal validity of self-determination. It then reverts to an embrace of particularism, where the alleged groundlessness of every determinate configuration gives way to a will to power, where no value can be affirmed that is not a perspectival imposition. In this fashion, the postmodern ironic distancing from every tradition becomes an invitation to fascism's promotion of the given particularity of a community over and against every aspiration of universal right. It should thus come as no surprise that the "master thinkers" of postmodernism could welcome Nazism.

VIII

Hegel and the Spirit of Comedy: *Der Geist der stets verneint*

Stephen C. Law

Hegel's *Lectures on Aesthetics* and its pessimistic "death of art thesis" have once again returned as focal points of scholarly criticism, but while many critics have focused upon the metaphysical, dialectical, or historical implications of Hegel's aesthetic views, few have taken more than a passing interest in his claim that comedy is the absolute telos of artistic expression. For Hegel comedy is a "telos" in the full sense of the word: it is not only the ultimate aesthetic experience, it is an art form that represents *die Aufhebung* of aesthetics as well. "Comedy," he declares, "leads . . . to the dissolution of art altogether."[1] Comedy is art that has the potential to render art "obsolete"; it is art that literally "transcends" the limits of aesthetic expression.

Most of those who have taken an interest in what Hegel says about comedy have concentrated on his ideas concerning dramatic comedy. The work of both Anne and Henry Paolucci is indicative of this approach, as are the writings of the Shakespearean scholar A. C. Bradley.[2] Slightly more focused are the interpretations of Jacob Loewenberg, George McFadden, and Gary Shapiro, all of whom are primarily concerned with the metaphysical underpinnings of Hegel's ideas on comedy.[3] Probably one of the most insightful analyses of the ideas that Hegel had about comedy is the recent work by William Desmond.[4] While deftly defending Hegel from a variety of ill-humored deconstructionist charges, Desmond offers a lengthy argument about the agapeic festival of metaxological thought that Hegel perceived in the writings of Aristophanes. What I propose here is that our understanding of Hegel's views on comedy need to be broadened somewhat: while it is indeed essential that his metaphysical system be brought to bear on the subject of comedy, it is equally important that we come to terms with the full range of comic genres and comic devices that he discusses. With a more complete picture of Hegel's perceptions of humor in general, we can better appreciate—or at least understand—his apotheosis of Aristophanes at the end of the *Aesthetics*.

While Hegel crowns "the hale spirit of comedy" as the pinnacle of man's artistic efforts, it should first be noted that his praise of comedy is tempered by an awareness of the dangers inherent within this aesthetic phenomenon. Like the dialectical processes of the universe itself, comedy achieves its aims through "negation": it reshapes our perspective on life by rendering impotent and obsolete whatever we laugh at. Comedy, therefore, is an art form in which our pleasure, to a large degree, is generated by seeing things undone. According to Hegel, so long as comedy restricts itself to negating things that are counterproductive to the human spirit, it serves its highest purpose, that is, it helps perfect the freedom that consciousness has bestowed upon us. But when the comic spirit is allowed to reign indiscriminately, then it becomes an antithetical force capable of negating not only art, but religion and philosophy as well. Thus for Hegel, comedy can be either constructive or destructive, depending on what it seeks to negate.

Hegel's ideas on comedy stem from a long-standing conviction that comedy is one of the truly pivotal inventions of the human spirit. Even in his discussions of *Kunstreligion* in the *Phenomenology* he betrays a profound respect for a power that can literally dethrone the gods of Olympus.[5] It is in the *Aesthetics,* however, that we find the fullest expression of his thoughts on comedy. Yet even here his discussions seems cursory. But when we focus upon the substance of what he says, an interesting vision emerges.

Hegel's discussion of comedy in the *Aesthetics* revolves around three main points. First, he establishes what the content of comedy is—that is, what is its "essential" nature, and what does it express? Second, he delineates the formal qualities of comedy; what are the comic genres, and how does each stand in relation to the goals of comedy? And finally, Hegel puts the existence of comedy into a phenomenological perspective. Why does comedy exist, and what does it say about the human spirit that such an art form was invented?

Hegel's answers to these questions are inextricably interwoven within the fabric of the *Aesthetics,* and, unfortunately, they are not as definite as one would like. A major problem is that Hegel, while purporting to give us a scientific or objective approach to aesthetics, succumbs to the *Weltanschauung* of this own day: he assumes that the *Quelle* of comedy—Old Comedy in the manner of Aristophanes—is the quintessential spirit of this phenomenon and that all subsequent forms of humor must necessarily be "inferior." Thus, other genres of comedy, such as New Comedy and satire, as well as romantic irony and other types of humor, are all cast in a negative light. Hegel maintains that their negations lead to destruction rather than transcendence. Yet another problem is that, even though Hegel's summation points to the importance of the comic spirit, his arguments are scattered throughout the *Aesthetics.* It is only with some effort that we are able to construct what might be regarded as Hegel's "theory of comedy."[6]

I. Comedy and the *Kunstformen*

Before turning to his ideas on comedy, it should be recalled that Hegel places comedy in the final phase of his tripartite dialectic, the *Lehre von den*

Kunstformen. Hegel posits three main phases, or *Kunstformen,* operational within the growth of aesthetics. Each of these phases represents a step in human ability to make the "form" of his work of art correspond to its "content." In the early or "Symbolic" phase, the form represents the content in an arbitrary or abstract way. In the middle or "Classical" phase, an artist learns to harmonize form and content so that they become ideally suited to each other and result in the phenomenon we call "beauty." Eventually, however, in the "Romantic" phase, an artist masters the manipulation of form to such an extent that the work becomes a mere vehicle for subjective reflection upon the content. The perceiver is torn away from the world of the senses—the true provenance of aesthetics—and is pushed forward into the world of ideas. Hegel asserts that when art loses touch with its sensual origins and metamorphoses into "ideas," it is fated to become *etwas Vergangenes* (a thing of the past). When this happens in a culture, aesthetics can no longer serve as a viable means for expressing the Absolute.

Hegel proceeds to construct an elaborate dialectic to show how each phase, or *Kunstform,* favors a particular medium of expression. The intricacies of his argument need not occupy us here. Suffice it to say that comedy, as a subset of poetry, falls within the romantic phase. Hegel sees poetry as the most subjective of all art forms because it uses only words—the very medium of thought itself. With the simplest of forms poetry creates its own inner world; a spiritual world free from the dictates of material necessity; a subjective world created by, and appreciated by, *Geist.*

Hegel postulates yet another dialectic within the confines of poetry; it moves from epic, to lyric, to drama. He sees this progression not only as a temporal, or historical development, but, more importantly, also as a spiritual development. These three forms of poetry are the products of the evolving phases of consciousness: epic is emergent, lyric is self-reflexive, and drama is rational. While the "form" of each of these types of poetry is different, their "content" remains essentially the same; that is, all poetry—in fact all art in Hegel's view—is an attempt to give expression to the complex and yet crucial relationship between humankind and the divine forces of the universe. While not all poetry need attend to this task, the most important and meaningful works invariably do. Indeed, the most profound poetry provides us with aesthetic answers to the very same questions posed by religion and philosophy.

II. Comedy and the Growth of Freedom

As Hegel sees it, one of the central issues of poetry is the problem of ascertaining our position in the cosmos. What are we, why are we here, and to what extent, if any, are we "free?" As consciousness evolves, so do our answers to these questions. In particular, our conception of divinity undergoes serious changes: the constant interference of the gods of epic eventually gives way to the remote—and perhaps even hostile—gods of tragedy. The Apollo who argues eloquently for the return of Hector's body is but a distant relative of the god who lets Oedipus stumble into patricide and incest. Indeed, says Hegel, the gods of tragedy are unacceptable to the human spirit and therefore must be laughed off the stage.

Similarly, as our concept of divinity evolves, so does our self-concept. As the powers of the gods wane, the human powers become crescent. Our early self-concept is one in which we conceive ourselves as relatively impotent in the face of powerful gods who offer little, if any, explanation for their behavior. Faced with this situation, we are forced, like the Homeric heroes, to create our own "ethical code" to render life meaningful. Later, as we become self-conscious, we assert that this *rational* and human code is at least as important as the inscrutable dictates of the cosmos. Having gained self-knowledge, Hegel argues that we realize the worthiness of our own individual spirits: it is we, not the gods, who are truly virtuous and honorable. Defiantly, we proclaim our own worth. We may be blind, but we have dignity. Finally, we come to see that our ethical code is the only thing that has any meaning at all. Humankind, truly, is the measure of all things, (and that which cannot be "measured" is essentially "unreal" and thus has no meaning). With this knowledge, we are on our way to becoming our own masters. Freedom, the foundation of Hegelian metaphysics, is also a primary concern of Hegelian aesthetics.[7]

The actualization of this freedom in the aesthetic sphere, is something Hegel sees as nascent in tragedy and fully developed in comedy. It is no coincidence, says Hegel, that these two art forms made their first appearance in ancient Greece; for it was there that the first meaningful sense of personal freedom arose. In Hegel's eyes, freedom is one of the most important requisites for the development of these art forms

> [T]ruly *tragic* action necessarily presupposes either a live conception of *individual* freedom and independence or at least an individual's determination and willingness to accept freely and on one's own account the responsibility for his own act and its consequences; and for the emergence of *comedy* there must have asserted itself in a still higher degree the free right of the subjective personality and its self-assured dominion.[8]

In tragedy we express our desire for freedom, but still concede that we are bound by the imperatives of necessity—imperatives not of our own making nor in accordance with our desires. In comedy the human spirit finally attains this freedom. In a grand gesture, comedy sweeps necessity aside, and rejects the restraints of the past as mere "clouds," illusions of no substance. The comic spirit declares that the objective world is really nothing but the subjective world we create for ourselves. It negates necessity and allows us to transcend the physical world by means of an act of will. Spiritual freedom is assured when we are able to remove any threat to our sense of well-being by sheer laughter.

Hegel argues that comedy is essentially "superior" to tragedy (in a dialectical sense) precisely because it has dispensed with the pity and fear that tragedy evokes. While these emotions do make for a successful drama, they also engender an Unhappy Consciousness.[9] Our fear is not merely of the Absolute and its power over us, but fear that our own rational code may prove insufficient to preserve us. Oedipus's tragedy is made all the more terrifying by the very fact that he acted as a reasonable man. For us, the ethical code itself is more meaningful than the ambiguous external forces that bring a good man to ruin. Therefore, we pity his misfortune because it is our own. Tragic doubt and uncertainty pave the way for comic iconoclasm and self-assuredness. The comic spirit knows neither pity nor fear.

III. Comedy vs. Tragedy

In the *Aesthetics* Hegel poses the important question: what constitutes the "content" of comedy? He asserts that the *dramatis personae* of any production—tragic or comic—are not merely "actors." They are the concretized representatives of *ideas*. These ideas may come into conflict with the apparent injustice of the cosmos, as in the case of Oedipus, or they may dialectically make war upon each other, as in *Antigone*. Even so, as concretized ideas these characters suffer from "particularization." They manifest what Hegel calls the limitations of "one-sidedness" (*Einseitigkeit*).[10] For example, neither Creon nor Antigone are the Idea, but rather each is a particular idea. Because these characters are particular, they cannot be expected to behave in an omniscient fashion. In tragedy such limitations lead to misfortune. A tragic hero is forced by *objective* circumstances painfully to recognize the inadequacies of his own *subjective* views. Yet, even in the face of this recognition the positive elements of the hero's behavior are preserved and our ethical code remains intact.

In comedy, on the other hand, not only does the code survive, the subjective views of the hero are preserved as well. This is not to say that the characters of comedy are any less "one-sided" than those in tragedy—far be it from the case, for, if anything, they are even more one-sided. Rather, the penalties for indulging in subjectivity are brought into accordance with our own rational code of ethics. In comedy it is we, not the gods, who decide which forms of behavior will be rewarded and which will be punished. Comedy needs no *deus ex machina* because we ourselves become the gods. We dispense justice as *we* see fit, and the penalty for nonconformity with reason is to be laughed at unmercifully.

Hegel says that comedy attains this stature by manipulating the relation between the "substance" of a character's actions (in other words, the relative worthiness of his goal), and the "subjectivity" of his reaction to the circumstances he creates. First, Hegel proposes that comic situations almost invariably grow out of three possible situations: (1) either the characters are contemptible in both the means they use and the end they pursue, in which case they are a contradiction to the values of the code and are therefore fit for ridicule; or (2) the characters are incongruous because they are admirable in their goals, but fail to possess the necessary means to attain their end; or (3) the characters possess those means, but find themselves subject to unexpected circumstances, and, hence, are unable to bring about the end they had in mind. Thus, their desires are frustrated despite their best efforts, just as they are in tragedy. But whereas tragedy admits defeat at this point (or at least acquiesces to misfortune), comedy demands an acceptable resolution

> [T]he comic action requires a solution almost more stringently than a tragic one does. In a comic action the contradiction between what is absolutely true and its realization in individuals is posed more profoundly. Yet what is destroyed in this solution cannot be either fundamental principle or individual character.[11]

This resolution, says Hegel, must preserve both the *substantive* code (or "fundamental principle") and the *subjective* autonomy of the individual's character. In comedy, it can be brought about in one of two ways: either the circumstances themselves can be brought into harmony with human wishes, or human wishes can be restructured in such a way that their abrogation has no effect on the harmony of the individual. The first situation is essentially what we find in New Comedy. In spite of the frustrations a hero endures in the development of the play, his wishes are gratified in the denouement.

The second type of comic resolution is preferred by Hegel. This resolution is less a product of aesthetic artifice than it is a sheer triumph of the human spirit. Here, we find no gratification of wishes; rather, the comic hero transcends the circumstances. "Failure" is no catastrophe for this type of hero, merely a mild disappointment, and one easily laughed away.[12] Such a hero is able to take anything in stride, says Hegel, because he is conscious that either his aims or his abilities are "self-contradictory" (*das an sich selber Nichtige*). Thus, the hero never really expects things to turn out the way he wishes, and when they do, he is genuinely surprised. Throughout all this, he maintains a cheerful disposition and refuses to indulge himself in the pessimistic attitudes of a cynic. The Hegelian comic hero is self-autonomous and self-assured; he himself decides what is important and what is not. Indeed, he and he alone is the measure of all things. He is able to do this, not through some supra-human stoic ability, declares Hegel, but precisely because he is granted a spirit that takes nothing too seriously—especially not himself.

IV. The Hegelian Comic Hero

Hegel's insistence that a truly comic hero be able to laugh at himself is one of commonplaces of the *Aesthetics,* thanks in part to the endorsement given by A. C. Bradley.[13] Although Hegel cites Falstaff as one of the archetypal examples, and certainly the premier example from the modern era, he argues that we must look to the ancients to find the poet who most successfully used this type of hero and this type of comic resolution.[14] Following the lead of Schlegel and other German literary critics, Hegel crowns Aristophanes as the master comedian of all time.[15]

> What is comical . . . is a personality or subject who makes his own actions so contradictory and so brings them to nothing, while remaining self-assured in the process. . . . On the whole this is the character of the old Greek comedy as it has been preserved for us in the plays of Aristophanes. In this matter we must very carefully distinguish whether the *dramatic personae* are comical themselves or only in the eyes of the audience. The former case alone can be counted as really comical, and here Aristophanes was a master. On these lines, an individual is only portrayed as laughable when it is obvious that he is not serious at all about the seriousness of his aim and will, so that this seriousness always carries with it, in the eyes of the individual himself, its own destruction.[16]

The Aristophanic hero, as Hegel sees him, is distinctive because he is a *parcipitator* in laughter, not merely the object of laughter.[17] Both he and the audience find his actions "ludicrous," with the pleasant result that we are able to laugh *with* him, not *at* him. This is not to say that the lack of seriousness on the part of a character implies a lack of seriousness on the part of either comedy or the comic poet. As genuine art, Hegel claims that comedy's goal is "to bring the absolutely rational into appearance."[18] The fact that it does so in a way that gives rise to laughter is not to be taken as an indication that the *issue* (that is, the content) is any less grave or serious that in those representations producing pity and fear. Although ridicule and persiflage are his medium, Hegel describes Aristophanes as "a true patriot" and a "man of most gifted intellect" who always held the welfare of the city of Athens foremost in his mind.[19] True comedy never attacks virtue, says Hegel, it attacks vice masquerading in the pretense of virtue. Aristophanes' goal, as Hegel sees it, is to point out the hypocrisy in Athenian society: the Athenians have correctly ascertained the true and substantive, but they refuse to take their own values seriously, and, so, have spiraled into a suicidal *reductio ad absurdum.*

According to Hegel, a comic poet must assure that the "lack of seriousness" on the part of his hero is directed towards worldly matters (that is, the highly subjective interpretations we give our values so that we can use them for our own selfish purposes), and not the substantive values themselves.[20] Aristophanic heroes, through their comic negations, transcend the trivialities of this world while reaffirming those values conducive to spiritual well-being:

> [T]hey reveal themselves as having something higher in them because they are not seriously tied to the finite world with which they are engaged but are raised above it and remain firm in themselves and secure in the face of failure and loss. It is to this absolute freedom of spirit which is utterly consoled in advance in every human undertaking, to this world of private serenity, that Aristophanes conducts us.[21]

Hegel declares that such poets are few and far between. According to his canon, the only other playwright who even comes close to Aristophanes is Shakespeare.[22] While there is some merit to his declaration, his strictures have an extremely adverse effect on all other manifestations of the comic spirit, at least as they appear in his system.

V. Aberrant Forms of Laughter

Hegel does admit that laughter is a complex phenomenon. "In general," he observes, "nowhere can more contradiction be found than in the things people laugh at."[23] Depending on how things are presented, we may laugh at the insignificant and tasteless, or at the profound and refined. Hegel notes that some people even find humor where they should not; such as in deadly serious matters. By only paying attention to some unimportant detail, a comedian can generate a contradiction that irresponsibly permits our attention to be diverted from the "truth." Such laughter, he says, is mere cleverness on our part, "an expression of self-complacent wit" (*eine Äusserung der wohgefalligen Klugheit*).[24] He also mentions in passing that there are other types of laughter: derision (*Spott*), scorn (Hohn), despair (*Verzweiflung*), and others (simply intimated by *usf.* or "etc.") that he chooses not to enumerate.

Hegel considers all of these "aberrant" forms of the comic, and relegates most of them either to satire or to "subjective humor"—both of which (as we shall see) he holds in very low esteem. Comedy, in his opinion, must always maintain "an infinite light-heartedness and confidence felt by someone raised altogether above his own inner contradiction and not bitter or miserable in it at all."[25] If freedom is the goal of human activity, then those emotions that have a negative effect on the human spirit should be avoided.

VI. The Drama of New Comedy

New Comedy, as seen by Hegel, departs from this "light-heartedness" in an attempt to mix laughter with serious emotion. Although mentioned twice in the closing arguments of the *Aesthetics*, Hegel's discussions of this type of comedy, and the traditions inspired by it, are both cryptic and somewhat biased. In both instances Hegel focuses on the inadequacies of this genre, rather than attest to any of its virtues. It appears that we are meant to compare this "lesser" art form with that glorious *Quelle* of the past, Old Comedy. To assure that we do so, Hegel predicates almost every observation he makes about this genre with a reference to Aristophanes.

Hegel's first mention of New Comedy emerges in his discussion of "drama," which for him is an intermediate form of poetry that dialectically tries to reconcile the difference between tragedy and comedy.[26] Although Hegel does admit that modern dramatic poetry (that is, the poetry of his own age) has been able to achieve such a synthesis, he rejects the notion that a "complete" synthesis occurred in antiquity. The "drama," or New Comedy, of the ancients is a synthesis of the "formal" qualities alone, while the "substantive" qualities are left unsynthesized. Hegel sees this as an artificial mixture of the serious and the comic, and cites both satyr plays and tragic-comedies as examples of what he means. He proposes that the action of a satyr play alternates between the serious proceedings of the central characters and the comic proceedings of the satyrs themselves.[27] In tragic-comedy the alternating contrasts are between the gods or kings and *hoi polloi*. Hegel believes that both of these types of drama are merely comic juxtaposition.

New Comedy, specifically "*die neue griechische Kömodie*," is also addressed in the closing paragraphs of the *Aesthetics*. After again reiterating his thesis that it is essential the *dramatis personae* find themselves laughable, (and once again reminding us that Aristophanes was "*der echte Komiker*"), Hegel turns to those whom he considers guilty of reversing this trend.

> But in the new comedy in Greece and later in Plautus and Terence the opposite tendency was developed, and this has acquired such universal prominence in modern comedy that a multitude of our comic productions verge more or less on what is purely prosaically laughable and even on what is bitter and repugnant.[28]

Here, it is interesting (but confusing from a dialectical standpoint) that Hegel makes "New Comedy" virtually synonymous with "modern comedy." He sees the latter as the direct descendant of the former, and discusses both at the same time, with each observation being applicable to both. Molière, whom he mentions immediately following the above passage, is reproved for including in his comedies characters who "are deadly serious in their aims." Tartuffe and Harpagon are cited as examples. Our laughter in such cases is not pure, says Hegel, but is mixed with "malice" (*Schaden*). On the other hand, he maintains, even when comedians avoid including such "serious" characters, they often exhibit a certain cleverness (*Geschicklichkeit*) for manipulating characters or plots, rather than provide their work with a dignified, substantive basis. Hegel infers that modern comedy knows how to please its audience, but not how to serve its best end.[29]

Hegel's displeasure with New Comedy derives from several sources. First, he says that we should have serious reservations about any art form that relies so heavily on plots involving deception. "A well-considered intrigue" (*eine wohlersonnene Intrigue*) may be ingenious, he insists, but it is also ingenuous. While Old Comedy certainly has its share of intrigue, there is an important difference between not taking things too seriously, and the intentional, consistent, and deliberate use of fraud to attain one's end. Even if a character's cleverness and trickery prove to be his own undoing, and even if we do take delight in seeing that "poetic justice" is served in the end, the elevation of this feature to the status of an inspirational force behind comic production is disturbing. Truth, claims Hegel, should never be approached through falsity.

Another aspect of New Comedy he finds unsettling is the inversion of the social order, what he calls "the laughable spectacle of masters being really the servants, or the servants masters."[30] A philosophical analysis of this phenomenon (Hegel's well-known dialectic on this subject) is one thing, making it the basis of an aesthetic representation of truth is yet another.[31] Seeing masters outwitted and frustrated by the deceptions of their slaves is not conducive to the growth of Spirit, regardless of how much enjoyment we might get out of such a mimesis. Hegel sums up his reservations by pointing to the dangers inherent in this precedent.

> But such a frank joviality as pervades the comedies of Aristophanes . . . does not animate this kind of modern comedy at all. Indeed these comedies of intrigue may be actually repulsive when downright evil, the cunning of servants, the deceitfulness of sons and wards, gains the victory over honest masters, fathers, and trustees when these older people have themselves not been actuated by bad prejudice or eccentricities which would have made them laughable.[32]

This situation is not "comic," observes Hegel, but "pathetic." When virtue, as a means to an end, proves inferior to vice, then the values of the ethical code are placed in jeopardy and society is no longer being served by its comedians. Although this art form may indeed be even more "subjective" than its predecessor, Old Comedy, (here the human spirit is not only free to choose its own destiny, but is also free to choose its own *means* to bring that destiny about), Hegel warns that art should never adopt a policy of subjectivity for its own sake.[33] If art is to serve the ends of spirit, then it must always maintain a sense of propriety. New Comedy, at least as Hegel conceives it, fails to measure up to the canon and thus cannot be considered truly "comical."

VII. The Specters of Satire, Irony, and Subjective Humor

What may have been reservations and reproof in association with New Comedy turns to bitter denunciation and revulsion when Hegel turns to satire. According to Hegel, satire is an unwholesome specter that runs counter to the spirit of comedy. He claims that this art form is not really "poetry" at all, but rather a form of prose. Its "prosaic" character—and Hegel uses *prosaisch* in the most derogatory sense possible—contributes, in his opinion, to the demise of the poetic or aesthetic aspects of comedy.[34] Losing its dramatic "persona," the comic spirit retreats to the private world of unrestrained and uninhibited self-consciousness: the satiric spirit throws away the mask to deal with things in the flesh. When this happens the mimetic barrier is torn down, and with it the aesthetic distance that Hegel deems necessary in order to keep comedy from becoming overly bitter. Hegel declares that satire is both dangerous to aesthetic sensibilities in general, and lethal to the ideals of the classical *Kunstform* in particular.

Hegel's attack on satire is couched in less than subtle terms. His intentions are threefold: first, to describe the destructive nature of this suprasubjective art form; second, to tie these same qualities to the romantic movement of his own day; and third, in a move that seems tainted with the politics of the early nineteenth century, to free the Greeks from the blame of having created this destructive force, and to fix it squarely on the Romans.

Although Hegel believes that satire is essentially antithetical to the spirit of comedy, he nonetheless sees it as an unfortunate (and yet rational) offspring of that force. The increasing subjectivity that comedy makes possible by allowing *serious* ideas to be rendered more palatable to the human spirit, finally confronts the contradiction inherent within its own efforts: indeed, we have learned to laugh, but that changes nothing. The gods have been replaced by our own rational code of ethics, yet the frailties of the human spirit render us woefully unprepared to cope with our own manumission. The satirist sees the pathos of this situation all too well and becomes the aesthetic spokesman of what Hegel termed the Unhappy Consciousness:

> [A] thinking spirit, a subject reposing on himself as subject in abstract wisdom with a knowledge of the good and the virtuous and a will to achieve it, is brought by art into a hostile opposition to the corruption of the present. . . . A noble spirit, a virtuous heart always deprived of the actualization of its convictions in a world of vice and folly, turns with passionate indignation or keener wit and cold bitterness against the reality confronting it, and is enraged with or scoffs at the world which directly contradicts its abstract idea of virtue and truth.[35]

In spite of the fact that satire may be a "rational" outgrowth of comedy, Hegel regards it as little more than a temporary aberration—temporary, but lethal. For Hegel, satire is nothing but a "transitional form (*Übergangsform*) of the classical ideal."[36] Hence, his analysis of satire is extraneous to his considerations of poetry or comedy. It is mentioned only once in that section, where it is criticized as being "crude" (*grell*) and "tedious" (*trocken*).[37] Rather, his discussion of this genre is found at the very end of the classical *Kunstform.* By placing satire in this emphatic position, Hegel implies that the beauty created by the classical ideal was dialectically "killed" by satire. This, I would argue, is another variation of the so-called "death of art thesis"; but this time it is not the death of art, but the death of beauty that Hegel laments. Why Hegel places satire where he does can be explained both in terms of the distinctions he makes between comedy and satire, and the *Zeitgeist* of early-nineteenth-century Germany.

One of the most important things contributing to Hegel's pessimistic view about the future of art is his own historical perspective. T. M. Knox suggests that, because Hegel witnessed the end of Germany's classical period—a relatively short moment of unparalleled brilliance in the arts and letters—he must have viewed the ensuing "degeneration" with displeasure.[38] The classical *Kunstform* was being abandoned once again: the "beauty" created by German idealism was being destroyed by the radical subjectivism of the romantics. Worse, the romantics' greatest weapon was itself an outgrowth of classical scholarship: Friedrich Schlegel's notion of poetic "irony."

Hegel carefully distinguishes between the ironic and the comic.[39] Though the two are related, he says, the comic will always "preserve" its content, while the ironic seeks to "destroy" it.

> [T]he ironical, as the individuality of genius, lies in the destruction of the noble, great, and excellent; and so the objective art-formations too will have to display only the principle of absolute subjectivity, by showing forth what has worth and dignity for mankind as null in its self-destruction.[40]

The notion of irony embraced by the romantics spawned its own manifestation of the comic spirit, which Hegel calls "subjective humor."[41] Here we find laughter in its most destructive form; and it is also here, I might add, that we can find the rationale for both Hegel's derogation of satire and his placement of satire within the framework of the *Aesthetics.*

Subjective humor, like satire, emerges from the tensions between reality and our idealistic notions of what that reality should be. But here an even more violent negation results: in satire the frustrated ego recognizes the good but is unable to actualize it; in subjective humor the frustrated ego, dissatisfied with the immutability of reality, decides to change the one thing that is within its power—the ethical code itself. By means of his subjectivity, the romantic denies his relative impotence and becomes his own demiurgos: he artistically remakes his world so that it will conform to his image of what it should be.

> [I]t is the artist himself who enters the material, with the result that his chief activity, by power of subjective notions, flashes of thought, striking modes of interpretation, consists in destroying and dissolving everything that proposes to make itself objective and win a firm shape for itself in reality, or that seems to have a shape already in the external world.[42]

Hegel has Jean Paul Richter in mind and he spares no words attacking him directly, declaring that his witty style is confused, disorderly, namby-pamby, and sentimental.[43] Such humor, through its radical negations, destroys the substantive without offering anything as a replacement. In a few brief remarks at the end of his discussion of romantic art, Hegel recommends that modern humorists try to reverse this process.[44] Instead of negating the substantive, they ought to try to reaffirm it. He prescribes something cryptically called *Objektiver Humor.* By means of "a deep feeling, a felicitous witticism, an ingenious reflection, and an intelligent movement of imagination," objective humor attempts to "vivify and expand" the smallest details of its subject rather than destroy it.[45] Even so, Hegel does not hold too much hope for this type of humor because, unlike its subjective counterpart, it tends to become boring rather quickly. Divorced from "negation" the comic spirit must necessarily lose its charm.

I propose that Hegel sets up an analogy between satire and subjective humor in the *Aesthetics.* These two "destructive" manifestations of the comic spirit are not exactly the same—satire is the product of an artist's love for the substantive, while subjective humor is a product of an artist's disenchantment with the substantive. Either way, the harmony, balance, and beauty that had been achieved in the classical *Kunstform* is dealt a mortal blow when subjected to the razor wit of these powerful demons. In Hegel's eyes they have the somewhat wretched distinction of being art that is antithetical not only to the spirit of comedy, but to the spirit of art as well. Most disturbing of all for Hegel is how the creators of both satire and subjective humor seem to relish their discontentedness. In his opinion, such attitudes are not conducive to the growth of Spirit.

Another consideration Hegel discusses in the section on satire is the historical origins of this "unhealthy spirit." He declares that it was not created in Greece, "the land of beauty" as he calls it, but in the Roman world, a place dominated by "abstraction" and "dead law."[46] Here again, I suspect, we should keep Knox's point in mind and remember the *Weltanschauung* of Hegel's age. In addition to the Teutonic preoccupation with *Quellenforschung,* there were the political rivalries of the period which were formulated in terms of the weak independent states of Germany versus the might of Imperial France. This partially explains, but hardly excuses, why Hegel holds the Romans in low esteem and dislikes Latin literature.

The Romans, Hegel maintains, had sacrificed the freedom of the individual to the good of the whole: abstract and impartial law replaced the more personal ethics of individual choice. In doing so, the Romans divorced themselves from the very source of creativity. Hence, proposes Hegel, they had to "borrow" their art from the Greeks. This is especially true, he observes, when it comes to comedy

> It is remarkable that what may be regarded as native in the case of the Romans is comic farces, Fescennine verses, and Atellan burlesques, whereas the more cultivated comedies of Plautus, and Terence too, were borrowed from the Greeks and were more a matter of imitation than of independent production.[47]

Regardless of whether there is any truth in Hegel's observation, it is clear that he views the indigenous creations with some contempt. The art in which the Romans excel is the very specter that Hegel is trying to exorcise

> What is peculiarly Rome's own is . . . above all satire. Here it is the spirit of a virtuous ill-humour about the surrounding world which strives to give itself some relief in hollow declamations. This form of art, prosaic in itself, can become poetic only if it so brings the corrupt shape of reality before our eyes that this corruption collapses in itself by reason of its own folly.[48]

In other words, satire can only be "poetic" if it conforms to Hegel's principles for comedy. This is something that it fails to do, of course, and only Horace, in his mind, even comes close. Even then, the *Satires* and *Epistles* only create a "joviality" that makes the bad appear laughable: "it may be exquisite and cultivated, but it is certainly not poetic."[49] Still worse are Persius and Juvenal, whom Hegel characterizes as harsh and bitter. Instead of "poetically" addressing the problems of the age, they launch into a tirade of "ill-humor, vexation, wrath, and hatred which expiate in abstract rhetoric about virtue and wisdom."[50]

Worst of all is Lucian. Hegel vehemently portrays Lucian as if he were single-handedly responsible for the demise of the classical value system. Any *Greek* (or even "Syrian Greek") who could turn his back on the aesthetic accomplishments of his own tradition, is, in Hegel's mind, a veritable "Judas." Lucian, he says, exchanged divine Beauty for a few cheap laughs:

> Later on, finally, we see Lucian, the Syrian Greek, turning with cheerful levity against everything, heroes, philosophers, and gods, and especially satirizing the old Greek gods on the score of their humanity and individuality. Yet he often fails to get beyond chatter about the externals of the shapes and actions of the gods, and therefore becomes wearisome, especially for us. . . . we know that these traits of the gods,

> considered in their beauty, have their eternal validity in spite of his jokes and ridicule.[51]

Lucian, the consummate satirist in Hegel's eyes, was more than antiquity could bear. This "Jean Paul" of the ancient world attacked art, religion, and philosophy with reckless abandon until there was little of substance left. As a result, the beauty of the classical *Kunstform* was destroyed, and subjectivity was set free to create its own inner spiritual world.

VIII. Conclusion

Thus, we can see that Hegel's views on comedy are multifaceted in both intent and application. Rather than maintain a strictly definitive dialectic of historical progression, Hegel reshuffles the comic genres to suit his particular needs. Satire, a relatively late comic genre, (and one, because of its highly subjective nature, we should expect to find discussed within the confines of romantic art), is used as a "transitionary form" at the end of the classical *Kuunstform.* New Comedy, on the other hand, traditionally viewed as the true "classical" archetype of comedy, is ambiguously characterized by Hegel as both intermediate and at the same time "modern." Finally, Old Comedy, the *first* to appear in the historical sequence, is elevated by Hegel to the status of the crowning aesthetic achievement of the human spirit.

The reason Hegel manipulates the genres in this way is, as we have seen, partially explainable in terms of the neoclassical biases of early-nineteenth-century Germany. More important, though, his structure is the direct consequence of his metaphysical convictions: those forms of humor that contribute to the growth of Spirit—to the growth of freedom—must necessarily be superior to those that either stunt such growth or divert it in an undesirable direction. Nevertheless, we would be amiss to underestimate Hegel's respect for the spirit of comedy. The "emphatic" position of his arguments, the fact that his concluding thoughts in this massive undertaking are on *comedy,* would tend to support the notion that he sees comedy playing a crucial role in the development of humankind. Importantly, although he touches on thousands of topics in the *Aesthetics,* we find the comic spirit at two critical transitions: it provides the final *Aufhebung* of both the classical and romantic approaches to art. Thus, comedy functions as a veritable *Geist der stets verneint,* and Hegel's aesthetic spirit, like Goethe's, is one with a devastating sense of humor.

Notes

1. G. W. F. Hegel, *Vorlesungen über die Ästhetik, Werke in zwanzig Bänden,* ed. E. Moldenhauer and K. Michel, 20 vols. and index, vols. 13–15, (Frankfurt am Main:

Suhrkamp Verlag, 1969ff), 15:572. English translation, G. W. F. Hegel, *Aesthetics: Lectures on Fine Art,* trans. T. M. Knox, 2 vols., (Oxford: Clarendon Press, 1975), 2:1236. Further references will be in the form: *Werke,* 15:572; *A,* 2:1236.

2. Anne Paolucci, "Hegel's Theory of Comedy," *Comedy: New Perspectives* (New York: New York Literary Forum, 1978), 89–108. A. Paolucci tries to construct a Hegelian "poetics" of dramatic comedy along Aristotelian lines. Although illuminating, her conclusions lead the reader to believe Hegel is being more systematic than he really is. Henry Paolucci, "The Poetics of Aristotle and Hegel," in *Hegel in Comparative Literature,* ed. Frederick G. Weiss, *Review of National Literatures,* vol. 1, no. 4 (New York: St. John's University Press, 1970), 201–9. H. Paolucci also expresses the notion that Hegel is the true inheritor of the Aristotelian tradition, and says that Hegel thinks of comedy as "the ultimate aesthetic catharsis." A. C. Bradley, "The Rejection of Falstaff," *Oxford Lectures on Poetry* (New York: St. Martin's Press, 1965), 247–75. Bradley's landmark essay, which focuses upon the nature of the comic hero, has influenced many literary critics, including the Paoluccis.

3. Jacob Loewenberg, *Hegel Selections* (New York: Scribner's, 1929); *Hegel's Phenomenology: Dialogues on the Life of Mind* (La Salle, Ill.: Open Court Publishing Co., 1965). Loewenberg makes the claim that one of the keys to understanding Hegel is to realize that comedy and dialectic are related: "The logic called dialectical is the logic of comedy par excellence. It is the logic by which ideals and beliefs are made to whip themselves, as it were, in the process of exhibiting their internal contradictions." (*Hegel Selections,* xxi). George McFadden, *Discovering the Comic* (Princeton: Princeton University Press, 1982). McFadden, perhaps arguing from the opposite direction, claims that Hegel's greatest contribution to the comic theory is the concept of dialectics (p. 91). Gary Shapiro, "Hegel's Dialectic of Artistic Meaning," *Journal of Aesthetics and Art Criticism* 35 (1976): 23–35. Shapiro, perhaps the scholar most sensitive to Hegel's views of comedy, focuses his attention on the dialectical tensions between tragedy and comedy. His arguments show why the existence of the former must necessarily give rise to the latter.

4. William Desmond, *Beyond Hegel and Dialectic: Speculation, Cult, and Comedy,* (Albany: SUNY Press, 1992). Desmond devotes two chapters of this book to Hegelian notions of comedy. In one he counters the "logocentric" charges mockingly made by deconstructionists like Derrida, showing that dialectic, like comedy, is essentially plurivocal and fosters a "breakthrough of consciousness" that stands (or dances) above the abyss of negation. In the other, Desmond provides an in-depth analysis of Aristophanic humor as made manifest to Hegel from both the comic plays and Platonic references.

5. Cf. G. W. F. Hegel, *Phänomenologie des Geistes, Werke in zwanzig Bänden,* ed. E. Moldenhauer and K. Michel, vol. 3, (Frankfurt am Main: Suhrkamp Verlag, 1969ff.), sections 744–47.

6. In deference to A. Paolucci, I think one must adopt a stance similar to that which Kaufmann expresses about Hegel's thoughts on tragedy: it is a misnomer, he says, to speak of "Hegel's theory of tragedy" when we really ought to be speaking about "Hegel's ideas about tragedy." Walter Kaufmann, "Hegel's Ideas About

Tragedy," in *New Studies in Hegel's Philosophy,* ed. Warren E. Steinkraus (New York: Holt, Rinehart, and Winston, 1971), 201–20.

7. The role of freedom—especially within the confines of the *Aesthetics*—is discussed by Andras Horn, *Kunst und Freiheit: Eine kritische Interpretation der Hegelschen Ästhetik* (The Hague, Netherlands: Martinus Nijhoff, 1969). Also see Warren E. Steinkraus, "The Place of Art in Hegel's System," *Pakistan Philosophical Journal* 10 (1972): 41–51. Cf. McFadden, *Discovering the Comic,* 98–99.

8. *Werke,* 15:534; *A,* 2:1205.

9. Cf. Shapiro, "Hegel's Dialectic of Artistic Meaning," 30–31.

10. Cf. Desmond, *Beyond Hegel and Dialectic,* 276. Desmond observes that even philosophers may exhibit a tendency towards "*der stiefe Verstand.*" Hegel, he suggests, is self-consciously aware of this phenomenon, and is capable of laughing at the absurdity of its implications.

11. *Werke,* 15:530; *A,* 2:1201.

12. Cf. Desmond, *Beyond Hegel and Dialectic,* 273–81. In his discussion of "the Comedy of Failure" Desmond notes that the Aristophanic hero negates all negations by adopting an "it is as nothing" attitude.

13. Bradley, "The Rejection of Falstaff," 261–70.

14. *Werke,* 14:210; *A,* 1:585.

15. Many of Hegel's ideas about comedy are similar to those expressed by Freidrich and August Wilhelm Schlegel. Particularly illuminating is Lecture II in A. W. Schlegel's *Vorlesungen über dramatische Kunst und Literatur* (1808) which discusses Old Comedy.

16. *Werke,* 15:552; *A,* 2:1220.

17. *Werke,* 15:569; *A,* 2:1233. Cf. Bradley, "The Rejection of Falstaff," 261–62; H. Paolucci, "The Poetics of Aristotle and Hegel," 207–08; Shapiro, "Hegel's Dialectic of Artistic Meaning," 31.

18. *Werke,* 15:530; *A,* 2:1202.

19. *Werke,* 15:554–55; *A,* 2:1222.

20. *Werke,* 15:535–36; *A,* 2:1206.

21. *Werke,* 15:553; *A,* 2:1221.

22. *Werke,* 14:210, 217–18; 15:572; *A,* 1:585–86, 591–92; 2:1235–36. Running close behind (or at least granted "honorable mention") are Ariosto and Cervantes. Cf. H. Paolucci, "Poetics of Aristotle and Hegel," 194–95, 202–9; A. Paolucci, "Hegel's Theory of Comedy," 101–2.

23. *Werke,* 15:528; *A,* 2:1200.

24. *Werke,* 15:528; *A,* 2:1200. It is interesting to reflect on how apropos these observations are when applied to the deconstructionist. Cf. Desmond, *Beyond Hegel and Dialectic,* 298.

25. *Werke,* 15:528; *A,* 2:1200.

26. *Werke,* 15:531–34; *A,* 2:1202–4.

27. One who has read Euripides' *Cyclopes* might wonder whether such a clear-cut division of the action is warranted—and still less so with *Alcestis,* which was performed in the "fourth position" (if the tradition is credible). Nevertheless, there is an awk-

ward, if not artificial, vacillation between the extremes of tragedy and comedy in these two plays, and Hegel's point can be well taken.

28. *Werke,* 15:569; *A,* 2:1233–34.

29. Hegel repeatedly insists that a comedian's goal should be to look to the good of his community. Comedy in his eyes (and in the eyes of many other theoreticians as well) is primarily a social phenomenon.

30. *Werke,* 15:571; *A,* 2:1235.

31. *PhG, Werke,* 3, sections 178–96.

32. *Werke,* 15:571–72; *A,* 2:1235.

33. This is, of course, a questionable position in itself, and one that many twentieth-century aestheticians and artists have rejected.

34. Hegel goes to great lengths in the *Aesthetics* to differentiate between poetry and prose. In fact, this is the first order of business in the chapter on poetry (*Werke,* 15:237–74; *A,* 2:971–99). Poetry is characterized as a manifestation of *Vernuft,* while prose is a manifestation of *Verstand.*

35. *Werke,* 13:122; *A,* 1:513.

36. *Werke,* 13:123; *A,* 1:514.

37. *Werke,* 15:528; *A,* 2:1200.

38. Cf. T. M. Knox, "Puzzle of Hegel's Aesthetics," in *Art and Logic in Hegel's Philosophy,* ed. Warren E. Steinkraus (New Jersey: Humanities Press, 1980), 7–9.

39. Cf. Desmond, *Beyond Hegel and Dialectic,* 277, 293–300.

40. *Werke,* 13:97 ; *A,* 1:67.

41. *Werke,* 14:229–31; *A,* 1:600–602.

42. *Werke,* 14:229; *A,* 1:600–601.

43. *Werke,* 14:230–31; *A,* 1:601–602. Cf. Rüdiger Bubner, "Hegel's Aesthetics: Yesterday and Today," in *Art and Logic in Hegel's Philosophy,* 15–33. Bubner not only discusses some of Jean Paul's own views on aesthetics, he provides an analysis of several nineteenth-century aestheticians who were inspired by Hegel's views on comedy as well.

44. *Werke,* 14:240–41; *A,* 1:609–10.

45. *Werke,* 14:240; *A,* 1:609.

46. *Werke,* 13:123; *A,* 1:514.

47. *Werke,* 13:124; *A,* 1:514.

48. *Werke,* 13:124; *A,* 1:515.

49. *Werke,* 13:124; *A,* 1:515.

50. *Werke,* 13:125; *A,* 1:515.

51. *Werke,* 13:125; *A,* 1:515–16.

IX

Squaring the Romantic Circle: Hegel's Critique of Schlegel's Theories of Art*

Judith Norman

Hegel was no fan of the artistic movement known as German romanticism; he thought it lacked taste, propriety, and theoretical acumen. In the introduction to his *Lectures on Aesthetics,* he targets Friedrich Schlegel, the chief spokesman of the Jena romantic circle, for particular criticism. The *Philosophy of Right* had already inveighed against Schlegel's novel, *Lucinde,* for its frank treatment and valorization of extramarital sexuality; here he criticizes the botched Fichtean metaphysical framework which, he believes, makes possible such a blatant disregard for moral law. I will look at Hegel's critique of Schlegel, and particularly of Schlegel's notion of romantic irony, an idea Hegel sees arising from the characteristically romantic misunderstanding of Fichte. I will defend Schlegel against Hegel's censure, and attempt to explain why Hegel got Schlegel so badly wrong. Hegel's critique of the romantic movement, I will argue, is quite telling; it is the inability of philosophy of art to recognize a ground between philosophy and art, and allow the logic of the concept to listen to the analogic of intuition.

I will follow Hegel in restricting my attention to the literary movement known as early romanticism. This short-lived movement was characterized by intense theoretical energy far more than by actual artistic achievement, and indeed, Hegel considers its historical import, such as it is, to be exclusively theoretical. The group formed in Jena, around 1797, amongst a close-knit social circle whose voice found collective expression in the *Athenaeum* journal. The group disbanded, coincidentally, at the same time Hegel moved to Jena. Prominent members included Friedrich Schlegel and his brother August, the dramatist Tieck, the poet Novalis, and Caroline Schlegel-Schelling, in whose hyphenated last name some of the causes of the group's dissolution can be discerned.

---

*I would like to thank Caroline Norman and Alistair Welchman for their support and advice while I was writing this essay.

Together with other theoretical movements of the period, German romanticism combined a view of modernity as somehow fractured or characterized by loss with an ambivalent nostalgia for a past that retained its wholeness at the price of naiveté. Like Hegel, the romantics thought this historical change had ramifications for the function of art; art could no longer properly reflect the Absolute in sensuous form. Unlike Hegel, however, romanticism tended to privilege artistic over discursive language as a vehicle for truth, despite the evacuation of the Absolute from the sensuous. This paper is primarily a study of this divergence.

I. Hegel's Critique of Romanticism

Hegel is quite critical of the Schlegels' theories, although he recognizes the proximity of their project to his. He praises them, vaguely, for their general post-Kantian theoretical orientation, as well as for their occasional displays of sound aesthetic judgment. But he believes they fail to theorize these insights with anything approaching philosophical rigor. Indeed, he believes, the Schlegels' were not philosophers at all, just critics whose speculative orientation was not thoughtfully assumed but rather unconsciously absorbed as part of the legacy of the age.

Yet to the extent that the Schlegels did attach their critical positions to a theoretical framework, Hegel thinks it was deeply problematic. He finds fault with two characteristically romantic notions in particular: romantic irony, and the idea of genius. As Hegel explains it, Schlegel's aesthetic theory results from the application of a Fichtean theory of subjectivity to the individual. According to Fichte's idealist metaphysics, the I (the absolute subject) establishes its own identity as subject by positing a not-I, a realm of exteriority opposed to it. All determination is negation, in other words, and the self-determination of the absolute subject is only secured by positing something outside itself. Since the formal I is autonomous, it will determine the content of this alterity. An opposition thus results between empty self and world, an opposition which the self immediately attempts to overcome, since the existence of this foreign world contradicts its supposed identity as absolute and autonomous.

Fichte does not intend this to be an account of the individual's relation to the world. Rather, the I which in positing itself posits a not-I—this I is subjectivity in general, a Kantian transcendental subjectivity. Yet, according to Hegel, Schlegel has privatized this I, made it the prerogative of genius. The genius, in Hegel's reconstruction of the romantic position, is the self-positing creator of the world, the absolute subject who has willed into existence a world whose content is determined by the genius's own caprice. Art, by extension, depicts an arbitrary and illusory world. According to Schlegel, Hegel writes,

> I live as an artist when all my action and expression in general, to the extent that it concerns any content at all, remains merely illusory for me and assumes a shape which is entirely in my power. . . . On the standpoint where the artist is the I that posits and dissolves everything out of itself, for whom no content of consciousness appears as absolute and in and for itself, but only as itself an artificial and dissoluble illusion, . . . only the formalism of the I is considered valid.[1]

Such an attitude, according to Hegel, has several consequences. For one thing, "the individual who lives as an artist indeed relates to others. . . but as genius, these relations to his determinate reality and particular actions, to what is inherently universal—these are as nothing; he relates ironically to them."[2] Irony, then, is the attitude of self-conscious value-positing, when the genius determines his situation, all the while knowing it is the product of his whims. But there is a less happy side to this life of ironic geniality: "the I can also find itself unsatisfied in its self-enjoyment, and instead finds itself lacking, and accordingly feels a craving for solidity and substantiality, for determinate and essential interests . . . and so [the I] falls prey to the longing that we have likewise seen emanate from the Fichtean philosophy."[3] In other words, the I can not be content in a world so radically unstable and malleable and longs for a source of solidity founded in something other than its own caprice.

Clearly, this would be a peculiar reading of Fichte. It simply does not make sense to individuate the Fichtean I, and to imagine each individual to have produced, at will, the content of their experience. Fichte made quite clear that the power to produce the not-I was the sole prerogative of the transcendental I, and that it occurred prior to any act of consciousness (indeed, it made consciousness possible). For any conscious individual, the world appears as given, in its principle respects at least. And to the extent that a striving arises, it is a striving to incorporate this alterity and become self-determining, not to find something objective outside of the subject.

We can distinguish two specific claims that Hegel attributes to the Schlegels: first, that the artistic genius is the Absolute I, and second, that irony is the attitude of the genius to the world it knows to be its own product. I will explore each of these claims in turn. In essence, I will argue that, although Schlegel did have a fundamentally Fichtean position, the first claim is false: he never associated the artistic genius with the absolute subject. Given this, irony cannot play the theoretical role Hegel believed it did, and it remains to be seen what role it actually played.

II. Romanticism and Genius

Looking at the *Athenaeum*, the journal in which the romantic theoretical self-explanations appeared, it is not hard to find statements that put into question Hegel's tidy Fichtean story. In one of the "Critical Fragments" Schlegel published, he writes that

> self-restriction . . . is, after all, for the artist as well as for the man, the first and the last, the most necessary and the highest duty. Most necessary because wherever one does not restrict oneself, one is restricted by the world; and that makes one a slave.[4]

Schlegel clearly thinks neither artist nor person has infinite powers in all spheres, as Hegel's interpretation would have it. Far from being the mere product of an arbitrary artisic whim, "the world" has the power to place certain constraints on the artist. Moreover, Schlegel continues the same fragment with a cautionary word to the artist:

> what appears to be unlimited free will, and consequently seems and should seem to be irrational or supra-rational, nonetheless must still at bottom be simply necessary and rational; otherwise the whim becomes willful, becomes intolerant, and self-restriction turns into self-destruction.

This contradicts Hegel's claims directly. Even the sphere in which the artist has infinite power (Schlegel has not said what it is) must still be governed by necessary law. It is unclear whether Schlegel's "must" is descriptive or normative, but it comes to largely the same thing: contrary to Hegel's interpretation, Schlegel recognizes the existence of necessary laws to which the artist is either advised or required to submit.

Indeed, Schlegel's scattered remarks concerning genius are cryptic in the extreme, and tend towards a strangely impersonal concept of artist creation. Schlegel writes that "Antiquity is the only genius that . . . can be called absolutely great, unique and unequal."[5] Benjamin goes so far as to indicate the impersonality of consciousness as precisely the essential distinction between Fichte and the romantics.[6]

Looking more closely at the notion of the artist Schlegel outlines, we might note that there is something oxymoronic in the notion of a Fichtean genius; there is not a contradiction, strictly speaking, in the conjunction of the two concepts, but there is an undeniable tension. To understand why this is so, it is necessary to review some principle elements of Fichte's epistemology.

Fichte's epistemology was derived from Kant's first and second *Critiques*. His notion of the I is the successor to Kant's transcendental unity of apperception, and the act by which it posits its other, the not-I, is the act of production of alterity. Now this not-I is considerably less mysterious than Kant's noumenal unknown. Kant's noumena played a (necessarily) undefined role in producing the particular empirical content of our experience. Presumably, it existed independently of the knowing act of the understanding. The idealists thought this very notion paradoxical; how could there be an object but for a subject? Fichte attempted to remove this source of incoherence in Kant; in Fichte's epistemology, the existence of the not-I was wholly dependent on and determined by its relation to the subject. This is why Hegel, when accusing the romantic genius of assuming the role of Fichtean subject, could conclude that the world would be entirely determined by the whim of the genius.

Kant's model of the production of nature (as a system of our experience) is, in a word, a type of transcendental hylomorphism,[7] where the material content given from some noumenal source is given form by the understanding. Fichte's idealism entails a reduction of matter to form, giving the spontaneity of the subject exclusive responsibility for the production of nature. As such, Fichte believed he was able to settle the inconsistencies left in the first *Critique* by Kant's dualistic epistemology.

Kant himself was not inclined towards Fichte's monistic solution. He recognized the weaknesses in his first *Critique* account of the production of nature, but his proposed resolution took him in a different direction, towards what might be considered an exacerbated dualism. In brief, he manifested growing concern that the tools with which he invested the productive subject in the first *Critique* were not sufficient to account for the system of nature we experience. In other words, the first *Critique* account of the production of order underdetermined the degree of orderliness we actually find in nature. For example, the first *Critique* explained why we experience causation in general, but failed to explain how particular empirical laws are possible. We can put it this way: Kant's ambition of defeating Humean skepticism and providing a foundation for Newton's laws was only half successful. Hume might be satisfied but Newton would not be, since the lawful behavior of particular natural occurrences was left entirely mysterious. If such laws could not be traced back to the spontaneous contribution of the subject, where did they come from?

The third *Critique* is, by and large, an attempt to reply to this question. Without getting into too many details, we can at least see how Kant positioned beauty and aesthetic judgment to function as part of the solution. An aesthetic judgment, according to Kant, arises from the feeling of pleasure which results from the harmony of the faculties of understanding and imagination. Such a harmony arises when the imagination presents to the understanding an object whose formal perfection was not already dictated by the concepts of the understanding. In other words, the form-giving faculty of the understanding finds an orderliness not of its own making. This instigates what Kant describes as a "free play" between the spontaneous and receptive faculties, resulting in the feeling of pleasure which causes us to call the object beautiful.

In contrast to the first *Critique*, then, the analysis of beauty in the third *Critique* suggests that there might be two sources of the production of order in experience. The understanding's job is co-opted by the imagination which presents an already orderly manifold. But this raises a question as to the source of this extraconceptual order. Unhelpfully, Kant says that nature itself gives the law. In natural beauty, nature presents us with an orderly manifold directly; and in artistic beauty, nature works through the agency of genius to impart a source of unintentional order to the beautiful object. As Kant writes, "artistic skill . . . is imparted to every artist immediately by the hand of nature."[8] As a being endowed with understanding, the artist can consciously give form to his artwork. But the production of material (not formal) order is not under our conscious control. It is nature working through the genius. Kant writes: "Genius is the innate mental disposition . . . through which nature gives the rule to art."[9] The artwork is not a conscious, intentional, rational product. Kant writes: "the author of a product for which he is indebted to his genius does not know himself how he has come by his ideas; and he has not the power to devise the like at pleasure or in accordance with a plan."[10]

I will not take the time to discuss this doctrine as it appears in Kant in greater detail. It is sufficient to note that it is a profoundly un-Fichtean direction of thought, as it suggests a productive capacity in nature, precisely that aspect of Kant's philosophy that Fichte impoverished to the point of nonexistence. Nature had no integrity in Fichte's system, no autonomy. It was mere not-I, an opposing principle to the subject, the condition of moral agency. A Fichtean genius would draw its productive capacity from an ideal source, the transcendental subject. The productive capacity of a Kantian genius is drawn from a real source, nature.

Schlegel has a notion of artistic production that draws on Kant's third *Critique* conception of genius. He writes, for instance "even if Homer himself had no intentions, his poetry and the real author of that poetry, Nature certainly did."[11] Other passages reveal a similar tendency: "A poem is only a product of nature which wants to become a work of art."[12] "Many so-called artists are really products of nature's art."[13] Schlegel does not fill out this notion of genius to any great extent. On the face of it, it is not immediately consistent with (what I will show to be) his Fichtean theoretical sympathies, and if he is to make it consistent, he will have to develop a less Kantian notion of nature, one which ultimately assigns the unconscious artistic processes to the subject. I am not interested in speculating about what this theory might involve. At present, it is most important to note that this model of artistic production is what we might call *irresponsible.* That is, the individual is not the ultimate and sole locus of the artistic intention. Rather, the artist is the tool of a greater power, a hidden source in which the intention ultimately lies.

Still, Schlegel does not have in mind a model where the artist is *merely* a mouthpiece of some muse; on the contrary, he frequently echoes Kant's instance that the artwork combine both the instinct and intention of the artist.[14] In this, he is also in agreement with Hegel, who writes that the artist must combine inspiration with industry. Still, Schlegel does give a strong account of the impersonal, unconscious drive which is required in the production of the artwork, and as such, his notion of irony cannot be what Hegel says it is. Schlegel's account simply does not accord the artist the freedom to form the work of art in a willful or lawless manner. This leaves open the question of what Schlegel meant by irony such that Hegel was not able to grasp its true philosophical significance.

III. Romantic Philosophy

We can look, to begin with, at Hegel's initial, dismissive judgment that the Schlegels' nature was "not philosophical but rather essentially *critical*."[15] This is an odd distinction in an age where philosophy meant critique, an age which, F. Schlegel writes, "deserves the humble but highly suggestive name of the Critical Age, so that soon now everything is going to be criticized, except the age itself, and everything is going to become more and more critical."[16] Everything will be criticized except the age itself. This points to an issue fundamental not only for Schlegel and the romantic movement but for the German anti-enlightenment in general. The basic insight was that the Enlightenment faith in the power of reason was just that: faith. Reason could support anything but itself, and the core of the anti-enlightenment lay in the recognition of this paradox. Kant, we might be tempted to say, did recognize this basic problem: witness his main text, the *Critique of Pure Reason*. But as Schlegel's remark indicates, Kant failed to criticize the nature of critique itself. The very first *Athenaeum* fragment reads: "nothing is more rarely the subject of philosophy that philosophy itself."[17] Later fragments hurl invective at those followers of Kant who failed to think critically about Kant's system. Schlegel makes one exception: He believes it was Fichte's great merit to have seen and responded to this critical crisis. He writes

> Fichte's theory of knowledge is a philosophy about the subject matter of Kant's philosophy . . . if the essence of the critical method is that the theory of the determining ability and the system of determined affective impressions should be intimately united in it . . . then it might very well be that even formally he is a Kant raised to the second power and the *Wissenschaftslehre* much more critical than it seems to be. Especially the new version of the *Wissenschaftslehre* is always simultaneously philosophy and philosophy of philosophy.[18]

And he ends the passage stating "one can never be too critical."

Now criticism, according to Schlegel, means presenting the ability of determination as united with the determined impressions. In more straightforwardly Kantian language, this means displaying the conditions of experience united with the experience it conditions. This is the type of criticism that Schlegel consistently praises, and which, as he concludes in the passage above, one cannot have enough of. In this sense, he would be proud to be a critic. Indeed, in his essay "On Incomprehensibility," a discussion of the nature of irony, he jokes about his plan to criticize Fichte as Fichte did Kant or in other words, he writes,

> to use the jargon that is most usual and appropriate to this kind of conception, [I will] place myself on Fichte's shoulders, just as he placed himself on Reinhold's shoulders, Reinhold on Kant's shoulders, Kant on Leibniz's, and so on infinitely back to the prime shoulder.[19]

Now there is a contradiction between notions of an infinite regress and a prime shoulder; Schlegel is paradoxically embracing both the thesis and the antithesis of Kant's first antinomy. Still he raises a serious issue in suggesting that historical progress elides with a conceptual one. History presents the spectacle of critique endlessly reapplied. And this relates directly to Schlegel's assertion that Fichte "is a Kant raised to the second power," Kant squared. Fichte's early philosophy can be seen as a reapplication of Kantian method to Kant's results. Rather than asking about the production of experience, he asked about the production of the categories of experience. Specifically, he traced their origin to the transcendental unity of apperception, as the supreme principle of subjectivity he called the I. The I is self-producing, or self-positing as he would say, but it is also paradoxical. It is both identical to and distinct from the not-I which is its product. Its mode of production is a "causality which is not causality," as Fichte would put it.[20] In a letter to Reinhold, Fichte writes that the positing of the I

> has no name, never occurs in consciousness, and cannot be grasped by means of concepts. . . . One enters my philosophy by means of what is absolutely incomprehensible. . . . Everything that is comprehensible presupposes a higher sphere in which it is comprehended and is therefore not the highest thing, precisely because it is comprehensible.[21]

Schlegel's taste for regress is well served. Fichte's critique of Kantian criticism has resulted in incomprehensibility. No true tortoise is to be found.

What does this have to do with art? Schlegel explains

> There is a kind of poetry whose essence lies in the relation between ideal and real, and which therefore, by analogy to philosophical jargon, should be called transcendental poetry. . . . But just as we wouldn't think much of an uncritical transcendental philosophy that doesn't represent the producer along with the product and contain at the same time within the system of transcendental thoughts a description of transcendental thinking: so too this sort of poetry should unite the transcendental raw materials and preliminaries of a theory of poetic creativity—often met with in modern poets—with the artistic reflection

> and beautiful self-mirroring that is present in Pindar, in the lyric fragments of the Greeks, in the classical elegy, and among the moderns, in Goethe. In all its descriptions, this poetry should describe itself, and always be simultaneously poetry and the poetry of poetry.[22]

Art, like philosophy, must give an account of the production of its product. The two accounts, clearly, are not analogous. The artwork might be the product of an artist, but experience is not the product of the philosopher. In other words, the philosopher can *argue* that experience is produced, and indeed trace the production process back to an incomprehensible prime mover, as did Fichte. But the artist can *present* experience as produced, as the phenomenal manifestation of some transcendental producer. This is a fairly tall order for any poem to fill, but Schlegel thinks that romantic poetry can accomplish this task. He writes

> Romantic poetry . . . alone can become like the epic, a mirror of the whole circumambient world, an image of the age. And it can also—more than any other form—hover at the midpoint between the portrayed and the portrayer, free of all real and ideal self-interest, on the wings of poetic reflection, and can raise that reflection again and again to a higher power, can multiply it in an endless succession of mirrors. . . . The romantic kind of poetry is still in the state of becoming; that, in fact, is its real essence: that it should forever be becoming and never be perfected . . . in a certain sense all poetry is or should be romantic.[23]

This passage has an implicit response to the question I posed earlier, on behalf of Schlegel and German anti-enlightenment in general: who will critique the age? The answer, it appears, is poetry. Transcendental romantic poetry (by which, to be etymologically rigorous, Schlegel means *das Poesie des Romans*) will "hover" between the portrayer and portrayed, which is to say that it will present an image of the age, but will present it as an image, as a portrait, as a product. It raises the presentation "to a higher power" just as Fichte had done to Kant, and by a similarly transcendental method. Just as in Fichte's philosophy, it shows the world to be a product and the producer to be incomprehensible.

But Schlegel does not simply claim that art can be used to illustrate Fichtean philosophical principles. His claim is more radical than that. He writes, "All philosophy is idealism, and there exists no true realism except that of poetry. But poetry and philosophy are only extremes."[24] And elsewhere, "Whatever can be done while poetry and philosophy are separated has been done and accomplished. So the time has come to unite the two."[25] In other words, it is time to synthesize Fichte and Goethe. Philosophy is one-sidedly ideal; it can talk about experience, but it cannot present it. Poetry has the opposite problem; it can present the object, but it cannot reflect on it. Schlegel calls for the unity of the two, a self-reflective art. And the mode of art's self-reflection is what he calls irony. He writes

> Every poem should be genuinely romantic, and every [poem] should be didactic in that broader sense of the word that designates the tendency toward a deep, infinite meaning. Additionally, we make this demand everywhere, without necessarily using this name. Even in very popular genres—the theater, for example—we demand irony; we demand that the events, the people, in short, the whole game of life actually be taken up and presented as a game as well.[26]

The subject can only be indicated by showing the object to be one-sided. In terms of Schlegel's theory, I have suggested, this means showing the object as a product of a transitive production relation. The trace of the presence of the subject is, as in Kant, a moment of reflexivity that accompanies all presentations. Irony, then, is the romantic successor notion to Kant's transcendental unity of apperception;[27] it marks the work as a production, it includes the subject in the presence of the object, revealing the illusory status of the object without displaying the presence of a subject. Kant wrote that the "I think must be able to accompany all representations," and this occasional awareness of supervenience exhausts our nontranscendental engagement with the theoretical ego. No intellectual intuition confirms the self-present subject for Kant or for Schlegel, who is here quite distant from Fichte; apperception is the echo of an intellectual intuition we are unable to perform. Schlegel will not leave the sphere of presentation, and if the subject is absent from this sphere, then that is the truth of the subject. If Pascal's hidden God was paradoxical, Schlegel's hidden subject is ironic.

Schlegel writes

> There are ancient and modern poems that are pervaded by the divine breath of irony throughout and informed by a truly transcendental buffoonery. Internally the mood that surveys everything and rises infinitely above all limitations, even above its own art, virtue, or genius.[28]

In other words, it shows that the truth of its object is finitude, and, in rising infinitely (which is to say rising to the infinite), points to it as such. This ironic act, a "rising," "hovering" or "reflecting" as we have seen Schlegel describe it, is a properly theoretical moment, a moment of immanent self-critique in the work of art. Irony raises poetry to a higher power, as Schlegel is fond of saying, and the higher power (or rather the raising) is what makes poetry into philosophy (or rather, unites the two). Irony, Schlegel writes, is an essentially philosophical gesture, through which poetry "can also reach the heights of philosophy," and this unity of poetry and philosophy is a task that Schlegel thinks is the most pressing issue for both disciplines.[29]

IV. Hegel versus Schlegel

With this notion of romantic irony in hand, let us return to Hegel. Hegel, it is clear, misunderstood the basic romantic theoretical position. Irony is not the attitude of a genius who knows the content of consciousness to be a personal whim. But irony does refer to the relation between the transcendental subject and the world it has produced, and Hegel was right to point to that. Moreover, Hegel correctly attributes to Schlegel the idea that, since the world is a product of the subject, it is subjective and illusory. Art, as Schlegel says, shows the game of life to be just a game. But as such, Schlegel has misrepresented the Kantian/Fichtean position he is drawing upon. For Kant, it is the categories applied by the subject that insure the objectivity of experience. That is, since the categories produce objects, they are objective—universal, discursive, conceptual. It is the manifold given in sensation that is subjective, particular, "less than a dream." (In the same way, the world of our experience is the only thing that can be considered "real," properly speaking, since "reality" is a category only applicable to possible experience in the first place.) In other words, Kant thought he had protected the status of experience by showing it to be a product, while Schlegel thought that this very production relation rendered it somehow illegitimate. On one level, Schlegel's reversal of terms is of little consequence, to the extent that the same idea is intended. On the other hand, it throws both Kant's as well as Fichte's epistemologies into a much bleaker light than is warranted, misrepresenting the very spirit of Kant's philosophy that each post-Kantian, it seemed, was so concerned to protect.

As such, Schlegelian irony implies a destructive attitude toward what Kant would call the empirically real, an attitude that Hegel did not fail to notice; indeed, Schlegel compares artistic production with sacrifice, which he defines as "the annihilation of the finite because it is finite."[30] But this is a sacrifice that affects the artist qua finite ego as much as it affects the artwork qua finite representation. Schlegel writes that "to become an artist means nothing but consecrating oneself to the gods of the underworld," which is to say "an eternal self-destination into the infinite." To add one more objection to Hegel's characterization of romantic genius, it appears that Christ rather than God is the model for the romantic artist. The artist must sacrifice himself to reveal that his truth is his finitude—and in so doing he indicates the infinite.

This points us back to the heart of Hegel's misunderstanding of Schlegel. To put it simply, Hegel thought irony was the attitude of the *subject* to the illusory object. In fact, as I have been concerned to argue, it is essentially the feature of the *object* by which it indicates its illusory status.[31]

Furthermore, irony is a function of the form, rather than the content of the artwork. As Benjamin notes, romantic art tended towards an evacuation of content. It was the form which was to break the surface as it were, to shatter the illusion, forcing reality to intrude into fiction or vice versa. And it was to achieve this, in the last analysis, by a mixing of genres. Schlegel has a complicated theory of genres and their mixtures which he attempted to put into effect in *Lucinde*, for one. The successful romantic work would combine the subjective aspects of the novel or poem with the objective features of classical works like the epic. *Lucinde* is an absolute hodgepodge of styles, and a second section, which would be composed of poems, was never written. Hegel mistook the philosophical significance of *Lucinde* to lie in its cavalier attitude towards sexuality; it lay instead, in *Lucinde*'s cavalier attitude towards itself.

V. Hegel's Critique of Romanticism Revisited

As I have argued, Hegel's critique of Schlegel's theories of art are not particularly well-informed. But it is not difficult to find Hegelian resources with which to construct a more accurate critique of Schlegel and his notion of the ironic auto-destruction of the finite. Hegel's discussion of finitude in the first book of the *Logic* is particularly relevant; finitude, he writes, "is the negation as *fixed in itself*."[32] Finite things know themselves to be nothing; they are essentially and irreconcilably cut off from the affirmation of infinity, and, as Hegel writes, "the truth of this being [finite] is their end."[33] In other words, their destiny is to cease to be; "there is no longer left in finite things an affirmative being *distinct* from their destiny to perish."[34]

Hegel points out the contradiction in this concept of finitude, whose endurance as finitude is at odds with its transitory nature, and we can see that this contradiction accrues to Schlegel's conception as well. This bears an obvious resemblance to the critique of Fichte implicit in Hegel's analysis of the "ought," which immediately follows the section on finitude in the *Logic*. In both cases, Hegel blames the understanding for clinging to finitude and failing to allow the category to develop into a more satisfactory one, a notion of infinity to which finitude is not opposed. Hegel would say, accordingly, that Schlegel has misunderstood the notion of the finite if he believes it to be ultimately opposed to the infinite.

For the purposes of this discussion, I am not concerned to resolve the dispute between Hegel and Schlegel so much as to understand its significance for aesthetics. Hegel and Schlegel would agree that the vocation of art is the (auto)presentation of the Absolute, a vocation it can no longer adequately fulfill. Both agree further that philosophy must now assume an increasingly dominant role in this task. They part ways, however, on the question of the enduring relevance of sensuous presentation. Given the evacuation of the Absolute from the realm of the sensuous, Schlegel will not admit that it can be followed elsewhere. Rather, it is the task of a philosophically sophisticated art to trace the lines of its flight.

Schlegel, in other words, remained committed to what Hegel would consider the philosophy of reflection. Against Hegel, Schlegel will not admit that the sensuous materiality of the given manifold can be exhaustively subsumed under (or developed into) the concept. Again, this ties in with his Kantian sympathies: any hidden affinity between sensibility and the understanding is beyond our ken. Accordingly, he considers the task of presentation to remain an essentially artistic, not an exclusively philosophical one. And so Schlegel will continue to hold fast to finitude, despite its contradictions and even because of them.

Hegel could not understand this strategy, and so he saw in the romantic movement only criticism failing to maintain its theoretical integrity (that is, to be philosophy), and enigmatic art offered up without explanation or propriety. Consequently, he necessarily also failed to comprehend the meaning and function of romantic irony, art's moment of immanent self-critique. Against Hegel's dismissal, we can pit Schlegel's comment that "one of two things is usually lacking in the so-called Philosophy of Art: either philosophy or art."[35]

Notes

1. G. W. F. Hegel, *Vorlesungen über die Ästhetik, Sämtliche Werke,* ed. Hermann Glockner, Jubilaeumsausgabe (Stuttgart: Frommann, 1927–30), 12:101–2. All translations of passages in Hegel's *Ästhetik* are my own.

2. *Sämtliche Werke,* 12:102.

3. *Sämtliche Werke,* 12:103.

4. Friedrich Schlegel, *Kritische Fragmente, Kritische Friedrich Schlegel Ausgabe,* ed. E. Behler and H. Eichner, 2 (Paderborn: Ferdinand Schöningh Verlag, 1958–), #37. The English translations of Schlegel's "Critical Fragments," "Athenaeum Fragments" and "Ideas" cited in this essay are from Friedrich Schlegel, *Lucinde and the Fragments,* trans. Peter Firchow, (Minneapolis: University of Minnesota Press, 1971). They will be cited by fragment number.

5. *Athenaeum Fragmente* (*Kritische Friedrich Schlegel Ausgabe,* 2), #248.

6. Walter Benjamin, *Der Begriff der Kunstkritik in der deutschen Romantik* (Frankfurt am Main: Suhrkamp Verlag, 1973).

7. This term suggested by Alistair Welchman.

8. I. Kant, *Kritik der Urteilskraft, Kants Gesammelte Schriften,* (Königlich Deutsche Akademie der Wissenschaften, Berlin: De Gruyter, 1902–), section 48. All English citations of this work which appear in this essay are taken from *Critique of Judgement,* trans. J. H. Bernard (New York: Hafner Press, 1951).

9. *Kritik der Urteilskraft,* section 46.

10. *Kritik der Urteilskraft,* section 46.

11. *Athenaeum Fragmente* (*Kritische Friedrich Schlegel Ausgabe,* 2), #51.

12. *Kritische Fragmente* (*Kritische Friedrich Schlegel Ausgabe,* 2), #21.

13. *Kritische Fragmente* (*Kritische Freidrich Schlegel Ausgabe,* 2), #1.

14. *Kritische Fragmente* (*Kritische Friedrich Schlegel Ausgabe,* 2), #23, *Athenaeum Fragmente* (*Kritische Friedrich Schlegel Ausgabe,* 2), #51.

15. *Sämtliche Werke* 12:118.

16. Friedrich Schlegel, "Über die Unverständlichkeit," *Kritische Friedrich Schlegel Ausgabe,* 2:364. The English translation cited is "On Incomprehensibility," from *Lucinde and the Fragments,* trans. Peter Firchow, 261.

17. *Athenaeum Fragmente* (*Kritische Friedrich Schlegel Ausgabe,* 2), #1.

18. *Athenaeum Fragmente,* (*Kritische Friedrich Schlegel Ausgabe* 2), #281.

19. "Über die Unverständlichkeit," *Kritische Friedrich Schlegel Ausgabe,* 2:367; Firchow, 264.

20. J. G. Fichte, "Über den Begriff der *Wissenschaftslehre* oder der sogenannten Philosophie," *Johann Gottlieb Fichte's Sämtliche Werke,* ed. I. H. Fichte, (Berlin: Veit, 1845–46), 1:65. The translation is from "Concerning the Concept of the *Wissenschaftslehre* or, Of So-called "Philosophy"" in *Early Philosophical Writings,* trans. and ed. Daniel Breazeale (Ithaca: Cornell Univ. Press, 1988), 134–35.

21. *J. G. Fichtes Briefwechsel: Kritische Gesamtausgabe,* ed. Hans Schulz (Leipzig: Haessel, 1930), no. 246. The translation is from: *Early Philosophical Writings,* trans. and ed. Daniel Breazeale, 399.

22. *Athenaeum Fragmente* (*Kritische Friedrich Schlegel Ausgabe,* 2), #238.

23. *Athenaeum Fragmente* (*Kritische Friedrich Schlegel Ausgabe,* 2), #116.

24. *Athenaeum Fragmente* (*Kritische Friedrich Schlegel Ausgabe,* 2), #96.

25. *Athenaeum Fragmente* (*Kritische Friedrich Schlegel Ausgabe,* 2), #108.

26. Friedrich Schlegel, "Gespräch über die Poesie," *Kritische Friedrich Schlegel Ausgabe,* 2. The translation is my own.

27. Lacoue-Labarthe and Nancy make a similar point where they indicate the structural relation between the historical conception of *Witz* (as Schlegel inherits it) and Hegel's Absolute Knowledge. Philippe Lacoue-Labarthe and Jean-Luc Nancy, *The Literary Absolute,* trans. Barnard and C. Lester (Albany: SUNY Press, 1988), 53.

28. *Kritische Fragmente* (*Kritische Friedrich Schlegel Ausgabe,* 2), #42.

29. *Kritische Fragmente* (*Kritische Friedrich Schlegel Ausgabe,* 2), #115; *Athenaeum Fragmente* (*Kritische Friedrich Schlegel Ausgabe,* 2), #451.

30. *Ideen* (*Kritische Friedrich Schlegel Ausgabe,* 2), #131.

31. In fact, Schlegel suggests that *Witz,* a concept quite close to irony, can only be conceivable in written form; *Athenaeum Fragmente* (*Kritische Friedrich Schlegel Ausgabe,* 2), #394.

32. G. W. F. Hegel, *Wissenschaft der Logik I. Erste Teil: Die Objektive Logik. Erstes Buch, Sämtliche Werke, Jubilaeumsausgabe* ed. H. Glockner (Stuttgart: Frommann, 1927–30), 4:148. The translation is from *Science of Logic,* trans. A. V. Miller (Atlantic Highlands, N.J.: Humanities Press International, 1991), 130.

33. *Logik, Sämtliche Werke* 4:147; Miller, 129.

34. *Logik, Sämtliche Werke* 4:147; Miller, 129.

35. *Kritische Fragmente,* (*Kritische Friedrich Schlegel Ausgabe*), #12.

X

Modernity and the Crisis of Aesthetic Representation in Hegel's Early Writings

Martin Gammon

In the fall of 1913, a young scholar named Franz Rosenzweig discovered a long forgotten document in Hegel's handwriting in the Berlin *Königlichen Bibliothek,* listed under the catalogue heading "Treatise on Ethics." Rosenzweig would subsequently edit and publish this fragment in 1917, and entitle it "The Earliest *Systemprogramm* of German Idealism."[1] Apparently written in late 1796, the fragment attempts to extend the theoretical reach of Kant's postulates of practical reason, in order to procure a "complete system of all Ideas." The author asserts that the "highest act of Reason is an aesthetic act," and dismisses the State as something "mechanical" which must be eradicated in the service of freedom. Such extreme convictions, Rosenzweig presumed, were not consonant with Hegel's own views in this period, and thus surmised that the fragment was Hegel's transcription from another document, most likely written by his colleague from the Tübingen seminary and rising philosophical star, F. W. J. Schelling, who would later defend what this fragment calls a "new mythology" in his 1802 lectures on the philosophy of art.

Since Rosenzweig's publication of this document, the controversy over its authorship has produced a virtual avalanche of scholarship.[2] Subsequent commentators have attributed the fragment to Hölderlin,[3] Schelling,[4] and Hegel himself.[5] However, since Otto Pöggeler's landmark defense of Hegel as the author of the fragment in 1969,[6] most commentators have taken his account to be definitive (albeit with some significant dissent).[7] One major consequence of Pöggeler's defense, however, has been a dramatic reappraisal of Hegel's early view of art, in light of this fragment's call for a new "aesthetic philosophy." A critical appraisal of this reformulation of Hegel's early aesthetic reflections will be the primary focus of this paper.

In his defense of Hegel as the author of this disputed fragment, Pöggeler turns to Rosenzweig's initial supposition—shared by Ernst Cassirer and Georg Lukács, among others—that Hegel could not possibly have expressed the views presented in the "Earliest *Systemprogramm.*" In Cassirer's words, everything we know since Dilthey's initial exposition of Hegel's early development "contradicts the assumption that Hegel actually could be the author of this fragment."[8] In the face of this conventional wisdom, Pöggeler argues that with the benefit of the full compendium of Hegel's *Nachlass,* unavailable in Rosenzweig's day, one can in fact relate each of the assertions in the fragment to associable convictions contemporary with it in Hegel's corpus. Until an original draft can be found from which Hegel would have made a purported transcription, it is purely gratuitous to suppose that Hegel is not the author.

Pöggeler initially disputes Rosenzweig's chronology, and argues that Hegel wrote this piece in early 1797, after moving to Frankfurt and falling under the influence of Hölderlin.[9] This would then help explain the "unmistakable" Hölderlinian imprint on the theory of beauty asserted in the fragment itself. Pöggeler presumes that Hegel did not find Frankfurt to be "*unglückselige,*" as is supposed by Dilthey and exploited by Lukács in his treatise on the young Hegel,[10] but rather that he found himself in the intimate company of young radicals like Hölderlin and Isaac von Sinclair, which fired his enthusiasm for "pointed political actions . . . and philosophical discussions." In this context, Pöggeler views the fragment as primarily informed by a new political enthusiasm, in which Hegel affirms a "mythology of Reason" as the basis for a practical philosophy of the future.[11]

At the outset of the "*Systemprogramm,*" the author attempts to extend the theoretical reach of Kant's doctrine of the postulates of practical reason, as elaborated in the *Critique of Practical Reason.* Kant defines a postulate in that work as "a theoretical proposition which is not as such demonstrable, but which is an inseparable corollary of an unconditionally valid a priori practical law."[12] For Kant, this procedure allows him to establish the immortality of the soul and the existence of God as corollaries of the universal applicability of the moral law. The author of this fragment hopes to extend this procedure in order to postulate a "complete system of all Ideas" as direct corollaries of moral premises. He proposes to determine the Idea of physics on the condition that the empirical world was created for a moral being, and to eradicate the State as something "mechanical" which frustrates pure moral actions. But following an apparent Schillerian perspective, the author would unite this set of moral postulates under the imprimatur of a supreme aesthetic idea.

> Lastly, the Idea which unites all the rest, the Idea of *Beauty,* taking the word in its higher Platonic sense. I am now convinced that the highest act of Reason, the one through which it encompasses all Ideas, is an aesthetic act, and *the truth and goodness only become sisters in beauty*—the philosopher must possess just as much aesthetic power as the poet. . . . The philosophy of the spirit is an aesthetic philosophy.[13]

As the embodiment of this new aesthetic philosophy, the author proceeds to insist on the need for a "new mythology," but one which is in "the service of the Ideas," and thus a "mythology of *Reason*." "Until we express the Ideas aesthetically, i.e., mythologically, they have no interest for the people, and conversely until mythology is rational the philosopher must be ashamed of it."[14] Pöggeler argues that Hegel's "new mythology" clearly anticipates the incipient Jena romanticism of Friedrich Schlegel's *Rede über die Mythologie* and Schelling's *Philosophy of Art*.[15] This fragment exemplifies Hegel's youthful desire to elevate art to the level of the Greek mythological ideal, but as a "new mythology" which suffuses sensuous presentations with the elixir of ideas, thereby creating a "mythological religion, which takes shelter under the guidance of poetry and yet safeguards Reason," making possible the "universal freedom and equality of spirits."[16] In Pöggeler's view, Hegel's resurrection of mythology resolves the problem of identifying a sensuous presentation of divinity that is in tune with the modern intellect.

> Religion is "beautiful religion" because it (mythologically) makes visible [*sichtbar*] the shining-forth of the eternal and the divine in the earthly and the worldly, and thereby no longer needs to be apolitical and withdrawn from the world (as was the Christian religion in Hegel's interpretation).[17]

On Pöggeler's account, then, Hegel's youthful flirtation with the Greek mythological ideal of a sensuous presentation of the divine makes him available to Hölderlin's quixotic vision of a *Vereinigungsphilosophie*, in which Reason succumbs to the dictates of Beauty in an all embracing "aesthetic philosophy."[18] Annemarie Gethmann-Siefert, who is perhaps the leading contemporary commentator on Hegel's Berlin lectures on aesthetics, also accepts Pöggeler's account of the authorship of the "Earliest *Systemprogramm*." She argues that the "*Systemprogramm*" fits comfortably into the continuity of Hegel's evolving philosophy in Berne and Frankfurt, specifically in regard to his "determination of art in the context of mythology."[19] According to Gethmann-Siefert, it was Schiller's influence on Hegel that was primarily responsible for his enthusiasm for an "Ideal of *Volkserziehung*," which could be attained only through the sensuous aesthetic presentation of ideas. However, in her view Hegel eventually developed an incipient critique of Schiller in "The Spirit of Christianity and Its Fate" of 1797, because of his burgeoning realization of the historical character of "factical existence." However, in the words of Richard Taft, who follows Gethmann-Siefert's scholarship on this issue, it was not until the early Jena period that Hegel "came to recognize that the Greek Gods were dead, are no longer capable of mediating truth by means of beauty, and thus that the modern world required a modern solution."[20]

Pöggeler and Gethmann-Siefert have provided some invaluable insight into that dimension of Hegel's early work which clearly anticipates his account in the Berlin lectures on aesthetics.[21] However, the provocative glare of an "aesthetic philosophy" as espoused in the "Earliest *Systemprogramm*" has tended to obscure the rather tentative nature of Hegel's concern with art prior to his move to Jena in 1800. Despite the enthusiasm expressed in this disputed fragment for a new aesthetic mythology, in those texts which we can be certain were actually written by Hegel in this period, a much more skeptical picture emerges of the possibility that art can procure a demonstration of divinity.

The argument of this paper returns to and reasserts Rosenzweig's initial hypothesis, that Hegel is simply not the author of the "*Systemprogramm.*" Without being primarily concerned with the authorship controversy which surrounds this fragment,[22] I will attempt to illustrate that the evolution of Hegel's view of art up through the early Frankfurt period elicits a striking continuity, concerning themes that are clearly autonomous of the framework proposed in the "*Systemprogramm*" itself. In the decade that precedes his arrival in Frankfurt in 1797, it is clear that Hegel came to harbor a progressively more profound skepticism as to the prospects for an aesthetic demonstration of divinity. In fact, it is precisely what Pöggeler and Gethmann-Siefert identify as the "mythological" demonstration of Reason heralded in this fragment that Hegel is driven to reject on the basis of his early studies in Stuttgart and Tübingen.

Under the influence of the leading *Popularphilosophen* of his day, including Johann Eberhard and Christian Garve, Hegel became tangentially embroiled in the German reception of the French *Querelle des Anciens et des Modernes* while still a student in Stuttgart.[23] In his earliest school essays and fragments, Hegel developed a relatively unique interpretation within this broad conflict: he aspired to identify the *independent* originality of the modern imagination. In this pursuit, he came to decisively reject the *mythological* structure of Greek poetry, in that it rested on what he identified as the immanent harmony of "*sichtbar und sittliche Natur,*" on the inherent coordination of the sensuous and the ethical dimensions of the Greek idiom. A crucial turning-point of his early reflections is the realization that modernity lacks an inherent "sensuous certainty" (*sinnliche Gewissheit*), which was the precondition of Greek mythological presentation. This early insight sheds some important light upon the opening movements of the *Phenomenology of Spirit,* as it illustrates that Hegel was originally employed with the problem of "sensuous certainty" as a mode of cognition peculiar to *antiquity*.

Furthermore, I will attempt to demonstrate that, although the "Earliest *Systemprogramm*" proclaims that "the highest act of Reason is an aesthetic act," and that "the philosophy of the spirit is an aesthetic philosophy," Hegel himself rarely used the term "*ästhetischen*" in his early writings, except in a negative or pejorative sense. Specifically, by "aesthetic" Hegel meant a "spectatorial" relation to the image of beauty, which segregates subject and object in an intellectual reflection. In contrast to this form of aesthetic reflection, Hegel would propose an alternative, nonrepresentational account of religious presentation, in which the image of beauty unites subject and object in the configuration of love (*gestaltete Liebe*). In fact, Hegel's earliest reflections on beauty are precisely gauged at undermining any "*aesthetic*" appropriation of the image of beauty.

Finally, I will argue that these early reflections on the problem of aesthetic presentation came to a head during Hegel's last days in Berne in the late summer of 1796. Hegel's disparate ruminations on the shortcomings of modern religious presentation culminate in an outright rejection of pictorial form itself as a mode of divine disclosure. In a compelling and widely overlooked *Tagebuch* entry of late July 1796, which recounts a voyage through the Alps, Hegel critiques the appropriating encroachment of the intellect upon the image of beauty, which segregates subject and object through an "aesthetic" spectatorial relationship. This *Tagebuch* entry precedes the purported date of the "Earliest *Systemprogramm*" by a matter of months; however, in this entry Hegel's skepticism concerning aesthetic presentations of the divine has never been more pronounced. This skepticism, I will argue, seriously draws into question Hegel's authorship of this disputed fragment, on aesthetic grounds alone. Even more so, it illustrates the paucity of our present understanding of the character of Hegel's earliest reflections on art and aesthetic experience.

I. Hegel and *Popularphilosophie*

Annemarie Gethmann-Siefert asserts that there are two principle foundations of Hegel's early philosophy of art: Hegel's evolving reception of the aesthetic theory of Schiller and Kant, and his concomitant dependence on a Greek model of "aesthetic education," which reached its apex in the early Frankfurt period, in the call for a new "mythology of Reason."[24] However, there is little evidence that Hegel was particularly employed with Schiller's aesthetic theory until after the "Letters on the Aesthetic Education of Man" were serialized in *Die Horen* in 1795.[25] Hegel's interest was presumably engendered by the enthusiasm Hölderlin had expressed for the "aesthetic part" of Kant's third *Critique* (and Schiller's appropriation of it) in a letter of July 1794.[26] Prior to this time, however, Hegel's interest in the *schönen Wissenschaften* was almost exclusively informed by the leading figures of *Popularphilosophie,* rather than by Schiller or Kant. In Stuttgart Hegel composed numerous excerpts from the *Berlinische Monatsschrift* and the *Neue Bibliothek der schönen Wissenschaften,* two of the leading periodicals of this disparate movement, and made excerpts from all its leading figures, including J. J. Engel, J. J. Eberhard, J. G. Feder, J. J. Dusch, Christoph Wieland, and Christian Garve.

The term *Popularphilosophie* arose in the latter half of the eighteenth century, and denoted a wide and diverse group of literati who hoped to further *Aufklärung* ideals through popular education and the translation of important works of the British and French Enlightenment. Although this group shared a common faith in the *Aufklärung* with Kant, they nevertheless emerged as the first serious opponents of the critical philosophy. As one of the leaders of *Popularphilosophie*, Christian Garve wrote the first review of the *Critique of Pure Reason* in 1782, which was simplified and distorted into a caustic diatribe by the editor of the Göttingen review in which it appeared, J. G. Feder, one of Kant's most vociferous critics. Another leader of *Popularphilosophie*, Johann Eberhard, would lead the most strenuous counterattack against the second edition of the first *Critique* in the *Philosophisches Magazin*. However, not all *Popularphilosophen* were so unambiguously opposed to Kant. Perhaps the leading unofficial spokesman of *Popularphilosophie* was Kant's longtime confidante, Moses Mendelssohn, whose widely-regarded essay on *Aufklärung* (rather than Kant's better known submission on this topic) became the benchmark for Hegel's earliest school essays.[27]

Hegel was first drawn into *Popularphilosophie* through a common Rousseauist enthusiasm for the ideals of *Volkserziehung*[28] He carefully studied J. G. Feder's *Neuer Emile* which led him to Christian Garve, as Feder depended heavily on Garve for his account of *Erkenntnisvermögen* or the faculty of cognition. Hegel subsequently made extensive excerpts from Garve's *Prüfung der Fähigkeiten* which contain his earliest references to the faculty of understanding (*Verstand*). Garve describes *Verstand* as the capacity to collect and distinguish between classes of similarities.[29] In the cultivation of the higher capacities of the soul, however, such as wit and genius, *Verstand* necessitates the counterpart of the imagination, that is, the capacity "to combine parts into new wholes."[30] Art and philosophy emerge as the highest products of these two primary faculties.

Following his reading of Garve, Hegel made a series of excerpts which further entertained the possibility of explaining the higher cultivated faculties in terms of a harmonious interplay of the intellect and the imagination, but he applied those insights to a reading of "myth" in antiquity. In 1787, Hegel transcribed some published lectures on philosophy and psychology by the well-known mathematician A. G. Kastner in the *Neue Bibliothek der schönen Wissenschaften* under the curious title, "Philosophy. Natural Theology. Providence." Kastner argued that our comprehension of things depends upon the organization of communal (*gemeinschaftliche*) classes of objects. This necessitates the construction of signs (*Zeichen*) which designate "similarity and distinction" among these objects,[31] and thus the analytic association of the intellect (*Verstand*).[32] In addition, for Kastner, even higher "cultivated" faculties, such as "wit" and textual interpretation, are merely extensions of this intellectual association,[33] as they establish ever more remote correspondences between concepts. This intellectual "communality" (*Das Gemeinschaftliche*) eventually sheds itself of the discrete peculiarities of things, and bounds itself into a complex unity, and thus "a providence which does not extend itself over singular things is only the providence of a weak and limited spirit . . . because it would not otherwise know the most necessary facts."[34] The significance of Hegel's title to this excerpt remains obscure, but presumably he finds that Kastner intimates the possibility of a "Natural Theology" through the providential extension of the discriminating faculty of the intellect into a proof of the complex natural unity of divinity itself.

This implicit valorization of the intellect in Hegel's earliest excerpts is partially borne out in his first school essays of 1787. Extending Garve's and Kastner's discussion of intellect and imagination, Hegel wrote these essays under the influence of Mendelssohn's important article on "*Kultur*" and "*Aufklärung*" in the *Berlinische Monatsschrift.* For Mendelssohn, enlightenment, culture, and education are all "modifications of social life." *Aufklärung* is the "theoretical" determination of persons as individuals in their rational knowledge and skill; *Kultur* is the "practical" cultivation of social and ethical life through beauty and elegance in the arts and handcrafts.[35] Together they combine to produce *Bildung* in general: "the more the social conditions of a people are brought into harmony with the determination of man, the more cultivation (*Bildung*] this people has." Nevertheless, this fusion of *Kultur* and *Aufklärung* in the formation of *Bildung* can become conflictual if one is excessively developed at the expense of the other: "Where *Aufklärung* and *Kultur* proceed at an equal pace (*gleichen Schritten*), there they are for one another the best protest against corruption."

It is precisely this imbalance of *Kultur* and *Aufklärung* which Hegel analyses in one of his earliest school essays. "On the Religion of the Greeks and Romans"[36] is primarily concerned with the deleterious effect of an excess of imagination in the maintenance of religious belief. Hegel apparently derived this judgment of antiquity from Christoph Wieland, who also provided him with his title. Wieland, in his commentary on Horace, argues that "the religion of the Greeks and the Romans were not bound by doctrinal concepts, but rather in their beliefs everything was indeterminate, vacillating, and voluntary," because the imagination enjoyed an unrestricted range of employment. Every individual would express their own peculiar relationship to the supernatural in personal imagery, which would eventually congeal into conflicting motifs and finally a riot of competing iconographies.[37]

Likewise, prior to fifth-century Athens, according to Hegel, the Greek religion "in its childhood" depended on "sensory representations" of God made from clay, wood, or stone, "everyone doing so according to the ideal he had formed of the most terrible being . . . without sensitivity to beauty or the arts. Inevitably, everyone had to bestow a special name to his god."[38] The sheer diversity within this primitive iconography, then, fragmented the communal core of ethical life. "The great confusion in mythology was enhanced by the efforts of scholars to find out the meaning of each fable."[39] The possibility of deriving clear ethical norms from this mythology was frustrated by the lack of a robust intellectual counterpart to imagination. "Without enlightenment (*Aufklärung*)," Hegel claims (following Mendelssohn), the unchecked imagination of these peoples ascribed direct supernatural causes for earthly effects, on the basis of a rampant "superstition."

In contrast, Hegel concludes that the "wise men of Greece" in the fifth century produce a "much more enlightened (*aufgeklärte*) and sublime concept of divinity" which checked these excessive sensuous views of the primordial being. Nevertheless, even here, these authors cannot avoid the "difficulty of arriving at pure truth undistorted by errors," as they equally deviated from the right path, "often blinded by a deceptive shape (*täuschenden Gestalt*)."[40] Hegel thus implies that the maintenance of a balance between *Kultur* and *Aufklärung* depends on the constant vigilance of the intellect over the "deceptive shape" of sensuous representation, even in the present day.[41]

However, Hegel's clear conviction here that the Enlightenment rudder of *Verstand* should guide aesthetic representations of divinity is radically revised in his subsequent work. In his school essays of 1788, Hegel is concerned with precisely the opposite problem: the reduction of sensuous representation to the dictates of the intellect, in contemporary society.

The reason for this reversal appears to be intimately related to two revelations he gained through his reading in the interim. On the one hand, excerpts Hegel made from Johann Eberhard's article on mythology and J. H. Kistenmaker's discussion of the Greek idiom convinced him that the "sensuous certainty" of Greek poetry possessed the virtue of a concrete particularity which was lost on modern sensibilities. On the other hand, through Wieland and Garve he recognized that the prevailing dogma of the "imitation of the ancients" proffered by Winckelmann, Christian Gellert, and others, was a prescription that entailed the mere dilution of this Greek virtue in an age to which it was now entirely alien.

In an essay on mythology in the *Berlinische Monatsschrift* in July 1787, Johann Eberhard had defined "myth" as a kind of poetry which provides supernatural guidance, but whose object exceeds the bounds of rational knowledge and experience. According to Hegel's own paraphrase of this essay,

> A whole system of such myths about religion is a *mythology;* and it is very natural that the philosophy and religion of every nation was originally a mythology. For the sensuous certainty [*sinnliche Gewissheit*] of the entire nation, just as much as for individual men, must precede rational [certainty], because in [sensuous certainty] the finite intellect [*Verstand*] can be guided to what is more perfect by at first following what is less perfect.[42]

In Eberhard's estimation, myth emerges as the predominant mode of religious and philosophical expression in early societies because rational distinctions depend on highly refined sensuous discriminations. "Sensuous certainty" is the precondition for developing abstract intellectual notions at the dawn of civilization because humankind has no prior intellectual models to follow. The finite intellect can only be guided by the immediate testimony of the senses, which therefore requires sensibility to develop a rich and sophisticated semantic register. Mythological constructions are the product of these intellectual refinements of sensuous certainty, which procure a system of archetypes as a scaffold for religious beliefs.

Taking Eberhard's contention one step further, however, Hegel asserts in a school essay of 1788 that it is precisely this "sensuous certainty" which is lacking in modern consciousness. In "On the Advantages which Reading the Classical Greek and Roman Writers Provide Us," Hegel stresses that among the Greeks, "taste [*Geschmack*] is cultivated through the blossoming epochs of the culture of their nation. Taste is [found] in the general feeling for what is beautiful [*Gefühl fürs Schöne*]."[43] The cultivation of Greek taste, however, had the advantage of resting on the immanent harmony of "*sichtbare und sittliche Natur*." "Their descriptions of both visual and ethical nature are out of sensuous grounds, and thus more lively and easier to grasp" than modern poetry.[44] This harmony of "*sichtbare und sittliche Natur*" in Greek life, in Hegel's view, accounts for the sensuous precision of their mythological creations. Hegel appears also to have been influenced here by another text he excerpted at the same time as Eberhard's work on myth: Johann Kistenmaker's study of Greek and Roman idioms. Kistenmaker argued that the sensuous fluidity of the Greek language expresses "the natural sagacity of the soul." The diversity of actions and transformations of worldly life "in and around us" are reflected in the "diverse formation of words" in Greek life.[45] Likewise, in his school essay on the advantages of Greek and Roman poetry, Hegel stresses the expressive fluidity of the Greek sensuous idiom, but as a linguistic quality lost to modernity.

> the different kinds and different passages and degrees of their culture which would be determined externally are so few, that were it necessary, they could generally consider things in other connections, and these references [of things] to one another is expressed in their language, and thus their concepts possess [qualities] which we cannot [grasp], because the words for them have been lost to us; one [may today] notice in an accidental way such a relation or mere similarity, but then the impression of the deficiency of a word is too fleeting for us to be able to fix the obscure concept.[46]

Although only a year earlier Hegel had derided the sensuous excesses of early Greek mythology, here he clearly praises this sensuous vernacular in the face of a rigidified conceptual apparatus peculiar to the modern intellect. Modern concepts lack precisely the sensuous certainty of the Greek idiom, which manifests similarity and relation without abstracting a universal quantifier out of the particularity of sense-objects. It is perhaps no coincidence then that Hegel would later adopt this concept of "*sinnliche Gewissheit*" as the inaugural shape of consciousness in the *Phenomenology of Spirit*, precisely to demonstrate the incapacity of achieving sensuous certainty through the filter of universal quantifiers like "this" and "now." Most commentators take "sensuous certainty" in the *Phenomenology* to refer to a primitive, demonstrative form of consciousness, that is, the naive standpoint of "common sense," in which the object is taken to be immediately given. However, in light of Hegel's earliest adoption of this phrase from Eberhard's account of mythology, it appears that "sensuous certainty" offered Hegel an account of how modern consciousness has broken free from the cognitive structures of antiquity. Hegel in fact alludes to this cleft between modern and ancient consciousness in the preface to the *Phenomenology*.

> The manner of study in ancient times differed from that of the modern age in that the former was the proper and complete formation (Durchbildung) of natural consciousness. Putting itself to the test in every aspect of its existence and philosophizing about everything that presented itself, [the natural consciousness] made itself into a thoroughly activated universality. In modern times, however, the individual finds the abstract form ready made. . . . Hence the task now consists not so much in purifying the individual of immediate sensuous modes of apprehension, and making him into a substance that is an object of thought and that thinks, but rather just the opposite, in freeing determinate thoughts from their fixity so as to give reality to the universal, and impart it to spiritual life.[47]

For Hegel, then, there is a basic epistemological cleft between antiquity and modernity, in that for the latter, intellectual concepts are not derived from the discriminations of sensibility. "Sensuous certainty" is no longer available to the "ready-made" abstractions of the modern intellect. This insight stems from Eberhard's account of myth, and is registered by Hegel's radical about-face in his treatment of Greek mythological poetry in his school essays in 1787 and 1788.

This fundamental view was further catalyzed for Hegel by Christian Garve's essay on the contrast of modern and ancient authors.[48] Garve's essay was specifically designed as a response to Winckelmann's influential account of Hellenism, and his insistence that modern art should pattern itself on the "imitation of the ancients." In Garve's view, the ancients were "original" because they possessed no other model than nature itself, and thus "their language was made to express sensuous images [*sinnliche Bilder*]." However, the modern poet can no longer be original, not only because so much has already been said, "but especially because [modern man] is introduced to descriptions [*Beschreibungen*] rather than descriptive objects [*beschreibenen Gegenständen*], they receive concepts of things rather than images of them."[49] The sensuous imagery of Greek mythology manifests only "descriptive objects," which concretely embody a transparent meaning within the ancient community. In contrast, the modern spirit is primarily conceptual rather than imagistic, and thus one should not mix "the colors of the ancients and the moderns."[50] Nevertheless, Garve claims that "we can still be original, in the subtler observation of the inner conditions and arrangements of the human spirit, of modes of thought, of morals [*Sitten*]."[51]

Following Garve, Hegel develops this critique of Winckelmann in another 1788 school essay, "On Some Characteristic Distinctions of Ancient Writers (in Relation to Modern Ones)." While the model Greek nation manifests the harmonious unity of the arts, religion, and the polis, for Hegel modernity is defined by the fragmentation of these realms.

> In our times the poet no longer has such an effective domain [*Wirkungskreis*] [as the ancient poets]. The famous deeds of our ancient, or even modern, Germans are neither woven into our constitution [*Verfassung*] nor is their memory preserved through oral tradition. We learn of them only partly through the history books of foreign nations, and even this knowledge is confined to the cultivated classes. The tales which entertain the common folk are adventurous traditions, connected neither with our religious system nor with true history.[52]

While the congruence of the arts, religion, and political life in antiquity may be observed by those who today possess a cultivated taste for this literature,[53] one cannot merely reproduce this harmonious model in modernity. The chief problem here is the incapacity of modern poets to ignite the imagination of the common people in the service of forging an ethical community, as contemporary religious works only appeal to the intellectual refinements of the cultivated classes. In contrast, Hegel here admires the ancient writers for their *Simplizität*, representing the thing itself (*Sache selbst*) with a simple image, rather than through learned hints and intimations. The ancient poets expressed complex perceptions (*Empfindungen*) simply, "without separating the manifold elements within it that the understanding (*Verstand*) can distinguish, nor dissecting out what lies hidden."[54] Here, in direct contrast to his essay on Greek and Roman religion one year earlier, the discriminations of the intellect would now *disturb* the sensuous immediacy of mythological presentations. In language that is highly reminiscent of Garve, Hegel contrasts this exemplar of Greek "simplicity" to the "book-learning" of modern people:

> Further, their whole system of education and *Bildung* was so constituted that everyone had derived his ideas from direct experience [*Erfahrung selbst*] and—"the cold book learning that is just expressed with dead signs in one's mind"—they knew nothing of, but for all they knew they could still tell "How? Where? Why? they learned it"; for this reason everyone had to have his own system of thought, his own peculiar form of spirit, each one had to be *original*.[55]

In striking contrast to his earlier work, here the sensuous diversity of Greek mythology is now praised by Hegel, as a celebration of the rich semantic register of the Greek idiom.

At the end of his studies in Stuttgart, then, Hegel had already begun to suspect that the problem of aesthetic experience in modernity arises from the lack of a mode of religious presentation that can accord with the direct experience and imagination of the common people. At the same time however, the simplicity of Greek mythological poetry could no longer recompense this lack, because intellectual distinction predominates over sensuous discrimination in modern consciousness.

Hegel's subsequent notes on art in Tübingen and Berne, therefore, are primarily concerned with clarifying this distinction between modern and classical art, in terms of their capacity to represent divinity for the common imagination. Taking a page from Kant's recently published *Critique of Judgment,* in 1792 Hegel would distinguish Greek and Christian art along the faultline of the *beautiful* and the *sublime.*[56] The architecture of the Greeks was everywhere designed to display "the highest ideal of beauty", and their divine images represented "the most beautiful human form . . . in the highest power of its existence and life [*Daseyns und Lebens*]." In contrast, in Christian cathedrals "the great works of art are usually buried in a corner and overwhelmed with childish and obfuscatory ornamentation, as a child who can not yet grasp something great, something sublime, whose soul has not yet achieved the maturity of [aesthetic] taste."[57] Here Hegel has significantly revised Kant's taxonomy. For Kant the "beautiful" is designated by a judgment of taste which provides an indeterminate concept of the understanding (*Verstand*) while the "sublime" is the intimation of a concept of Reason (*Vernunft*) which exceeds the bounds of sensibility as such.[58] For Hegel, however, the experience of the sublime in Christian art is the intimation of divinity forever withdrawn behind the crenelations of Gothic ornament. While the Greeks "embroider" the veil of divinity with sensuous images, and manifest divinity in human shapes, the Christians obscure divinity behind the ornamental veil. In Hegel's view, then, the ornamental sublimity of Christian art is a mark of the immaturity of the common imagination and the weakness of the imagery in contemporary religion. Ideally, one must ascend from the "childish" state of a sublime experience with God to the "maturity" of apprehending Him directly in the image of beauty. This ascension to the beautiful, then, must overcome the sublime veil, and approach God in sensuous form. The conundrum, however, is that this ascension to the beautiful cannot be a mere return to the Greek Ideal, because the modern world precisely lacks the immanent harmony of "*sichtbare und sittliche Natur*" characteristic of Greek mythology.

The problem with fostering the *Bildung* of religious sense in modernity, then, is that Christianity has effaced any remnant of an indigenous German imagery. In the "Positivity of Christian Religion" (1795), Hegel bitterly stresses that the older pagan mysteries have been demoted into "superstitions" which the cultivated classes now wish to extirpate altogether. As a result, "it has become totally impossible to ennoble these remnants of mythology and thereby refine the imagination and sensibility of the common people."[59] Without an indigenous imagery that can ignite the common imagination, the renewal of mythology in modernity is impossible.

In his Tübingen essay (1792–93), therefore, Hegel decisively concludes that the archetype of Greek art is now lost; in an ironic rejection of Winckelmann's major thesis, Hegel asserts that the "genius" of the Greek nation now remains only in *mere* reproductions: "We have only a few traces on a handful of surviving reproductions that enable us to contemplate and lovingly admire his likeness; and these can but awaken a painful longing for the original." Hegel thus clearly rejects the plea for an imitation of the ancients as the manner of revitalizing religion. In contrast to the sensuous expressivity of the Greek nation, modernity precisely lacks the immanent harmony of "*sichtbare und sittliche Natur.*" As a result of this verdict, Hegel is progressively concerned with precisely defining an alternative form of imagery in the face of this Christian effacement.

For Hegel, the chief problem lies with the cultivated classes, who have co-opted religious imagery into a repository of intellectual refinements which exclude the imagination of the common people. In the Tübingen essay, Hegel notes that "the spirit of our religion has banished all the beautiful colorations of sense as well as everything that has charm, even while we have become far too much men of words and reason to take much delight in beautiful images—it may well lapse into childishness."[60] The imposition of an intellectual veil over religious imagery is precisely what maintains the sublime withdrawal of Christian imagery from popular taste. In the fragment "*Aber die Hauptmasse . . .*" (1793) Hegel locates this suppression at the heart of the religious decline:

> Christian religion grants the imagination [*Phantasie*] a wide scope, out of which our great Christian epic poets have created more majestic paintings, more thrilling scenes and more moving dispositions [*Züge*] than as they appear beforehand in a poet's soul. (But these [productions] do not descend to the common folk; they could not be sanctioned through anything, they are not publicly recognized.—Moreover, a rationality [*Vernunft*] is able to fasten itself to the idea of the poems—a sympathy which is susceptible to fine materials and possesses a deep sentiment for the poetry, but which further alienates many others; this sentiment is tolerable for coarser men, is credible but they would pass over the higher forms of the beautiful [*höhern Schönheiten*] which are present for cultured reason [*Vernuft*] and sentiment.) In contrast, the imagination [*Einbildungskraft*] of the people has no guidance, no beautiful representations of images are placed before them,

> neither through painting, nor sculpture—nor poetry, which they follow, on which they could depend, and also which teaches them to worship a religion, God in spirit and in truth.[61]

While great poets and cultured men already possess a developed imagination in which to contemplate the beautiful images of the divine, the common people have no such preternatural skill. The common people's incapacity to comprehend the intellectual refinements of Christian art results in a breach within the religious community, as the rational, reflective sentiment necessary for appreciating this work is the exclusive domain of the educated elite. Thus, while in his earliest study of Greek religion the "wise men" of fifth-century Athens shored up the rampant superstition of their forebears with enlightenment and Reason, here Hegel finds the opposite: that modern folk religion requires a mode of aesthetic representation which can excite the common imagination.

As we have seen, then, Hegel's major concern with art in Stuttgart and Tübingen is narrowly focused on two issues: the cleft between the mythological presentations of antiquity and the modern intellect, and the failure of Christian imagery to ignite the common imagination. He draws a strict distinction between the Greek model of beauty, as the evocation of ideal perfection in human form, and the modern condition of Christian art, which withdraws the sensuous image of divinity behind a sublime curtain which only rational sentiments can appreciate. Far from proposing a regeneration of a "mythology," therefore, which depends on the harmonious unity of "*sichtbare und sittliche Natur,*" Hegel recognizes that modern religious imagery must appeal to an intellectual (*verstandliche*) register that is at odds with the sensuous certainty of Greek myth. Rather than turning to a new "mythology of Reason," then, as the "Earliest *Systemprogramm*" proposes, Hegel on the contrary is concerned precisely with this grafting of rational sentiments onto primitive Christian imagery, which subverts its public function as the symbolic bond of the Christian community. On these grounds, then, the hypothesis of Gethmann-Siefert and other commentators—that Hegel condoned a revival of the Greek model of mythological presentation for modernity, prior to his move to Frankfurt—stands in striking contrast to Hegel's own deliberations on the cleft between the ancient and the modern in this period.

II. Hegel's *Alpenwanderung*

For Hegel, as we have seen, the key problem of modern art rests on the reduction of sensibility to the conditions of the concept, which segregates subject and object in an intellectual reflection. These discriminations of the understanding (*Verstand*) do not allow for an imaginative union with divinity in Christian art.

Toward the end of his time in Berne (1796), however, Hegel came to recognize that this inadequacy rested less on the expressive offerings of Christian artists and epic poets, than with the very nature of pictorial representation itself. We can in fact date Hegel's initial determination of art as a philosophical problem to his final days in Berne. Prior to this point, Hegel had taken only a pragmatic interest in art as a mode of divine disclosure, which could help promote a "subjective" religion. In his final days in Berne, however, aesthetic representation as such becomes the target of his investigations.

In the late summer of 1796, Hegel made an excursion through the Swiss Alps, which he recorded at length in his *Tagebuch*.[62] This lyrical meditation concerning his *Spaziergang* through the Alps is important for our present concern, in that it was written a matter of months before the purported date of the "Earliest *Systemprogramm*," and is the only document we possess from this period other than the poem "*Eleusis*," which Hegel sent to Hölderlin in August. Towards the end of his diary entry, Hegel describes what might be termed an "epiphany," in Joyce's sense of the term, when coming upon a waterfall and observing the play of the waves in the descending stream. In an extended theatrical metaphor, Hegel describes the spectacle before him:

> From [above] one enjoys the spectacle of the falls where one can broadly oversee it, and the majestic theater certainly held for us compensation for the pains of an unpleasant day. Through a narrow stone cleft the water issued forth, then falling vertically below into broader waves; the waves constantly drew the eyes of the spectator ever downward, and yet are never fixed, can never be pursued; therefore their image [*Bild*], their form [*Gestalt*], dissolves at every moment [*alle Augenblicke*] as each moment is thrust aside by a new one, and *in these falls one sees eternally the same image, and yet sees at the same time that it is never the same* [*in diesem Falle sieht er ewig das gleiche Bild, un sieht zugleich dass nie dasselbe ist.*][63]

In the image of the falls, there is a perpetual instantiation of likeness, of sensuous similarity, which perpetually dissolves and is renewed at each instant. However, the power of this spectacle of similarity resides precisely on its dissolution of any configurational fixity, of any determinate vantage point. The spectator is perpetually drawn downward into the spectacle, displacing his position as a disinterested observer, and implicating him in the fluctuations of the scene.

This experience had a profound effect on Hegel, as he would return to it again in the fragment, "Religion, a Religion Endowed" (mid-1797) as an exemplar of the embodiment of divinity in an image.

> To observe a stream, how according to the law of gravity it must fall to deeper regions and is limited and pressed by the ground and its banks,

> is to comprehend it [*begreifen*]—[but] to give it a soul, *to take part in it as one's equal* [*als an seines Gleichen Anteil an ihm nehmen*]—is to make it into a God.[64]

Hegel here contrasts the conceptual apprehension (*begreifen*) of the stream to that of a religious intuition, in which one participates in the spectacle, and thereby overcomes one's spectatorial relationship to it. Likewise in his *Tagebuch* entry some eight months earlier, the fluctuations of the scene implicate the spectator in the image, drawing the eyes "ever downward" into the spectacle. In "Religion, a Religion Endowed," however, Hegel warns that the appropriating spectacle of the stream, in which the observing subject is intimately connected with its object, is *also* capable of conceptual apprehension by the intellect. The stream is both an ensoulment of the divine, and a cognitive object:

> yet because a stream, [or] a tree can at the same time also be an object, [it is] subjected to sheer necessity. . . . [Only] where subject and object—or freedom and nature, are thought as united, so that nature is freedom, so that subject and object are not separated, *there is the divine*—such an Ideal is the object of every religion.[65]

The unification of subject and object in an image, which Hegel finds to be an ideal mode of divine presentation, can also be open to the conceptual encroachment of the intellect. The conundrum that Hegel faces then is to identify an aesthetic mode which can capture this integral compact of subject and object without reverting to intellectual reflection. He requires an aesthetic image that is thoroughly nonrepresentational. In his *Tagebuch* entry, following his description of the falls, Hegel in fact turns to the possibility of capturing this spectacle aesthetically. He is emphatically clear, however, that pictorial representation in particular is inadequate to this task

> My impression has correctly drawn attention to these falls, but a description can compensate so little, as a painting [*Gemälde*] which only partially captures one's point of view [*Selbstansicht*]. With a description, the imagination [*Einbildungskraft*], when it already has similar images [*ähnlich Bilder*], can paint the whole [*sich das Ganze hinmalen*]. But a painting, when it is not painted very large, cannot fail to be a poor reproduction, and only give an inadequate presentation. The *sensuous presence of paintings* [*sinnliche Gegewart des Gemäldes:* Hegel's emphasis] does not allow the imagination to stretch out [*ausdehnen*] to the presented object, but rather apprehends the object only as it appears on its face [*sich dem Gesicht darstellt*]. Even more so, it is hindered from the object's extension [*Erweiterung*]: if we hold the painting in our hands, or find it hanging on a wall, then its sense can only be a measure of our own dimensions [*an unserer Grösse*] against the dimensions of the sur-

rounding objects, in which it is found to be small. Such a painting must be brought so near the eyes that it has difficulty giving a survey [*überblicken*] of the whole. It cannot displace the neighboring objects, and thus completely abandon all measure [*und so völlig allen Maasstab verlöre*]. Moreover, that which is most alluring [*Anziehendste*] in the best paintings, must also lose that which is most essential [*Wesenlichste*] in such scenes [*Schauspiels*]: the eternal life, and the powerful alertness [*die gewaltige Regsamkeit*] of that eternal life. A painting can give only a part of the total impression, namely, the equality of the image [*die Gleichheit des Bildes*], which must give it determinate outlines and allotments [*Partieen*]; on the other hand, the other part of this impression, the eternal, irresistible fluctuation [*Veränderung*] of every part, the eternal dissolution of every wave, every spume, which perpetually draws the eyes down [*die das Auge immer mit sich herniederzieht*] is lost; there is no higher third [*Terze*] [uniting these parts] which allows the eye the same [*gleiche*] direction of its glance: all this power, all this life, is entirely lost.[66]

In this passage, Hegel is struck by the fact that a spectatorial relation to the pictorial representation can only capture its formal equivalence or adequation with the object. For a mere spectator, the equality of the pictorial image with its subject loses precisely the eternal fluctuations of the stream, in which it manifests "eternal life." The problem with the pictorial image is that it restricts the parameters of the presentation to a static frame. It cannot "abandon all measure," which is the decisive characteristic of divinity in sensuous form. The "sensuous presence of paintings" cannot manifest divinity, because they lack three decisive qualities: (*a*) they do not allow the imagination to extend out (*ausdehnen*) to the object, but only discern its face; (*b*) they enframe the view and thus reduce it to a definite object that is comparable with other objects, thereby undermining its infinite proportions; and (*c*) they restrict the lively fluctuations of the view to a static image. In this characterization, then, Hegel's finds that the painting itself precisely embodies the conditions which reduce an observation of the divine to an intellectual cognition. It imposes reflection and the separation of subject and object by its very form. The only aspect that a painting can proffer is that of formal equivalence of the conceptual adequation of its image with the petrified object.

This revelation is of utmost significance, for it is precisely in these terms that Hegel will deride what he calls the "aesthetic" appropriation of the image of beauty. Despite the testimony of the "Earliest *Systemprogramm,*" this term occurs with extreme infrequency in Hegel's extant early writings. In his earliest writings at the Gymnasium, he makes one rather conventional use of the term when he refers to the "aesthetic power of the soul" (*ästhetischen Seelenkräfte*) among the Greeks, in a school essay of 1788.[67] However, the term does not reappear in his vocabulary until "The Positivity of the Christian Religion," (1795) in which it is employed in a decidedly pejorative sense. Hegel attempts to describe the Last Supper in terms that capture the sense of unification of subject and object which he later identifies in the experience at the falls. In describing Christ's distribution of the bread and wine, Hegel states, "This sensuous picture [*Sinnbild*]in which he imaginatively conjoined his memory with the serving of the meal they would enjoy in the future was very easily apprehended from the things on the table in front of them; but if they are observed merely aesthetically [*bloss von der ästhetischen Seite*],it may seem something of a play on words [*spielend*]."[68] While Christ would "imaginatively conjoin" his divinity with the bread and wine, a merely "aesthetic" apprehension of this scene would reduce his words to a simile or "play on words." Hegel would later develop this insight in "The Spirit of Christianity and its Fate," in which this parable is treated as an exemplary contrast to the mode of aesthetic apprehension. In the Last Supper, the objectification of divinity is not at the disposal of a "spectator" who merely reflects on the comparison from outside the action: "a spectator sees nothing but the breaking of a useful thing and its division into useless and valueless pieces." Furthermore, the spectator can only conceive of the relation of bread and the body of Christ as a *simile,* "by a mere 'just as' [*gleichwie*]." On the contrary, the mystical action dissolves the very difference between the objectivity and the act, between the distribution of bread and the participants.

> [T]he connection of objective and subjective, of the bread and the persons, is here not the connection of allegorized with allegory [*Verglichenen mit einem Gleichnis*], with the parable in which the different things, the things compared, are set forth as severed, as separate, and all that is asked is a comparison, the thought of the likeness of dissimilars [*Gleichheit Vereschiedener*]. On the contrary, in *this* link between bread and persons, *difference disappears* [*Verscheidenheit fällt*], and *with it the possibility of comparison.* Things heterogeneous are here most intimately connected [*verknüpft*].[69]

In this passage, Hegel articulates a mode of aesthetic demonstration that collapses the difference between subject and object. The spectator is implicated in the "beautiful" act of distribution. However, following on his earlier insights in the "Positivity" essay, this unification is not accessible to the "aesthetic" observer, removed from the beautiful configuration which Christ's words are meant to animate.

> "He and the father are one"; "he is bread come down from heaven," and so forth. These are hard words [*harte Ausdrücke*] [*sklhroi logoi*] σκλήροι λόγοι, which are not softened by being interpreted as imagery [*für bildliche*], or misunderstood as the uniting of concepts, instead of being taken in spirit as life [*mit Geist als Leben*]. Of course, as soon

> as intellectual concepts are opposed to imagery [*Bildlichem*] and taken as dominant, every image must be set aside as only play [*nur als Spiel*], as a by-product of the imagination without truth; and, instead of the life of the image [*des Leben des Bildes*], nothing remains but objects.[70]

Echoing his earlier revelations in the "Positivity" essay and his *Tagebuch,* here the aesthetic or merely symbolic appropriation of Christ's words indicates a subordination of the image to intellectual concepts, which efface the "life" of divinity embodied in the images as such. In this regard, then, "aesthetic" apprehension is only a form of conceptual appropriation, which segregates the image from its divine embodiment, making of the aesthetic configuration [*Gestalt*] nothing but an "object" for the contemplative subject. In contrast, Hegel aspires to a modern imagery that implicates the spectator in the image, as he would later detail in his account of the Christian parable in "The Spirit of Christianity and its Fate" in Frankfurt.

Taken as a whole, Hegel's specific references to art in Stuttgart, Tübingen, and Berne are clearly impelled to a progressively more skeptical terminus: that modern art is incapable of manifesting divinity because aesthetic form itself conforms to a mere intellectual determination of its object. On the basis of Hegel's early recognition of the cleft between modern and ancient forms of consciousness and the irredeemable character of mythology as a product of sensuous certainty, as well as his explicit repudiation of "aesthetic" representation in the "Positivity" essay and his *Tagebuch* entry in the late summer of 1796, it seems to be the height of implausibility to suppose that a few months later, in the "Earliest *Systemprogramm,*" Hegel would triumphantly proclaim that the true "philosophy of the spirit is an aesthetic philosophy," and the need for a "new mythology" which merges aesthetic demonstration and rational apprehension. As I have tried to illustrate, there is simply no convincing precedent for these remarks. In fact, Hegel's concern with art in the first decade of his literary career has focused on themes that are almost antithetical to the proposals outlined in the "*Systemprogramm.*" As we have seen, Hegel's deliberations on art up through the Berne period are primarily concerned with the abstract character of modern consciousness, the obsolescence of mythological forms of presentation in modernity, the failure of Christian art to ignite the common imagination, and the reduction of sensibility to conceptual determination. Furthermore, it is particularly significant that only at the end of July 1796 does he suppose that the problem lies with the nature of aesthetic form itself, in that it reduces the image to an object of display for a contemplative subject. Since this revelation occurs just months before the "*Systemprogramm*" was written, rather than marking the height of his faith in an "aesthetic synthesis," I would argue that Hegel in his final days at Berne first identifies art as a philosophical problem, which shall continue to have a deliberative impact on his discrimination between art and speculation in the early Jena writings.

Notes

1. Franz Rosenzweig, "Das alteste Systemprogramm des deutschen Idealismus. Ein handschriftlicher Fund," in *Sitzberichte der Heidelberger Akademie der Wissenschaften*, Phil.-hist. Klasse, 1917, 5; reprinted in *Mythologie der Vernunft: Hegels 'alteste Systemprogramm' des deutschen Idealismus*, ed. Christoph Jamme and Helmut Schneider, (Frankfurt: Suhrkamp, 1984); hereafter, *MV*. The "alteste Systemprogramm" is also printed in G. W. F. Hegel, *Werke in zwanzig Bänden*, ed. E. Moldenhauer and K. M. Michel, 20 vols. and Index (Frankfurt am Main: Suhrkamp Verlag, 1969ff.), 1: 234. Further reference will be in the form: *Werke*, 1:234. A facsimile of the actual manuscript can be found in *MV*, 9–10; translation of the manuscript can be found in H. S. Harris, *Toward the Sunlight: Hegel's Development 1770–18:* (Oxford: Clarendon Press, 1972), 510–12; hereafter *Toward*.

2. For a convenient survey of this literature and its evolution, cf. Frank-Peter Hansen, ed., *"Das Alteste Systemprogramm des deutschen Idealismus": Rezeptionsgeschichte und Interpretation*, (Berlin: Walter de Gruyter, 1989).

3. In 1926, the editor of Hölderlin's *Gesamtausgabe*, Wilhelm Bohm, argued that Hölderlin was in fact the author of this fragment. Cf. "Hölderlin als Verfasser das 'Altesten Systemprogramms des deutschen Idealismus,'" in *Deutsche Vierteljahrschrift* 4 (1926). Bohm supposed that Hölderlin was underappreciated for his philosophical predilections and was in truth a "strong, systematic, and intellectual poet" (341). The pronouncement in the fragment of an "aesthetic philosophy" which overcomes the diremption between sensibility and spirit, Bohm surmised, fit well into Hölderlin's attempt to revive the Platonic notion of a "philosophy of naivete" (351). A year later, Ludwig Strauss countered Bohm's contentions in the same journal with an argument on stylistic grounds. He noted Hölderlin's antipathy towards theoretical formulation, apart from his early fragmentary attempts in, for example, "Urtheil und Seyn." These initial theoretical energies were ultimately diverted into projects like "Hyperion," Strauss argued, because Hölderlin was uncomfortable with philosophical demonstration. This antipathy towards theoretical formulation made Hölderlin an implausible candidate, in Strauss's view.

4. Most early commentators took Rosenzweig's argument as definitive, including Ernst Cassirer, Georg Lukács, and Karl Jaspers. Cf. Frank-Peter Hansen, 21–174.

5. Herbert Marcuse had noted significant associations between the concept of the State in the "*Systemprogramm*" and Hegel's early political sentiments in *Reason and Revolution* in 1941.

Cf. *Vernunft und Revolution: Hegel und die Entstehung der Gesellschaftstheorie* (Darmstadt: Neuweid, 1972), 22; *Reason and Revolution: Hegel and the Rise of Social Theory*, (Oxford: Oxford University Press, 1941), 12. Also, Boris Jakowenko argued in favor of Hegel in 1943, in *Über die Hegelsche Philosophie* (Prague, 1943). However, the first definitive case for Hegel was presented by Otto Pöggeler in 1969.

6. Otto Pöggeler, "Hegel, der Verfasser des altesten Systemprogramms des deutschen Idealismus," *Hegel-Studien* 4 (1969); reprinted in *MV*, 126–43. Pöggeler's contentions were first presented at the Hegel conference in Urbino in 1965.

7. In recent years, many scholars have renewed the defense of Schelling,

specifically in regard to his convictions concerning the new mythology and its influence on the incipient romanticism of the *Atheneaum.* Most notable here is Manfred Frank, in *Der kommende Gott: Vorlesungen über die Neue Mythologie,* (Frankfurt am Main: Suhrkamp Verlag, 1982).

8. Ernst Cassirer, "Hölderlin und die deutsche Idealismus I," *Logos: Internationaler Zeitschrift für Philosophie der Kultur* (1917/8): 262–82; cited by Pöggeler in *Die Frage nach der Kunst* (Freiburg: Karl Alber, 1984), 54.

9. *MV,* 127.

10. Dilthey argues to this effect in his seminal work on the young Hegel, *Die Jugendgeschichte Hegels, Gesammelte Schriften,* 4:40–43; this context is exploited by Georg Lukács in his rejection of this fragment from Hegel's corpus, in *Der Junge Hegel: Über die Beziehung von Dialektik und Ökonomie, Werke,* 8, (Neuwied & Berlin: Luchterhand, 1967), 61ff.

11. Pöggeler alights on the modifier *künftig* in the first line of the fragment in order to orient Hegel's general philosophical outlook in this period. Pöggeler sees a link to the theistic predilections of the Tübingen seminary, where Hegel's teachers C. G. Storr and J. F. Flatt had attempted to adopt Kant's "postulates of practical reason" as the basis for justifying the necessity of future providence. While Pöggeler does not presume that Hegel shared these views, he nevertheless argues that Hegel revised this sentiment along Fichtean lines, so that philosophy must be inherently "practical" in the sense that the Self is constituted on the basis of an "infinite striving" after the object of cognition. Philosophy should change its essence into a "metaphysics of morals," as the "Earliest *Systemprogramm*" claims, in that it is always becoming the future (*künftig*), is always a practical striving for total cognition. In Pöggeler's view, "this is the only kind of philosophizing that interested the young Hegel" (*MV,* 131).

However, reducing Hegel's philosophical outlook to the dictates of Kant's "postulates" and the premise of a theoretical "futurity" (*Künftigkeit*) seems to run against the grain of Hegel's critique of Kant in this period. The "postulates of practical reason," as they appear in Kant's second *Critique,* emerge in the context of asserting the "primacy" of practical over theoretical reason. This primacy rests, in Kant's account, on suppressing the degree to which practical reason is "pathologically conditioned," that is, as applicable to regulating sensuous inclinations. Rather, for Kant, practical reason maintains its primacy to the degree that it conforms to the purely formal principle of the universal moral law. Cf. Immanuel Kant, *Kritik der Praktischen Vernuft,* in *Werke in Zwölf Bänden* (Frankfurt: Suhrkamp, 1956), 7:251ff; *Critique of Practical Reason,* trans. Lewis White Beck (New York: Macmillan, 1989), 125ff. As early as 1792–93, however, in his Tübingen essay, Hegel recognizes that there is an analogous moral sentiment in the realm of sensuous inclination, specifically in the condition of love (cf. G. W. F. Hegel, *Frühe Studien und Entwurfe,* ed. Inge Gellert [Berlin: Akademie Verlag, 1991], 43–44.) This sentiment was implicitly superior to the rational calculation of the moral law, in that it did not depend on a heteronomous authority, nor proposed a merely theoretical postulate of future providence. This initial formulation is the germinal core of Hegel's emerging critique of Kantian morality, as it emerges most fully in "The Spirit of Christianity and its Fate," in 1797. In that essay,

Hegel will reject the heteronomous authority implied by Kant's notion of duty to the moral law, in favor of the unifying effects of love elicited in Christ's Sermon on the Mount. In this period Hegel was striving to affirm the moral virtue of immediate sensuous inclinations against the universalizing postulates of Kant's moral law. On this basis, Pöggeler's assertion that Hegel strove to ground a subjective religion on the purely theoretical conjecture of future providence, predicated on Kant's postulates of a moral law, appears implausible in light of Hegel's incipient critic of Kantian morality in this period. It is the sensuous immediacy of love, not the theoretical futurity of the Kantian postulates, which guides Hegel's thinking; cf. my article, "Dynamic Resemblance: Hegel's Early Theory of Ethical Equality," *Review of Metaphysics* 50 (December 1996): 315–49.

12. Immanuel Kant, *Critique of Practical Reason,* 127.

13. *Werke,* 1:235; *Toward,* 511.

14. *Werke,* 1:235; *Toward,* 511.

15. Otto Pöggeler, *Die Frage nach der Kunst,* 54.

16. Otto Pöggeler, *Die Frage nach der Kunst,* 53.

17. *MV,* 140.

18. *MV,* 135–36.

19. Annemarie Gethmann-Siefert, "Die geschichtliche Funktion der 'Mythologie der Vernuft' und die Bestimmung des Kunstwerks in der 'Ästhetik'," in *MV,* 226. Cf. also her important study, "Die Funktion der Kunst in der Geschichte," in *Hegel-Studien, Beiheft* 25 (Bonn: Bouvier, 1984).

20. Richard Taft, "Art and Philosophy in the Early Development of Hegel's System," *The Owl of Minerva* 18:2 (1987): 161.

21. See also, Otto Pöggeler, "Die Entstehung von Hegels Ästhetik in Jena," in *Hegel-Studien, Beiheft* 20, ed. D. Henrich and K. Dusing, (Bonn: Bouvier, 1980); Annemarie Gethmann-Siefert, "Hegels These vom Ende der Kunst und der 'Klassizismus' der Ästhetik," in *Hegel-Studien* 22 (1986).

22. My purpose here is not to dispute Pöggeler's contentions root and branch, but rather to construct an independent scaffold that supports Hegel's early view of art and aesthetic experience at the same time that it renders the "*Systemprogramm*" superfluous on that account. An adequate discussion of the authorship question would amount to an investigation in its own right.

23. For further discussion of the impact of the *Querelle* on Hegel and his contemporaries, cf. Walter Jaeschke, "Early German Idealist Reinterpretation of the Quarrel of the Ancients and the Moderns," *CLIO* 12:4 (1983): 313–31.

24. Annemarie Gethmann-Siefert, "Die Funktion der Kunst in der Geschichte," 18ff.

25. Hegel briefly affirms in an April 1795 letter to Schelling that he finds the first installment a "masterpiece," (*Briefe von und an Hegel,* ed. J. Hoffmeister and F. Nicolin [Hamburg: Felix Meiner Verlag, 1969], 1:25; *Hegel The Letters,* trans. Clark Butler and Christiane Seiler [Bloomington: University of Indiana Press, 1984], 36). However, as H. S. Harris points out, he confuses the title with Lessing's "Education of the Human Race" (*Toward,* 253). Prior to this time, however, Hegel's interest in Schiller appears to be fairly minimal, and restricted to his poetry as such. He wrote a short an-

alytic summary of Schiller's *Fiesko,* for example, in the same period that he transcribed virtually all of Horace's epistles and Klopstock's odes. See *Dokumente zu Hegels Entwicklung,* ed. Johannes Hoffmeister, (Stuttgart: Frohmanns, 1936), 398–99; hereafter *Dok.*

26. Hegel first illustrated his engagement with the *Critique of Judgement* in the notes to his study of "Transcendental Psychology" in 1794; cf. G. W. F. Hegel, *Gesammelte Werke,* ed. Rheinisch-Westfälischen Akademie der Wissenschaft, vol. 1, (Hamburg: Felix Meiner Verlag, 1989), 189–90, hereafter *GW.* See also the distinction between the beautiful and the sublime in "Schon in der Bauart," *GW,* 1:81.

27. In May 1787, Hegel excerpted from Mendelssohn's "Über die Frage: Was heisst aufklären?" in the *Berlin Monatsschrift* of September 1784; he returned to the relation of *Kultur* and *Aufklärung* in August 1787 in an excerpt from Nicolai's *Beschriebung eine Reise durch Deutschland und die Schwiez,* (1785); cf. *Dok.,* 140–43, 145–47. These sources inform his discussion in "On the Religion of the Greeks and Romans," discussed below.

28. Hegel was probably first drawn to the discourse of *Popularphilosophie* from theological coincidences. In diary entries of August 1785, he remarks on the novelty of Catholic services in Protestant Germany. Some months earlier an exchange of letters appeared in the *Berlinische Monatsschrift* between Christian Garve and the editor, Johann Biester. There, Garve likewise noted that figures like Nicolai had grown up entirely in a Protestant land and were thus overly astounded by the recent profligacy of Catholic worship in Germany. Cf. *Dok.,* 404–5.

29. *Dok.,* 125.

30. *Dok.,* 119.

31. *Dok.,* 137.

32. *Dok.,* 139.

33. For example, Wit (*Witz*) "is the ability to perceive the similarity of things," and the interpretation of texts depends on perceiving connective chains which "ease the transition from one truth to another" (*Dok.,* 138).

34. *Dok.,* 137.

35. *Dok.,* 141, "*Aufklärung* relates to *Kultur* as theory relates to praxis."

36. *GW,* 1:42–45. "On the Religion of the Greeks and Romans," trans. Christiane Seiler, *CLIO* 9:1 (1979): 69–74.

37. Christoph Wieland, *Horazens Breife,* ed. Paul Stachel, in *Gesammelte Schriften* 2, Abteilung 4, (Berlin: Weidmann, 1987), 328–29. According to Rosencranz, Hegel had made especially large and comprehensive excerpts from Wieland's three hundred page commentary; cf. *Dok.,* 398n.

38. *GW,* 1:42; Seiler, 71–72.

39. *GW,* 1:43; Seiler, 72. Hegel's diagnosis of the failure of "interpretation" here echoes Kastner's assertion in an earlier excerpt that for any "interpretation" the intellect is necessary to connect and unify images into a coherent system. In Hegel's view in this essay, the excess of imagination in Greek mythology can only depend on "superstition" as a guide to moral action: "These [superstitious] beliefs are, moreover, the strongest rein on their passions; rational grounds and those of a more pure religion are not effective enough against these passions" (*GW,* 1:44; Seiler, 73.

40. *GW,* 1, 45; Seiler, 74.

41. "We learn from their history how common it is through customs and the limitations of certain representations [*Vorstellungen*] to regard the greatest nonsense as rational, disgraceful foolishness as wise. *This will make us aware of our inherited and propagated opinions . . . that they might perhaps be completely false or only half-true.*" *GW,* 1:45; Seiler, 74.

42. *Dok.,* 144.

43. *GW,* 1:53.

44. *GW,* 1:51–52.

45. *Dok.,* 148; J. H. Kistenmaker, *De origine ac vi Deponentium et Mediorum Graecae linguae* (Munster, 1787).

46. *GW,* 1:52.

47. G. W. F. Hegel, *Phänomenologie des Geistes,* in *Sämtliche Werke,* ed. Herman Glockner (Stuttgart: Fromanns, 1951), 34–35; *Phenomenology of Spirit,* trans. A. V. Miller, (Oxford: Oxford University Press, 1977), 19. Hegel identifies "natural consciousness" and the condition of "sensuous certainty" in *PhG,* 89–90; *PS,* 64.

48. *Betrachtung einiger Verscheidenheiten in den werken der ältesten and neuern Schriftsteller, insbesondere der Dichter;* cf. *Dok.,* 407.

49. *Dok.,* 410.

50. *Dok.,* 409.

51. *Dok.,* 410.

52. *GW,* 1:46; *Toward,* 36. In a passage from the Tübingen essay of 1792–93 Hegel describes the "spirit of the nation" among the Greeks in exactly the terms that he here finds lacking in modern society. The Greek spirit appears as a personification of genius: "The father of this genius is *Chronos,* on whom he remains more or less dependent all his life (the circumstances of the time)—his mother is the πολιτεια the constitution [*Verfassung*]—his midwife, his wet-nurse [is] religion—who accepts the fine arts into her service to aid his education—especially music, physical and spiritual motion. . . . With the flowers of her fine [*schöne*] free imagination [*Phantasie*] she adorned the impenetrable veil behind which divinity withdraws from our view—conjuring behind it a realm peopled with living images, from which he carried forth the great ideas of his own heart with all the fullness of higher and beautiful feelings" (*Toward,* 506–7).

53. Hegel claims that for a select few, "from the distant days of the past, a picture radiates the soul which has a feeling for human beauty, the greatness of the great, a picture of the genius of the people—a son of fortune, of freedom, a pupil of beautiful imagination" (*Frühe Schriften und Entwürfe,* 56–57).

54. *GW,* 1:46; *Toward,* 36. As H. S. Harris correctly points out, this is the first occasion in which Hegel refers to the understanding, *Verstand,* as a faculty of analysis and dissection which kills life (36). However, as I have tried to show, the *positive* role of *Verstand* in earlier excerpts, and in controlling the spread of imaginative excess in Greek religion in his 1787 essay, suggest that the rejection of *Verstand* here is a deliberate revision of his earlier views.

55. *GW,* 1:46–47; *Toward,* 37. The quotations are taken from Lessing's *Nathan.*

56. "In einer Republik . . . " 1795: "Greek and Gothic architecture, the former beautiful, the latter sublime . . . ," *GW,* 1: 203.

57. "Schon in der Bauart . . . ," 1792/3–4, *GW,* 1:81.

58. Immanuel Kant, *Critique of Judgement,* trans. J. C. Meredith (Oxford: Oxford University Press, 1991), pp. 90–91.

59. G. W. F. Hegel, *Early Theological Writings,* trans. T. M. Knox, (Philadelphia: University of Pennsylvania Press, 1975), 147.

60. G. W. F. Hegel, *Three Essays,* trans. Peter Fuss and John Dobbins (Notre Dame: Notre Dame University Press, 1984), 53.

61. *GW,* 1:79.

62. "Bericht uber eine Alpenwanderung," 25 July 1796, *GW,* 1:388.

63. *GW,* 1:388. Hegel's emphasis.

64. *Frühe Studien und Entwürfe,* 387.

65. *Frühe Studien und Entwürfe,* 387, emphasis added.

66. *GW,* 1:388–89.

67. *GW,* 1:53.

68. *Frühe Studien und Entwürfe,* p 239; *Early Theological Writings,* 90

69. *Early Theological Writings,* 249; *GW,* 1:366.

70. Frühe schriften und Entwürfe, 536; *Werke,* 1:377; *Early Theological Writings,* 261.

XI

Aesthetic Education and the Aesthetic State: Hegel's Response to Schiller

Andrew G. Fiala

Schiller's *Letters on the Aesthetic Education of Man* explore the possibility of an aesthetic utopia in which human beings play freely with their aesthetic sensibilities. In this utopia, human life would neither be infected with the fears and dangers of the savage state of nature nor be subject to the constraints of the rigid bourgeois state. For Schiller, aesthetic experience is both the means to this aesthetic utopia and the end to be enjoyed in it. Given Hegel's debt to Schiller and Hegel's own understanding of aesthetics as a mode of Absolute Spirit, we wonder what happened to this vision of an aesthetic state in Hegel's writings on aesthetics and politics.[1] While Schiller makes a case for aesthetics as the political savior of the world, Hegel's conception of aesthetics does not have any immediate political significance. Rather, Hegel emphasizes the limits of both aesthetics and politics.

Schiller maintains that aesthetic experience is a means toward higher ends, including among these ends truth, duty, scientific reflection, and even political action. However, for Schiller, aesthetic experience is also an end in itself that surpasses all of these. In the last of his letters, Schiller gives us a picture of his ideal in the following: "In the aesthetic state [*in dem ästhetischen Staat*] is everything—even the tool which serves—a free citizen who has equal rights with the noblest."[2] With this move, Schiller announces that his theory of aesthetics has all along been a utopian political theory. Hegel partially agrees with Schiller's understanding of the pedagogical function of aesthetic experience, but by separating ethical life and aesthetics as different realms of truth, Hegel distances himself from Schiller's utopian project of a seamless synthesis of the aesthetic and the political. Hegel's reason for keeping aesthetics and politics separate as realms of inquiry involves his recognition that there are different ways in which the true manifests itself. Hegel tries to balance the aesthetic between the political, on the one hand, and the religious and philosophical, on the other, without collapsing the difference between these different realms in the way that someone like Schiller does.[3] To collapse this difference is to fail to recognize the significance of the form with regard to the way in which the content is thought.[4] Hegel's system rejects the utopian conclusions of Schiller's *Letters* by remaining cognizant of the differences between Objective and Absolute Spirit.

In what follows, we will look closely at Schiller's *Letters* in an effort to see the relation between politics and aesthetics that Hegel is simultaneously adopting and transforming. We will compare this to Hegel's own definitions of aesthetics in the *Encyclopedia* and the *Lectures on Aesthetics* and Hegel's criticism of utopian thinking in the *Philosophy of Right* in an effort to show how Hegel responds to Schiller's theory of the relation between aesthetic experience and political utopia. In the end we will attempt to articulate the difference between art and politics in Hegel's system.

In *On the Aesthetic Education of Man,* Schiller maintains that social alienation can be solved by aesthetic education. This can occur in two ways. In the first, aesthetic education facilitates development from immersion in immediate nature to the higher reflected or mediated unities of ethics and science; in the second, aesthetic experience itself is the highest unity possible for man, that is, the unity of sensuousness and rationality which itself overcomes all alienation. These two aspects of aesthetic reconciliation revolve around an ambiguity inherent in any theory of education.

On the one hand, a theory of education must consider specific methodologies and media of teaching. For Schiller, the medium and the method are aesthetic—the appeal to taste and to the universal, subjective experience of beauty is the method by which Schiller would show us the path from immediacy to reflection.[5] Hegel, as we shall see, agrees with this account of the experience of beauty as a way of articulating the Absolute Idea that can lead us toward a comprehension of the true.

On the other hand, a theory of education must have a goal toward which it is directed. For Schiller, this goal is freedom and the creation of a state and society in which absolute freedom appears. What is most interesting is that this state of freedom is understood by Schiller as an aesthetic state. It is here that Hegel differs with Schiller, by keeping the state separate from aesthetics. For Hegel, aesthetic experience is an end in itself which has no political consequences. We will now examine both of these aspects in detail, showing the way in which Hegel agrees with the first part and disagrees with second part of Schiller's theory.

I. Aesthetic Experience as a Means toward Higher Truth: Aesthetic Education

Schiller claims that "we must indeed, if we are to solve that political problem in practice, follow the path of aesthetics, since it is through Beauty that we arrive at Freedom."[6] Schiller maintains that beauty shows us the way toward freedom and that the resolution of contemporary social problems requires a step into the supersensible realm disclosed in aesthetic experience.

It is clear from the context of the first few letters that Schiller's goal is political freedom. The letters themselves were written directly after the French Revolution and were originally addressed to the Duke of Augustenberg. In the early letters, aesthetics appears as merely the means to the social and political ends of unity, equality, harmony, and freedom. Here, at the beginning of Schiller's account, aesthetic education already aims at ethical and political ends. Schiller can thus be seen as a revolutionary who maintains that to change political life our whole manner of existence must be changed.

Aesthetic experience is the catalyst for political change because it is able to facilitate the achievement of freedom. Most obviously, aesthetic experience frees us from seemingly contradictory aspects of human life, synthesizing the rational and the sensuous, the immutable and the mutable in a unified whole.[7] This synthesis occurs by either the "melting" (*schmeltzende*) or "energizing" (*energische*) properties of art.[8] The melting property of art relaxes the tensions in us, while the energizing property lifts us out of lassitude.[9] The goal of both of these is the same: the experience of beauty leads us to a middle region between sensuality and rationality, between lassitude and frenzy, between form and content. As the middle ground between these extremes, the experience of beauty is a unifying harmony which first and foremost brings sensuous experience to thought, thus freeing us from the particularity of natural life. The primary goal of aesthetic education is to lift us out of sensual immediacy by way of the experience of beauty.

At the same time, however, Schiller recognizes an opposite function of aesthetic experience: to bring the overly spiritual thinker back to sensuous experience and thus to qualify ethical experience with a dose of reality. Both of these movements occur by an *Aufhebung* which cancels the oppositions between intellect and sense while also preserving them.[10] Schiller describes the resolution of the contradiction between the sensual and the spiritual in human beings as following from the ambiguous nature of beauty itself.

> But the former [sensual men] do not reflect that the freedom in which they quite rightly place the essence of Beauty is not lawlessness but harmony of laws, not arbitrariness [*Willkürlichkeit*] but the utmost inner necessity; the latter [intellectuals] do not reflect that the definiteness [*Bestimmtheit*] which they equally rightly demand of Beauty consists not in the exclusion of certain realities but in the absolute inclusion of them all, so that it is therefore not restriction but infinity.[11]

Beauty is the absolute inclusion of all realities—an infinity. The experience of beauty thus reconciles the one-sidedness of both the sensual and intellectual ways of viewing the world. Aesthetic education as a means of education is a path which attempts to overcome our finite, one-sided perspectives by acquainting us with the infinite truth of beauty. On the one hand, aesthetic experience lifts us from out of our immediate immersion in the sensuous world and enables us to freely see the rational world and its interaction with the world of sense. On the other hand, aesthetic experience can remind the pure intellect of the sensual world which it inhabits. The first of these is what Schiller is primarily concerned with in his account of aesthetic education because human beings begin from immediate immersion in the world of sense. However, by remembering the dialectical opposition of this way of education we can see that this is a method of synthesis which does not completely reject either the sensual or spiritual perspectives. Aesthetic education is an antidote to both savage sensuality and over-weaning intellectualism.

Hegel shares Schiller's conception of the aesthetic as the synthesis of the sensual and the spiritual. He defines art as the presentation of the Absolute in sensual terms. In his own words: "the content of art is the Idea, while its form is the sensuously formed configuration [*sinnliche bildliche Gestaltungen*]."[12] Hegel thus considers the beautiful in fine art to be a synthesis, just as Schiller did. In fact, Hegel, in explicitly acknowledging his debt to Schiller, maintains that Schiller himself had attained to the level of a scientifically valid theory of art.

> This unity of universal and particular, freedom and necessity, spirit and nature, which Schiller grasped scientifically as the principle and essence of art and which he laboured unremittingly to call into actual life by art and aesthetic education, has now, as the Idea itself, been made the principle of knowledge and existence, and the Idea has become recognized as that which alone is true and actual.[13]

The chief problem with regard to Schiller's theory of aesthetics, as Hegel subsequently indicates, is that Schiller did not articulate the relation of art to an entire theory of the philosophical idea as Hegel himself did.

In addition to this shared theory of the logic of aesthetic experience, Hegel also shares Schiller's understanding of the educational role of art. According to Hegel, there are two ways in which art functions as education. First, art can curb desire and soften rudeness by lifting us out of particularity. This can be roughly equated with Schiller's account of melting beauty. For Hegel, art uplifts crude consciousness and mitigates the brutalizing power of immediate passions by objectifying those passions and thereby making them less immediate. When art represents the passions, it mediates them and allows us to reflect upon them. As Hegel says; "Now such rudeness and untamed force of passion is indeed already softened [*mildert*] by art, in that it represents [*vorstellig macht*] to man what he feels and achieves in such a situation."[14] Ultimately, Hegel concurs with Schiller that this process of representation and mediation leads us to freedom, in this case, freedom from the immediacy of the passions. Hegel and Schiller agree most obviously and fundamentally on this point.

The other way in which aesthetic experience can educate, according to Hegel, is by presenting the spiritual idea before us in sensible form.[15]

Hegel says explicitly that "the aim in relation to teaching could only consist in bringing into consciousness, by means of the work of art, an absolutely essential spiritual content."[16] Here Hegel is trying to get beyond a theory of art that would reduce art to mere moral edification. In fact, while not denying that art can be understood as a tool for education, Hegel is trying to found a theory of art that would go beyond art as mere tool for anything. Rather, Hegel wants to understand art as an end in itself. This end is to display the truth of man's "amphibious" nature.[17] Hegel concludes with what seems at first to be an explicit rejection of a Schillerian type of "aesthetic education." In the following passage, Hegel is trying to preserve the purity of aesthetic experience against an instrumental account of art.

> Against this [theory of art as useful for another end] we must maintain that art's vocation is to unveil the truth in the form of sensuous artistic configuration, to set forth the reconciled opposition just mentioned, and so to have its end and aim in itself, in this setting forth and unveiling. For other ends, like instruction, purification, bettering, financial gain, struggling for fame and honor, have nothing to do with the work of art as such, and do not determine its nature.[18]

Schiller agrees that aesthetics is such an unveiling of the truth in sensuous form. But for Schiller, this leads to further political ends. Once we have made the jump from purely sensuous experience to aesthetic experience, we are already far along on the path toward rationality and freedom. In this way, for Schiller, ethics and science are made possible by aesthetic education which provides us with our first glimpse of the mediated truths of reason and which shows us the possibility of a self-determining morally free will. Still, Schiller is careful to avoid the kind of corrupt view of art which Hegel rejects above. In addition, throughout the letters, Schiller is very careful to point out that beauty does not actually interfere with the truth of morality or science. In fact, he maintains the Kantian position that "the pure logical form—the concept—must speak immediately to the understanding [*Verstand*], the pure moral form—the law—immediately to the will."[19] Beauty and aesthetic experience may lead the sensual person to the concept and the moral law but the moral law and the concept determine themselves purely and rationally. While wanting to preserve this purity, Schiller also maintains that each of these ways in which the truth can occur—the moral and the logical—is only one-sided. Thus in the last few letters Schiller moves to a position that Hegel would agree with, namely that aesthetic free play is a higher form of truth than either natural science or morality insofar as the experience of beauty expresses the duplicitous nature of the human spirit.[20] Thus, Hegel and Schiller would agree that aesthetic experience leads us from immediacy to higher truth. Moreover both agree that the truths of science and morality are themselves overcome by a return to the experience of beauty in which true unity and absolute freedom occur.

Now we must turn to the place in which Hegel and Schiller most vehemently disagree, namely with regard to the aesthetic state.

II. Aesthetic Experience as an End in Itself: The Aesthetic State

On the Aesthetic Education of Man has an explicit political content. Schiller concludes with a description of the stages of progress toward the ideal state in which equality and justice will prevail. This progress goes from the dynamic state of rights (*dynamischen Statt der Rechte*) in which persons interact on the basis of power and force to the ethical state of duties (*ethischen Statt der Pflichten*) in which persons interact on the basis of law and external restrictions of will. The final stage which surpasses both of these is the aesthetic state (*ästhetishcen Statt*) in which human beings interact on the basis of free play: "To grant freedom by means of freedom [*Freiheit zu geben durch Freiheit*] is the fundamental law of this kingdom [*Reichs*]."[21] This final state, according to Schiller, will be governed by the natural order of human taste and the natural harmony of beauty. Schiller concludes: "Though need may drive Man into society [*Gesellschaft*], and Reason implant social principles [*gesellige Grundsätze*] in him, Beauty alone can confer on him a social character [*geselligen Charakter*]. Taste alone brings harmony into society, because it establishes harmony in the individual."[22] In the aesthetic state, each human being will freely and harmoniously play with its own faculties in harmony with its world and with other equally harmonious human beings; the social character will grow and humanity will flourish. The aesthetic state is the highest manifestation of freedom, the place where freedom will not be restricted or in conflict, a place where human freedom plays in harmony with itself. The aesthetic state thus resolves the social and political problem of alienation (alienation of each individual from each other, as in the dynamic state, or alienation of the individual from the general will as in the ethical state).[23]

The goal of aesthetic education thus seems to be to create a society in which the most beautiful human beings can live the most beautiful lives. Thus aesthetic education has an explicitly political goal. With aesthetic education, human being becomes an aesthetic formation, a work of art that is formed according to the ideal which is beautiful, harmonious, social, and free.[24] This aesthetic human being will then create a new state in which freedom and harmony can be played with freely. Neither the dynamic state of rights nor the ethical state of duties is able to manifest this ideal. The dynamic state is restricted to plays of force in which human beings confront nature and each other in an effort to establish order. The ethical state is the subsequent manifestation of order by the imposition of the general will which prohibits and restricts individual freedom. Only in the aesthetic state will human beings be free and unconstrained while also having a common taste and a social feeling that binds them in harmonious union. Schiller equates the dynamic state with the sensuous good and realizes that the dynamic state (which is perhaps analogous to the feudal state) will make only one person happy because it is "based on appropriation" and aims at establishing exclusivity in property.[25] The ethical state is equated with the absolute good (analogous perhaps to the French state after the revolution) and is better than the dynamic state in that it aims at the universal, but that universality is only achieved by "renunciation" (*Verläugnung*) (which Schiller perhaps equated with the Jacobin terror).[26] Schiller concludes that the aesthetic state alone promises a true synthesis of the universal and particular because the experience of the beautiful is the only truly free and universal experience. Schiller concludes, "Beauty alone makes all the world happy, and every being forgets its limitations as long as it experiences her enchantment."[27]

The final goal of aesthetic education is thus the creation of an ideal state, a political work of art, a utopia; or as Schiller calls it in the last letter "a state of beautiful appearance [*Staat des schönen Scheins*]."[28] This utopia is to be achieved by aesthetic education which will lead us to the harmonious middle ground which synthesizes the duplicitous essence of humankind. By way of aesthetic education, Schiller believes that human beings can be formed into a perfect image of themselves with the result being the formation of a state based on this image. This education must be aesthetic because human nature is duplicitous in the same way that aesthetic experience is duplicitous, that is, a mixture of reason and sense. The merely ethical state is not adequate to the ambiguous essence of human nature because it one-sidedly emphasizes the objectivity of law. The perfection of human being requires the sort of harmonizing that is only seen in the essence of beauty: as Schiller describes it, "the happy equilibrium which is the soul of Beauty and the condition of humanity."[29] In harmonizing within duplicity, humankind can be formed into the work of art which Nature intended us to be, and the state can become a beautiful appearance.

Thus for Schiller, aesthetic experience is both a means to morality and ethics and the end in itself that overcomes ethics. Thus all of the various determinations of rational scientific, ethical, and political organization are subordinate to the harmony of the aesthetic state as the final end of the process of education. For Schiller, life in the aesthetic state would exhibit the perfect reconciliation of the sensual and the rational. Sensual existence is equated with the savagery that exists before the coming of any state whatsoever, while reason is the basis of that form of ethics and politics which restrains freedom. Schiller maintains that human beings need to go through aesthetic education in order to overcome their particular finite sensuousness and to be able to enter into the realm of universal rationality and ethics. And yet Schiller claims that this ethical universal order is alien to the nature of human being, that human being is not meant for duty alone, but that we also need the freedom of play. Thus Schiller subsequently proclaims that the rational ethical order must eventually be sublated by the aesthetic realm of freedom at play with itself. Ethics and politics are thus uplifted and combined with aesthetics in this utopian theory.[30]

Hegel of course aims at a synthesis that is higher than a mere aesthetic state. In the *Phenomenology*, for example, revealed religion and absolute knowing are placed beyond the artistic religion and above ethical life. This progress is schematized more thoroughly in the *Encyclopedia*. Ethics and politics occur there as Objective Spirit while art, religion, and philosophy occur (in this order) as Absolute Spirit. In both of these accounts, aesthetics, religion, and philosophy are beyond politics insofar as they involve a more complete synthesis and manifestation of the Idea. In the *Encyclopedia* especially, the types of disclosure that occur in politics and in art are quite different. Although they contain the same content (free spirit), they disclose this content in quite different ways. Thus Hegel rejects Schiller's attempt to combine aesthetics and politics and create an aesthetic state.

It is the utopian character of Schiller's theory which Hegel most vehemently rejects, although this rejection comes as a result of Hegel's theory of politics and not his theory of aesthetics. As we have seen, Hegel agrees with Schiller about the type of truth that aesthetics discloses. Hegel and Schiller agree about the synthetic component of beauty, about the unity and life exhibited in the beautiful, and even about the way in which the pure experience of the beautiful must be a free end in itself, not directed at some further moral usage.[31] However, Hegel's understanding of the relation between aesthetics and the state is quite different from Schiller's. Although Hegel does recognize the need for Spirit to go beyond ethical life and enter into the realm of Absolute Spirit, aesthetics is never proclaimed as a replacement for ethical life. Aesthetics is a mode of Absolute Spirit and the ethical life of the state is a mode of Objective Spirit. Hegel wants to keep these two modes separate.

The relation between aesthetics and the state is difficult to grasp because of the structural ambiguities of Hegel's system. On the one hand, Hegel does place aesthetics higher than ethics and politics. On the other hand, this structure is not rigidly hierarchical, but rather involves a series of reciprocal and even circular determinations.[32] In Hegel's *Encyclopedia* we can recognize a distinctive split between the real ethical state and the aesthetic ideal. And yet within the totality of the system, this split cannot be too radical. Objective Spirit must have some relation to Absolute Spirit.

Hegel's specific rejection of Schiller's aesthetic state is not articulated in the *Aesthetics*. This rejection can be found, however, in Hegel's general rejection of utopian thinking in the Preface to the *Philosophy of Right*. For Hegel, Schiller's description of the aesthetic state is, at best, a confusion of different modes of presentation of the Absolute Idea. At worst, it is a rampant misuse of the powers of the imagination which has no right to claim to be scientific. As Hegel warns in the Preface to the *Philosophy of Right*, if a philosopher's theory "does indeed transcend his own time, if it builds itself a world as it ought to be, then it certainly has an existence, but only within his opinions—a pliant medium in which the imagination can construct anything it pleases."[33] It is not much of a leap to suggest that Hegel may have had Schiller in mind in this passage. Schiller's own aesthetic state admits to being the imaginative construction of a "visionary" or "zealot" [*Schwärmer*] that is perhaps only actual in "a few select circles."[34] Despite Hegel's sympathetic agreement with Schiller's theory of the beautiful, he is not sympathetic to Schiller's imaginative attempt to leap over Rhodes and create an ideal state.

It is not only with regard to utopian thinking that Hegel disagrees with Schiller. More important is Hegel's theory of the relation between ethical life and art. In Hegel's theory, the ethical state does not overcome itself in an aesthetic state as it does in Schiller's theory. Rather, the ethical state is a necessary way in which Spirit discloses itself: *Sittlichkeit* is one of the necessary forms that the Absolute must take. Spirit requires the objectivity of ethical life and law and cannot overcome politics completely with a move to the aesthetic.

Art does give form to the ethical idea of a nation (as Hegel indicates in the *Phenomenology*) but so can religion and philosophy. These different forms each articulate the content in importantly different ways. Thus, for Hegel, the aesthetic state is an oxymoron. Art is one way in which Spirit is disclosed; ethics and politics is another. The specific form of politics must not be confused with the quite different form of aesthetics.

In order to make this clear, let us briefly recapitulate the location of both ethical life and aesthetics within the whole of Hegel's system. In the introduction to the "Philosophy of Spirit", the third part of the *Encyclopedia,* Hegel says that the three stages that Spirit encounters on its path to liberation are one and the same: "the finding of a world as presupposed, the production of that world by Spirit, and the liberation from it and in it."[35] These three are roughly equivalent to the three major divisions in the third part of the *Encyclopedia* itself. Subjective Spirit finds a world presupposed—the anthropology and psychology treat Spirit as something found existing as a natural object. Objective Spirit produces a world for itself—natural law, morality, and ethical life are the processes of Spirit determining itself freely by giving itself laws. And finally, Absolute Spirit is freedom coming to know itself in and for itself—art, religion, and philosophy are modes of Spirit's coming to freely play with its own freedom. These three stages can be seen as roughly equivalent to Schiller's three states, the dynamic, the ethical, and the aesthetic. However, Hegel denies that either the first or the third can rightly be applied to the concept of the state. What Schiller calls the dynamic—the mere play of forces—is not properly called a state according to Hegel, nor is the aesthetic—the pure play of freedom. Rather, as Hegel makes clear in the *Philosophy of Right,* "the state is the actuality of the *ethical* Idea."[36] While the state gives concrete form to the ethical idea, the aesthetic has its own Idea, namely the idea of the beauty of art which is the Absolute

Idea expressed in concrete form.[37] While these share the content of free Spirit, their forms are quite different and must remain distinct as unique ways that Spirit comprehends itself.

Given this differentiation of aesthetics and ethics in terms of form, let us ask how the sphere of Objective Spirit, that sphere which Hegel characterized above as "generating a world as our own creation," is related to the sphere of Absolute Spirit, the sphere which is characterized as "gaining freedom from [that world] and in it." Given the structure of the *Encyclopedia,* we would assume that there would be a connection between politics and art because *Sittlichkeit* is the final determination of Objective Spirit and *Kunst* is the first determination of Absolute Spirit. What occurs in the transition between ethical life and art?

The transition from Objective Spirit to Absolute Spirit involves a rearticulation of the truth of Objective Spirit in three different ways, the religious, the philosophical, and the artistic. The Protestant religion appears to be the self-understanding (in representational thought) of contemporary *Sittlichkeit.* In the same way, Hegel's own philosophy is the self-understanding in scientific *Nachdenken* of this same *Sittlichkeit.* Art can thus be understood as the immediacy of *Sittlichkeit* in intuition or images. Hegel states this all succinctly at the beginning of the final part of the *Philosophy of Right* where he introduces the concept of world history: "The element of the universal Spirit's existence which is intuition (*Anschauung*) and image in art, feeling and representational thought (*Vorstellung*) in religion, and pure and free thought in philosophy, is, in world history, the spiritual actuality in its entire range of inwardness and externality."[38] Thus we see that the determinations of Absolute Spirit do not change or transform the determinations of Objective Spirit. Rather, they merely re-present the truth of these determinations, the same spiritual element, in a higher and more transparent form. It is the form of presentation that is crucial here. Art is the re-presentation in sensuous images of the truths of Spirit, while ethical life is the lived truth of Spirit in the *Sittlichkeit* of the community. The crucial distinction here is that *Sittlichkeit* itself does not involve a re-presentation of the Idea. Art on the other hand is always a mediated re-presentation of the Idea. That is why there can be art that makes manifest the spiritual idea of an ethical community: such art re-presents the truth that is merely lived by that community.

Whatever they may have in common with regard to content, the truth presented in the ethical Idea is thus presented differently in the Idea of the beautiful artwork because in the artwork this presentation is a re-presentation of that truth. Art's ethical or political impact occurs merely as sensuously displaying the truths that the ethical Spirit itself has already experience in lived objective forms. While the content of both the aesthetic and ethical Ideas is free Spirit, the manner in which this Idea is manifest is unique to each mode of presentation. Moreover, the form of presentation determines the content in a unique and necessary manner. Hegel states this succinctly: "we are expressly rejecting the above-mentioned idea which assumes that art is useful for some varied ulterior subject-matter [*Inhalt*] or other interests foreign to itself."[39]

Hegel thus agrees with Schiller that the truth as presented in the ethical state is one-sided. In a significant passage in the introduction to the *Aesthetics* Hegel writes that the state is an organic whole but that

> the principle itself, the actualization of which is the life of the state and wherein man seeks his satisfaction, is still once again one-sided and inherently abstract. . . . It is only the rational freedom of the will which is explicit here; it is only in the state—and once again only in this individual state—and therefore again in a particular [*besondere*] sphere of existence and the isolated reality of this sphere, that freedom is actual. Thus man feels too that the rights and obligations in these regions and their mundane and, once more, finite mode of existence are insufficient; he feels that both in their objective character, and also in their relation to the subject, they need a still higher confirmation and sanction.[40]

This higher confirmation is the confirmation of the realm of Absolute Spirit in which truth is presented in its absolute form. Thus Hegel is undoubtedly sympathetic to Schiller's call for a move beyond the merely ethical state. He admits, as quoted above, that humankind is still not satisfied with the objective truth as found in the state. This objective truth is still too particular, too finite. And perhaps it still involves a bit of alienation. Thus, Hegel realizes that Spirit can only find itself fulfilled in the realm of Absolute Spirit which he describes as "the region of a higher, more substantial, truth, in which all oppositions and contradiction in the finite can find their final resolution, and freedom its full satisfaction."[41] But that spiritual fulfillment will not result in a utopian aesthetic state. Rather, it is a quite different manner of fulfillment: "This is the region of truth itself, not relative truths."[42]

III. Conclusion

Thus we can conclude that Hegel shares all of Schiller's main concerns with regard to aesthetic education, including most significantly the recognition of the need for a way of overcoming alienation even as it still occurs in the ethical state. Both Hegel and Schiller also recognize that the experience of beauty, as a synthesis of the sensual and rational, plays a significant role in the overcoming of alienation. However, Hegel rejects Schiller's utopian vision of an aesthetic state that would rearticulate the higher synthesis of aesthetic experience back into political terms. Collapsing the difference between objectively lived ethical life and the artistic re-presentation of the truth of Spirit can only result in confusion and the type of utopian zealotry that Schiller's last letter gives way to.

The truth as it occurs in art cannot have a revolutionary impact on the truth as it occurs in the state because these truths are limited by the mode of disclosure that occurs in these different realms. While art does involve a higher reconciliation of Spirit with itself, it does not therefore have any immediate political effect. Rather, the truth of politics plays itself out on an entirely different stage than the truth of the artwork.

We might want to condemn Hegel here as conservative and unnecessarily limited by the rigidity of his system, but we must also agree that Schiller's aesthetic state is fantastic and superficial. The rigidity of Hegel's system seems to limit him from saying anything about the way in which art might transform politics. This is troubling because it seems on the face of it that art does have political implications and that the type of aesthetic experience which Schiller describes could be the foundation for a harmonious community. The virtue of Hegel's account, however, lies in the fact that the very rigidity of his system prevents Hegel from leaping toward a utopia such as Schiller's. While Schiller's poetic vision is beautiful in its own right, it seems to actually interfere with serious contemplation of the problems of ethical life. While Hegel and Schiller would both agree that many of our social problems could be resolved by aesthetic education, Hegel realizes that this alone is not enough. Ethical and political alienation must be overcome in their own realm via ethical and political education such as that offered by the *Philosophy of Right*. Schiller's vision fails to offer any concrete ethical and political solutions. Such solutions must take the form proper to the concerns of ethics and politics, with the aesthetic realm offering solutions of its own to a related, yet different, series of problems.

Notes

1. Cf. Hegel's letter to Schelling of April 16, 1795 where he calls Schiller's essay a "masterpiece" (in Walter Kaufmann's *Hegel* [Garden City, N.Y.: Doubleday, 1965], 303). Hegel's debt to Schiller is considered in detail, to cite but a few well-known examples, in Kaufmann's *Hegel*, 46–58; in Charles Taylor's *Hegel* (Cambridge: Cambridge University Press, 1975), 26–42; in Philip J. Kain's *Schiller, Hegel, and Marx* (Kingston: McGill University Press, 1982); and most recently in Robert Wicks's *Hegel's Theory of Aesthetic Judgment* (New York: Peter Lang Publishing, 1994), 41–56. None of these directly address the issue of the relation between aesthetics and politics.

2. My translation, *Schiller's Werke* (Weimar: Hermann Böhlaus, 1962), 20:412; *On The Aesthetic Education of Man*, ed. and trans. E. M. Wilkinson and L. A. Willoughby (Oxford: Clarendon Press, 1967), 140.

3. This last description is taken from William Desmond, who criticizes the left-Hegelian move of interpreting art politically by seeing this as a failure to maintain the purity of the sphere of Absolute Spirit. Desmond concludes his essay on "Art as 'Aesthetic' and 'Religious'" (in *Hegel's Philosophy of Spirit*, ed. by Peter G. Stillman

[Albany: SUNY Press, 1987]) with the following remarks: "It is true, of course, that just as art and religion were deeply intertwined for Hegel, so also were religion and politics. But here a distinction essential to the Hegelian balance vanished in the Left-Hegelian appropriation. In this latter, putting the point in Hegel's own terms, Absolute Spirit tends to be collapsed into objective spirit; or rather, objective spirit, in the shape of the 'political', is elevated into the absolute and comes to possess something of the ultimacy and centrality previously possessed by art and religion. In Hegel art and religion may be deeply rooted in the political but they are marked by a dimension not entirely reducible thereto, as we must grant if we acknowledge some truth in his distinction between objective and Absolute Spirit" (Art as 'Aesthetic' and 'Religious'," 189–90). The present paper is an attempt to examine this very distinction between Objective and Absolute Spirit.

4. Cf. *Encyclopedia,* sections 1–3 where Hegel maintains that there is one truth that appears in a variety of forms of thinking.

5. Schiller is of course drawing on Kant's third *Critique* throughout his work. Although space will not allow a full account of Kant here, three recurrent themes need to be mentioned. First, for Kant, the judgment that a thing is beautiful is subjective, but also made as if it were universally true (cf. section 7 of *Critique of Judgment*). Second, Schiller borrows the idea of aesthetics as free play from Kant (*Critique of Judgment,* section 9). Third, Kant already talks of the aesthetic experience in social terms (*Critique of Judgment,* section 9). Schiller merely takes up these Kantian themes and turns them toward an explicitly political context. In so doing, he also transforms these from Kant's own concern with a theory of judgment to his own concern with a theory of art (cf. Gadamer, *Truth and Method,* trans. Weinsheimer and Marshall [New York: Continuum, 1993], 56). Hegel too, in his work on aesthetics, is more concerned with art than with judgment, perhaps borrowing this concern from Schiller (cf. Gadamer, *Truth and Method,* 59).

6. *On the Aesthetic Education of Man,* 27; *Schillers Werke,* 20:312.

7. Cf. *On the Aesthetic Education of Man,* 86–88 *Schillers Werke,* 20:364–66.

8. *On the Aesthetic Education of Man,* 82; *Schillers Werke,* 20:361.

9. *On the Aesthetic Education of Man,* 83; *Schillers Werke,* 20:361–62.

10. *On the Aesthetic Education of Man,* 87–88. Here Schiller uses the word *aufgehoben,* foreshadowing Hegel's usage of this term (*Schillers Werke,* 20:366); cf. Wick's account (48–50) of Hegel's appropriation of dialectic and the term *Aufhebung;* also Kaufmann, 51–53. Deric Regin states this *Aufhebung* as follows: by aesthetic experience Schiller means "reconciliation or unity . . . a synthesis suspending the polarity of the sensate and the intelligent forces in man's mind" (*Freedom and Dignity,* 118). Deric Regin, *Freedom and Dignity* [the Hague: Martinus Nijhoff, 1965].

11. *On the Aesthetic Education of Man,* 90; *Schillers Werke,* 20:367.

12. My translation, G. W. F. Hegel, *Vorlesungen über die Ästhetik, Werke in zwanzig Bänden,* ed. E. Moldenhauer and K. M. Michel, 20 vols. and Index, (Frankfurt am Main: Suhrkamp Verlag, 1969ff), 13:100; G. W. F. Hegel *Aesthetics: Lectures on Fine Art,* trans. T. M. Knox, 2 vols. (Oxford: Clarendon Press, 1975), 1:70. Further references will be given in the form: *Werke,* 13:100, *A;* 1:70.

13. *Werke,* 13:91 *A,* 1:62–63.

14. My translation, *Werke*, 13:73–74; *A*, 1:48.

15. This may be roughly equated with Schiller's conception of "energizing" beauty which brings the intellect back to life. Hegel does emphasize the fact that the concept must be concrete. Art presents the idea in concrete form. However, Hegel nowhere mentions explicitly this "energizing" function of art. Moreover, for Hegel, as is well known, art is inadequate to express certain concepts; religion and philosophy represent even higher modes of presentation of such ideas.

16. *Werke*, 13:76; *A*, 1:50.

17. Cf. *Werke*, 13:80; *A*, 1:54.

18. *Werke*, 13:82: *A*, 1:55.

19. My translation, *Schillers Werke*, 20:384; *On the Aesthetic Education of Man*, 108.

20. Of course, if science is understood as philosophy, then Hegel would disagree. If Schiller is to be credible in this regard, he must have natural science more in mind than he does the all-inclusive science of philosophy.

21. *On the Aesthetic Education of Man*, 137; *Schillers Werke*, 20:410.

22. *On the Aesthetic Education of Man*, 138; *Schillers Werke*, 20:410.

23. In the fourth letter, Schiller indicates that alienation is the problem that he will be confronting throughout the rest of the text (*On the Aesthetic Education of Man*, 30–34). Regin indicates that the goal of the aesthetic state is to overcome this alienation: "The nature of the individual being freedom, it follows that on the esthetic level of state organization, the conflict of society and citizen, of community and individual is resolved" (Regin, *Freedom and Dignity*, 142). Kain indicates that alienation takes a number of forms: "Fragmentation must be overcome at the cultural, the social, and the political level, The question we must ask is how well Schiller succeeds in this project" (Kain, *Schiller, Hegel, and Marx*, 15). This is in part our current question as well.

24. This ideal is borrowed from the Greeks (cf. Regin, *Freedom and Dignity*, 122–23) and is seen as a return to the Greek experience of unity and harmony but on a higher level (cf. Kain, *Schiller, Hegel, and Marx*, 13). As Schiller says, "The Greeks put us to shame not only by their simplicity, which is alien to our age; they are at the same time our rivals, often indeed our models, in those very excellences with which we are wont to console ourselves for the unnaturalness of our manners. Combining fullness of form with fullness of content, at once philosophic and creative, at the same time tender and energetic, we see them uniting the youthfulness of fantasy with the manliness of reason in a splendid humanity" (*On the Aesthetic Education of Man*, 37–38).

25. *On the Aesthetic Education of Man*, 138; *Schillers Werke*, 20:411.

26. *On the Aesthetic Education of Man*, 139; *Schillers Werke*, 20:411.

27. *On the Aesthetic Education of Man*, 139; *Schillers Werke*, 20:411.

28. My translation, *Schillers Werke*, 20:412; *On The Aesthetic Education of Man*, 140.

29. *On the Aesthetic Education of Man*, 125; *Schillers Werke*, 20:399.

30. That the aesthetic state is merely a promise or a utopia is made clear by Philip J. Kain in his criticism of Schiller. Kain's main complaint, coming from a Marxist perspective, is that Schiller's account is not sufficiently revolutionary in the political sphere. Schiller's emphasis throughout the *Letters* is upon changing the subject via

education and not upon changing the objective institutions. If this is true, then Kain contends that the aesthetic state must remain an ideal and that there is nothing that can move us beyond the merely rational ethical state to the aesthetic state (cf. Kain, 29–33). Regin also declaims Schiller's project as idealistic and politically naive; however, he is more sympathetic and tries to make Schiller more palatable by denying that Schiller had any larger political program. He concludes that "Schiller's intentions were simply to develop in mankind a harmonious conscience" (*Freedom and Dignity,* 144).

31. Cf. *Werke,* 13:145–50; *A,* 1:106–15.

32. As Hegel says at the beginning of the *Encyclopedia,* there is a circulation between all of the determinations within the system: "Each of the parts of philosophy is a philosophical whole, a circle that closes upon itself; but in each of them the philosophical Idea is in a particular determinacy or element. Every single circle also breaks through the restriction of its element as well, precisely because it is inwardly [the] totality, and it grounds a further sphere. The whole presents itself therefore as a circle of circles, each of which is a necessary moment, so that the system of its peculiar elements constitutes the whole Idea—which equally appears in each single one of them" (G. W. F. Hegel, *Encyclopedia Logic,* trans. Garaets, Suchting, and Harris [Indianapolis: Hackett, 1991], section 15.

33. G. W. F. Hegel, *Elements of the Philosophy of Right,* trans. Nisbet (Cambridge: Cambridge University Press, 1991), 22; G. W. F. Hegel, *Grundlinien der Philosophie des Rechts, Werke in zwanzig Bänden* (Frankfurt am Main: Suhrkamp Verlag, 1970), 7:26.

34. *On The Aesthetic Education of Man,* 140; *Schillers Werke,* 20:412.

35. My translation, *Encyclopedia* section 386.

36. *Philosophy of Right,* section 257, Nisbet trans., 275; *Philosophie des Rechts,* 398.

37. Cf. *Werke,* 13:104; *A,* 1:73, emphasis added.

38. My translation, *Philosophie des Rechts,* section 341.

39. *Werke,* 13:140; *A,* 1:102.

40. *Werke,* 13:137; *A,* 1:99.

41. *Werke,* 13:137; *A,* 1:99.

42. My translation, *Werke,* 13:137; *A,* 1:99.

XII

THE LOGIC OF ART: BEAUTY AND NATURE

Edward Halper

Everyone knows that Hegel thinks the real is rational and the rational real. And nearly everyone knows that Hegel also thinks that art, religion, and philosophy have the same object, the Absolute: art pursues the Absolute through sense, religion through feeling, and philosophy through reason. We have only to combine these two claims to see a problem: if the rational is real and art is not a matter of reason but of sensation, then art is unreal. In other words, insofar as art pursues the Absolute through *sensation*, it fails to be fully rational. But if it lacks rationality, it must also lack reality. Is the result of Hegel's aesthetics, then, that art cannot exist? This question about the reality of art resembles Plato's concern in the *Sophist* with how art objects, nonbeings, can exist. Insofar as such products of the sophist are unreal, they ought not to exist; insofar as they do exist, they must be real. Likewise, Plato's solution of this problem by referring to otherness is similar to Hegel's, as we will soon see. But the question of the reality of art is but one formulation of the issue that will occupy us here, for Hegel's solution generates a new problem or, rather, a new formulation that is intelligible within his system. More specifically, for Hegel the question of the reality of art is tantamount to the question of the place of art within his philosophical system and this latter to the questions of the nature of artistic categories and the processes of conceptual transition among them. These last are the issues that this chapter will address. My discussion will not provide much insight into questions about the plausibility and success of Hegel's account of art, but it should elucidate the well-recognized dependence of Hegel's aesthetic theory on his metaphysics (or logic).

I. The Reality of Art

What, then, is Hegel's solution to the problem of the reality of art? Hegel indicates his answer to this question in at least two places in his lengthy introductory remarks. In each, he is responding to an issue that I take to be a formulation of this one. In the opening pages he asks whether art admits of a philosophical treatment, and, for discussion's sake, he proposes that it does not because art appeals to sensuous feelings in contrast with reason. It lacks rules and regularities, and it is, seemingly, infinitely diverse in its particularity.[1] Of course, to ask whether art admits of philosophical treatment is to ask whether or not it is rational and, thus, real. Hegel's response is important: he insists that art is a sensuous manifestation of the Absolute. An art object itself might seem to be *merely* sensuous, but it is not. Rather, an art object is such precisely because it manifests something beyond sensuousness, the thought or spirit of the artist who created it. A philosophy of art is thus possible because there is an intelligible principle that generates art, and the task of this philosophy is to understand why thought manifests itself sensuously in this way. In short, the philosophy of art is possible because art really is rational. It falls within Hegel's system of philosophy. It is somehow a branch of *Realphilosophie*. The art object is sensuous, but it does not stand on its own; it is part of a larger totality.

Just what that totality is becomes clearer when Hegel considers for a second time in the introductory remarks whether there could be a philosophical treatment of art.[2] Here the objection turns on the particularity of art: since only the universal is intelligible and since art is intrinsically particular, in trying to understand art, we seek to make it something other than it is. Hence, attempts to think art must necessarily fail.

This formulation of the issue has a certain contemporary resonance; for attempts to think music and poetry would seem to miss their point entirely. But, of course, much the same can often be heard about ethics, history, and religion as well. The distinctive mark of Hegel's system is that it purports to bring all these under thought. One of his key moves to achieve this is the recognition that particularity is not an obstacle to intelligibility. Since something can be particular only if there is a universal for it to instantiate, the particular is thinkable through the universal, and particularity is itself a category of thought. Hence, the particularity of art is not an obstacle to its philosophical treatment; on the contrary, art falls under the system because it is a particular and particularity is a category of thought.

Where does art fall in the system? Neither logic nor nature, art clearly falls in the third part, Spirit. As physical, human beings belong to the second part, nature; but our physical needs "pass over" into a spiritual development.[3] This development attains one type of completion in the state where it realizes itself as freedom, for Hegel takes freedom to lie in a will for those practices and institutions that constitute the state. Inasmuch as the state is constituted by an exercise of will, the will for the state is a will for itself. Yet, this will remains "one-sided": it is an abstract will embedded in the particular institutions that constitute the state. The particularity requires some higher justification, and this it acquires through art, religion, or philosophy.[4]

Art is, then, a determination of Spirit, and it appears in the *Encyclopedia*'s final section, "Absolute Mind" (sections 556–63), after the analogue of the material discussed in the *Philosophy of Right.* Hence, not only is art real, but inasmuch as it belongs near the end of the system, it realizes rationality more fully than nature and other, earlier categories of the system. Though sensuously perceived, art manifests the Absolute. Philosophy of art is not concerned with the merely sensuous but with the way that the Absolute appears *through the sensuous.* As such, it is rational and real; indeed, more so than philosophy of nature.

II. The Idea of Beauty

Hegel, thus, solves the problem of the reality of art by locating it as a category in his system. But this solution creates a new problem. Having answered the question *whether* art is real, Hegel needs now to say just *how* it is real, and this means explaining how it differs from the other categories that constitute the system. What sort of conceptual category is art, and how does it differ from the categories of logic and nature and from the other categories of Spirit? After answering this question, we will need to consider what sort of conceptual transitions occur within the category of art and how they differ from purely logical transitions.

Part of the characteristic conceptual content of the category of art can be surmised from the distinction Hegel draws between the logical Idea and the artistic Ideal.[5] The former is "the Idea as such" or the "Absolute Idea"; it is true "in and for itself." As Hegel defines it, the artistic Ideal, the Idea as the beauty of art, consists of this (Absolute) Idea "with the nearer determination *[Bestimmung]* to be an essentially individual actuality *[Wirklichkeit],* as well as an individual formation of actuality with the determination to let the (Absolute) Idea appear essentially within itself" (my translation.) Hegel explains that this actuality must be "adequate" to the (Absolute) Idea, which latter appears through the actuality. Whence, "the Idea as an actuality formed according to its Concept *[Begriff]* is the Ideal."

As I read this text, Hegel identifies the Idea of beauty with a complex consisting of the Absolute Idea, the culminating category of the *Logic,* and an additional component, an actuality through which the Idea somehow appears. That is to say, the Idea of beauty is a complex consisting of the Absolute Idea with an additional category, "actuality," and each category is a determination of the other. In an idealism such as Hegel's, an additional determination can only be another logical category or complex of logical categories: there simply is nothing besides the categories. The development of logical categories is completed in the *Logic,* and the only way that I see for Hegel to sustain his claim that later portions of the system add nothing logically new is for him to reuse logical categories. Of course, Absolute Idea does not admit of additional determinations that transform it into another category; it is already fully realized. So any additional determination that it receives is simply added to it. Thus, "actualization" does not change Absolute Idea into another category. It continues to be Absolute Idea but is now, as Hegel speaks of it, present with an additional determination. He refers to Absolute Idea and its determination as a "totality."[6] The additional determination ought to be adequate to the Absolute Idea; that it is not is the basis for a development within the Ideal of beauty.

There is support for this interpretation later in the introductory remarks when Hegel speaks of truth and existence as two sides of the Concept:[7] the former is Absolute Idea or another manifestation of Idea; the latter is a separate finite determination of Absolute Idea that can come into opposition with truth. Still more conclusively, the first chapter of the *Lectures*, "The Concept of the Beautiful in General," delineates the Idea (*die Idee*) of the beautiful as "the Concept, the reality of the Concept, and the unity of both."[8] Hegel explains that though the reality is generated out of the Concept, reality and Concept do not merge into a single entity, as an acid and a base would produce a salt. Apparently the "reality of the Concept" must remain independent of the Concept, to some degree; it constitutes a second side of the Idea.

This interpretation of the Idea of beauty allows us to see at once why art falls within the system and how it relates to the system's other parts. Again, art is not the merely sensuous; it is the Absolute Idea that manifests itself as sensuous. And the rationality of art depends upon the art object's being a manifestation of some universal. It is the complex of the universal and its sensuous manifestation that is rational, and the adequacy of the manifestation to what it manifests forms the basis for conceptual development. Moreover, the manifestation, the sensuous art object, is itself an instance of logical categories; it is an actuality and an individual.

Other parts of Hegel's system contain categories with a parallel bipartite structure. Thus, nature is constituted by Absolute Idea and additional determinations from the logic of being. The philosophy of right arises from Absolute Idea determined by categories from the logic of Concept. In general *Realphilosophie* develops additional determinations of Absolute Idea, and it follows the sequence of the *Logic*. It constitutes a kind of second unfolding of the logical categories, this time as determinations of Absolute Idea. Insofar as art falls near the end of *Realphilosophie*, it should consist of the Absolute Idea taken with an additional category from the end of the *Logic*. So my interpretation of Hegel's distinction of the logical Idea and the Idea of beauty fits well with my interpretations of other portions of the system. But I shall not rely on interpretations of other Hegelian works here. My concern is rather to understand specifically what additional determination Hegel adds to Absolute Idea to get beauty and then to see how he effects transitions in the philosophy of art.

III. Beauty and Life

An art object exists in the first instance as a physical entity, a painted canvas, chiseled stone, and so forth. But it is not merely a physical entity; what makes such objects works of art is precisely their deeper significance. They are physical objects that somehow make manifest the Absolute, and the mystery for the philosopher is how the merely physical could convey something that is nonphysical. Part of Hegel's solution, as I have already indicated, is that the Idea of beauty has both dimensions: one side is the Absolute Idea, the other its sensible, physical manifestation. We know the Absolute Idea from the very end of the *Logic* as what is in and for itself; more concretely we know it in the realm of Spirit as freedom, the in and for itself that manifests itself as in and for itself. What is puzzling is how to understand the other, more concrete side of the Idea of beauty. What additional determination is present with the Absolute Idea to constitute the Idea of beauty? What counts as the "actuality" or "existence" of the concept?

We might, at first, suppose that "determinate being" (*Dasein*), "actuality" or some other category from the logic of being were good candidates. But the work of art is more complex. It is not a mere physical object, but a physical object whose existence, shape, and material depend upon the artist; it is a physical object whose very existence depends upon the mediation of Spirit.

My contention is that the concrete side of beauty consists of the logical category of life, a category from the very end of the logic. In other words, the Absolute Idea manifests itself in art as a living thing. Once we see that this is so, the problematic of the opening chapters of the *Aesthetics* will become clear. First, though, let me set out more of my interpretation. The third and final section of the final portion of the *Logic,* the "Subjective Logic," is "The Idea." It has three chapters: "Life," "The Idea of Cognition," and "The Absolute Idea." These correspond to, respectively, art, religion, and philosophy. When Hegel claims that each of these disciplines has the Absolute as its object, he means that each aims to grasp the *Absolute Idea.* So, too, there are three disciplines because Absolute Idea manifests itself as life, as cognition, and as Idea. Clearly, the last one, philosophy, is the highest and most adequate manifestation. But art and religion approach it and are proportionately important.

What supports identifying the actuality or existence side of the Idea of beauty with life? Before we can look at the text of the *Aesthetics* we need to ask, what is the concept of life? Hegel answers this question in the *Logic* by distinguishing the logical Concept of life from the life of nature and the life of Spirit.[9] In nature, life has an external existence that is conditioned by inorganic nature. In Spirit, life also has a determinate externality, the life of nature, to which it opposes itself and its own ends and activities. In contrast, the moments of the logical concept of life remain "enclosed within the form of the Concept"; and this Concept contains its externality within itself as a diverse multiplicity that is "permeated throughout by the Concept." That is, life remains an "omnipresent" unity throughout a multiplicity. These two aspects of life, the *multiplicity* in which the Concept is one and the *Concept* that retains its simple self-relation in the multiplicity, are more commonly termed "body" and "soul." It is obvious from Hegel's understanding of them that they are two aspects of the same category. However, it remains puzzling how the Concept can be one and yet be omnipresent as a unity to a plurality of diverse parts—indeed, Hegel calls this an "incomprehensible mystery" as long as we remain at the level of the type of thinking he terms "reflection."[10] What we need to realize, though, is that Hegel is operating in the realm of Concept. A Concept itself gives itself a plurality of diverse elements while remaining present and self-identical in all of them. The Concept with such a relation to its own parts is an instance of life.

Hegel makes no appeal to experience, but the Concept of life that he develops in the *Logic* captures well what we usually take to be characteristic of living entities. They have a plurality of parts, each of which, despite its diversity, manifests the identity of the organism. That is, the parts are all connected together, each functions with the others for the sake of the whole, and the organism is manifest in every part. Most of us would be unlikely to refer to this Concept of an organism as a Concept that "contains multiplicity as its own externality and negates this externality in self-identity," but the characterization is apt. Moreover, the Concept is also related to itself in the sense that it excludes the external multiplicity. This Hegel refers to as the "living individual."

With this understanding of life, we can now look at the evidence that it is part of the Idea of beauty. There are some suggestions to this effect in the first chapter of the *Aesthetics,* "The Concept of the Beautiful as Such." There Hegel claims that this Idea consists of a Concept and its real or objective existence; and, most characteristically, these two sides are one. That is to say, the abstract Idea of beauty consists of the adequacy of the objective manifestation to the Concept it manifests.[11] And Hegel describes the Concept by using the same terms that he used in the *Logic* to characterize life: the Concept is a self-identical unity that permeates a multiplicity; its relation to itself is a negativity that is also a self-determination.[12] Now this Concept ought to manifest itself in some adequate actuality, but the multiplicity it contains lacks specification and genuine diversity. Multiplicity remains implicit (*an sich*) within the Concept. Thus, the abstract Idea contains life but not an adequate manifestation of life. I shall have more to say about the transition to the next chapter later.

It is really in chapter 2, "The Beauty of Nature" that we see most clearly the Idea of life. Indeed, Hegel begins his treatment of natural beauty with a lengthy exposition of "The Idea as Life." Here he identifies the soul, "the substantial unity and all-pervasive universality which is simple relation to itself and subjective self-awareness," as feeling.[13] That is, feeling does not belong to one part of the organism; it permeates every member, and it is the same organism that feels throughout its frame. The identity of feeling at once unifies the multiplicity and defines the organism as an organism. Here, too, Hegel denies that the organism contains *parts* defined in relation to each other; its constituents are rather *members* that could not exist apart from the whole. Thus, a hand severed from the body is no longer a hand.[14] The very same idea is expressed in the *Logic*'s treatment of life.[15] Both the idea and the example come from Aristotle's *Metaphysics*.[16] Aristotle is describing the relation of the material parts to the whole sensible substance, a living thing. The point is that in a living thing the constituent parts are so closely connected that they have their forms and functions only within the whole. In contrast, an artifact, such as a house, contains parts like stones and boards that retain their identities and properties (such as weight and solidity) whether or not they are functioning as parts of the house. What this means is that the living thing has a stronger unity than an artifact.

It is just this type of unity that belongs within the Idea of beauty. Hegel discusses the beauty of nature immediately after the section "The Idea as Life," and a reader could suppose (incorrectly) that the beauty of nature is a concomitant to the treatment of nature and a mere part of the treatment of beauty. But Hegel insists that nature "foreshadows" (*geahnt*) the concept of beauty.[17] The reason is that the relation between the natural object's form and matter is the same as the relation between the art object's Concept and appearance. Just as the nature's form is a unity present to a plurality of material parts which prove unable to exist as such without form, the Concept of beauty is a unity that is present to every bit of the multiplicity of the appearance which cannot exist as such without it. That is to say, the Idea of beauty contains the relation that is the defining mark of life.

This is part of the reason that Hegel recognizes some beauty in nature. The unity of material body, the joint functioning of its members, is a manifestation of its form, the self-identical soul. As Hegel puts it, "life in nature is *beautiful* because, truth, the Idea in its earliest natural form as life, is immediately present there as individual and adequate actuality."[18] However, Hegel also claims that the living thing fails to be truly beautiful because its material parts do not make the soul fully manifest. Though soul is an inner principle of unity that explains why the members can function together, the soul itself does not appear. Hence, its actuality in the body fails to be fully adequate to it. In other words, insofar as soul is some inner hidden principle of unity, the body whose unifying organs are internal and hidden is an adequate expression of it, and nature is beautiful. But insofar as the soul remains hidden, the unity of the body fails to be fully apparent, and the natural object fails to be beautiful. Significantly, in either case, whether or not nature is beautiful, the assumption is that the parts of whatever is beautiful are unified by some self-identical principle. This is the soul of a nature, or some other principle. Since, life is defined as a multiplicity that is permeated by self-identical principle, every beautiful thing satisfies the criterion of life.[19]

Let us consider more carefully the respect in which a nature fails to be beautiful. Though it is clearly alive, it fails to be beautiful because the soul fails to be manifest. Why, though, should we expect soul to appear? Soul was the inner to which the *body* was adequate. When Hegel maintains that the living thing is deficient in beauty, he is apparently measuring it, as a whole of body *and* soul, against another Concept. That is, the living thing would be beautiful if it, as a whole, were a manifestation of the Concept of beauty; and it would manifest beauty if this Concept permeated every part of it. Again, the presumption remains that something beautiful will be living—it will be a multiplicity permeated by a self-identical unity. Hegel's claims that a nature is and is not beautiful turn on which Concept it is measured against: in respect of its own soul the nature is an instance of life, but in respect of another Concept (the Concept of beauty) it is not living. It fails to be alive in the sense that its parts appear to lack the proper degree of unity, a deficiency that could perhaps be remedied with the appropriate principle.[20] In short, the presumption here is that something beautiful is alive, but the Concept of life can be understood in reference to soul or in reference to a higher principle of unity. We can see why it is that Hegel rejects the Greek notion that art imitates nature. Art encompasses nature and life, but goes beyond them. Art is even more alive than nature.

The Concept to which the art object should be adequate is that of beauty or, as Hegel sometimes says, freedom. But we have already seen that the Concept of beauty is itself a manifestation of the Absolute Idea, the final category of the *Logic.* So is freedom. I suggest that it is the Absolute Idea that the artist seeks to make manifest in the work of art. The artist does so by producing something that is alive in the Conceptual sense that "life" has in the *Logic.* In short, the realm of art can be understood as Absolute Idea's manifesting itself through life. In the *Logic* Hegel calls life the immediacy of the Idea, and there he means that life is the first, immediate development of the Idea;[21] but life is also the immediacy of the Idea in aesthetics in that it is a sensuous manifestation of the Absolute Idea.[22] While the Absolute Idea of the *Logic* is manifest as a living thing in art, it is manifest as cognition or feeling in religion, and fully or absolutely, in philosophy. Each of these represents a doubling, Absolute Idea determined as one of the three Ideas from the logic—life, cognition, or Absolute Idea.

Once we see that life is part of the Idea of beauty, the problematic of the opening chapters of the *Aesthetics* becomes clear. Hegel's extensive discussion of natural things is neither irrelevant nor arbitrary. Nature and art fall under the same logical category, life. Hence, nature is a good candidate to illustrate the conceptual relations intrinsic to art, but it is also a competitor with art. Showing how life exists in living things, Hegel shows why they have some degree of beauty and enables us to understand beauty's first concrete manifestation. But art must be distinguished from nature if we are to grasp its more adequate manifestations.

In sum, in logic the category of life, the immediate Idea, consists of a multiplicity of members united by a self-identical principle that is present to each member. In nature, life, the immediacy of the Absolute Idea, lies in a multiplicity of members that exist physically in space and time, conditioned by inorganic nature; life consists of the Absolute Idea determined by other categories from the *Logic*. In art, life is itself the determination of the Absolute Idea; Absolute Idea manifests itself as something living, and the truth of the manifestation, its adequacy to the Absolute Idea, is its beauty. In nature, the multiplicity of a body is united by an internal principle; in art, the multiplicity that constitutes all of life, the body and the soul, must be united by some other principle, perhaps, harmony or law. Thus, while nature meets some of the criteria of beauty, art itself is richer and higher than nature. Whereas every member of a living organism manifests the unity of soul, every member of an art object ought to manifest the Absolute. The conceptual differences between nature and the beautiful in art should now be clear. I have explained them as instances or combinations of the logical categories. (As noted earlier, I distinguish the realms of nature and spirit from that of logic by additional logical determinations present with Absolute Idea; these determinations and Absolute Idea constitute an irreducible complex.) In this way, beauty can be a distinct category without adding any conceptual determination that is logically new.

IV. The Dialectic of Art

It remains to broach the question of the dialectic of art. How are conceptual transitions effected in this realm? Do they differ from transitions in other realms? In *Logic,* transitions between categories depend on self-determination. By showing that a category is an instance of itself, one shows that it has additional content that was not immediately apparent; and this new content makes the category be a different category. In *Realphilosophie,* the transitions to new categories are different. In nature, the transitions are effected by showing that a category negates itself; this is a process of self-othering. In the *Philosophy of Right,* transitions between categories depend upon showing that a category includes its contrary within itself; I call this self-identification. Since philosophy of art belongs to the realm of Spirit, transitions among its categories should be similar to those among categories of right. We will see, though, that Hegel's dialectic here is proper to the treatment of art.

To understand the way Hegel's dialectic of art works it will be necessary to present his reasoning. I shall proceed only through the first few chapters of the first section, and even here it will be necessary to be selective because the categories are developed in much detail. It will be necessary to repeat here some of what I have already said when I argued for the definition of beauty. However, my concern now is not with defining the aesthetic categories but with showing how the definition of beauty emerges from nature and transforms itself into art. Besides working through the reasoning of this text, I want to show that the reasoning processes in aesthetics are not less rigorous than those in other portions of the system. I shall follow Hegel's organization of the sections of his first two chapters and the first section of his third chapter, though where possible I shall abbreviate the argument. (Throughout the rest of this section, I shall use Roman numerals to designate Hegel's chapters and his own numbers and letters to designate his sections and subsections.)

I. The first chapter of the *Lectures* begins with the Idea of beauty. We have seen that Hegel understands this Idea as the Concept, the existence or actuality of the Concept, and the unity of these two. The component of existence belongs because we are in *Realphilosophie,* and the unity of the two components because the Idea is that of beauty. These components do not merge, as acids and bases do to form salts; they retain their integrity within the composite.[23] The existence component, as Hegel first describes it, is life, the immediacy of the Absolute Idea, as we have seen.

1. (a) The Concept, Absolute Idea, contains within itself all the logical categories and thus all the determinations through which it could acquire objective existence as a work of art. However, the determinations remain implicit (*an sich*) within the Concept. These determinations are not distinct parts of Absolute Idea; the latter exists in all of them as the ego exists in all its own ideas. Standing in this relation to its own content, Absolute Idea is a *universal,* and its content is its own *particularity;* further, it is the *totality* of its particular specifications. In giving itself such determinations, Absolute Idea has ceased to be simply Absolute; Hegel designates it as "Concept," and its determinations give it "objectivity."[24]

(b) Objectivity is the determination of the Concept (Absolute Idea); it is its particularization. The determinations that the Concept gives to itself are those that are included within it, namely, all the logical categories; but these are also distinct from it. However, inasmuch as each determination is a determination of the Concept, *it* includes the Concept.

(c) The Concept is, thus, one and the same in each determination it gives itself: it is a unity that gives itself a plurality but maintains itself as a unity in the plurality. It is, thus, an instance of (the logical category of) life. Insofar as Concept's subjectivity corresponds to its objectivity, it is also truth. The totality of Concept, its determinations, and their unity constitute the Idea.

2. Truth is, thus, the reality that corresponds with and is adequate to the Concept. This reality has truth insofar as it is the *existence* of the Concept. Since the totality of existence and Concept is the Idea, the Idea alone is true and real.

3. The truth of the Idea is the correspondence of its constituents, the adequacy of Concept's determinations to Concept. It is grasped and measured through Concept. On the other hand, the correspondence can also be viewed through the determination, that is, through Concept's existence. When the Concept exists not as mere thought but immediately, the totality of Concept and existence is beautiful. But immediate existence is sensuous existence. Hence, the Concept must have a sensuous manifestation if there is to be beauty.

(a) The understanding cannot apprehend beauty because it cannot overcome the distinction between the Concept and the immediate or sensuous.

(b) Nor could any finite, one-sided intelligence apprehend beauty because such an intelligence takes its object to exist independently of it and attempts to grasp its *activity* by *passively* receiving sensations. Likewise, a finite will aims to fashion beauty by *acting* upon something *passive,* but it cannot convey its own freedom and activity to it. In neither case is the manifestation adequate to what it manifests—neither can be beauty. And finite will and understanding contradict each other in taking their objects as exclusively active or exclusively passive.

(c) Beauty must overcome their opposition and unify both points of view. It does so because beauty is the Concept's *own* sensuous manifestation and, ideally, the manifestation is one with the Concept. The rational and sensuous are somehow united through the Concept's activity. The activity is, as it were, the result of beauty's own will, and the desire (or will) of the subject withdraws before it. It follows that beauty exists independently of our apprehension of it. It is free insofar as it gives itself its own determination, necessary insofar as its particular aspects are linked to one another. As such, beauty is withdrawn from finitude and raised to Idea and truth.

II. The Idea of beauty, as thus derived, is an independent entity, the unity of Concept and its existence; the Concept manifests itself in its own sensuous appearance. As such, this Idea is nature, and beauty is natural. That is to say, the Idea of beauty develops, as we have seen, by including within itself the distinctions and the relations among its parts. Because it is both a Concept that manifests itself in its existence and the existence that manifests the Concept, its parts are, in principle at least, adequate to each other. Its existence is, thus, independent of human subjectivity. But a Concept whose existence is other than every other existence is a nature. Hence, the Idea of beauty manifests itself first as nature.

A. 1. The Concept, however, takes on different types of existence as a nature.

(a) Its first manifestation is as the simplest determinations of nature, inorganic bodies. The unity of such bodies is merely the uniformity of their qualities. This unity is inadequate to the Concept and, indeed, the negation of the latter's diverse multiplicity.

(b) The second manifestation of the Concept is, accordingly, the negation of the uniformity of the first, non-uniform bodies. These bodies exist in relation to each other, as in the solar system; but their unity is something distinct from them. In beauty, though, the Concept is one with its existence; hence, dissimilar bodies, existing apart from their unity, fall short of beauty. The latter is, thus, the negation of the differences of non-uniform bodies. These bodies must exist not merely in relation to each other but essentially with each other: not as "parts" but as "members" of a whole, as organs of a *living* being.

(c) The third manifestation of the Concept is the only one that counts as the Idea of beauty: it consists of the Concept manifesting itself as life. (Here, life is a category of nature.) Unlike non-uniform bodies, the bodies that constitute living things, the organs, contain within them their principle of unity; for they are organs only insofar as they exist together in one living thing. The living body contains within itself the Concept's distinctions; for the Concept (Absolute Idea), too, is a unity constituted by negating the plurality of its constituents and so, as we saw, an instance of (the logical category of) life. Hence, the living body is a manifestation of Concept. The Concept, however, does not, as such, exist in space and time; it remains distinct from body even though it shows itself through body. The body's unity is soul. Now the relation between body and soul is a long-standing problem. In one sense, they are identical: the body could not exist as such without a principle, like feeling, that unites its members in a common function, and the function could not occur without the bodily members. On the other hand, body and soul differ because the distinct bodily members exist in different places while the soul is equally in all places. The overcoming of this contradiction is the organism's process of life: the organism uses its own diverse parts *for itself.* Likewise, limitations that spatial existence imposes on individual living things are overcome by reproduction, a process in which the individual uses what is external *for itself.* The existence of such a living subject is termed by Hegel the "idealism of nature."

2. Nature is beautiful insofar as the Idea of beauty is present in an individual living thing, and to the extent that this latter is a multiplicity permeated by a unity, this Idea is present. However, nature does not grasp itself in this way; nature appears beautiful *to us.* Hence, its beauty is not *for itself* but *for us.* Insofar as this beauty depends upon something external, it fails to be genuine beauty.

(a) Each of an animal's motions is conditioned by its particular circumstances. It does not grasp what unites them, but we can. Only this principle is recognized by thought. Hence, the Concept does not *appear* in the living thing, and it lacks beauty.

(b) Each of an animal's bodily parts has its own shape, and all together constitute a single bodily shape. Here a unity of the organism does appear, but it is not this spatial unity that makes the bodily parts members of a single organism. It is rather soul that unites them. Hence, though the unity of shape appears, it does not manifest soul.

(c) An animal's bodily parts are, however, a manifestation of its soul insofar as the parts are so structured as to perform functions essential to the animal's life. This is a beauty that the biologist perceives, rather than a beauty of which the animal is aware. Insofar as the appearance of beauty depends upon someone else, it is not a manifestation of Concept. Hence, the animal is not *in itself* beautiful.

3. Nonetheless, nature is beautiful insofar as the harmony and necessary relations of its sensible parts presuppose a single inner principle of unity. Nature "foreshadows" the Concept; but the Concept, the principle of unity, remains merely inner.

(a) The beauty of nature is the ensouled harmony of material parts, and the principle of unity, soul, is the matter's own activity.

(b) But harmony of an animal's shape, of a landscape, and of the emotion (the animal's appropriate response to the landscape) depends upon conscious awareness of just the sort lacking in nature.

(c) Since nature lacks the conscious awareness to recognize its own harmonious parts, Concept is not in nature, and nature is not the existence of the Concept. It follows that nature is not beautiful.

B. The material unity of the parts of nature is not a manifestation of Concept, as beauty would require. The outer, *material* unity falls short of the inner unity of Concept, and the former unity results instead from a different inner, configurating form, one whose unity does not permeate nature. This form remains other than and distinct from the matter of nature and, as such, abstract.

1. Insofar as this form is an external determinacy and unity imposed upon matter, it is regularity or symmetry. (a) Regularity is the most primitive and external unity; it is simple sameness and repetition of form. Because it fails to manifest the self-identity of Concept, it is a kind of negation of beauty. The latter, then, is some sort of negation of regularity. The first negation of the repetition of identical form is the repetition of non-identical but similar form; this is symmetry. This, too, fails to manifest Concept, and beauty is some sort of negation of it. (b) The negation of the repetition of similar elements is a totality of dissimilar elements; this, Hegel, thinking of the construction of an ellipse, terms "conformity to law." Again, this latter fails to manifest Concept. (c) Its negation consists of dissimilar elements in opposition with each other; this is harmony. Harmony is still an external positing of differences that does not manifest the Concept's self-identity through difference. Hence, the unity that should be manifest in nature cannot exist in abstract forms.

2. With the failure of form, we might look to the matter to make manifest the inner principle of unity. Indeed, the abstract purity of matter has an aes-

thetic effect on consciousness, but it is not itself a subjective principle of unity: it cannot recognize its own unity.

C. The first manifestation of beauty is nature; but, on closer consideration, nature shows itself to lack beauty. What needs to be explained is why nature is imperfectly beautiful. As an Idea, beauty must actualize itself in individuals. It does actualize itself in natural individuals, but inadequately.
1. The manifold activities that constitute an individual animal's outward existence do not make visible the inner nature from which they spring. Only in the case of human beings does the life force show itself in the color and sensitivity of the skin, the pulsation of the blood visible through the skin, and the expression on the face. However, these manifestations fail to be adequate because the skin is porous, wrinkled, and non-uniform, unlike the sensitive soul it can express—a soul uniformly one throughout the body—and because nature does not manifest higher spiritual entities like freedom, state, and will.
2. An individual animal is also necessarily related to and limited by other individuals. It can be sustained by water, land, climate, and so forth, but also harmed. Humans, too, are sustained and limited by such individuals and by other people. Such limitations prevent a natural individual from fully manifesting the freedom of Spirit.
3. The individual human is also limited by species, race, ethnicity, family, occupation, and, even, its own experience. Such finitude of existence is at odds with the inner essence of Concept which is free, individual, and infinite. Even our knowing, willing and acting are necessarily subject to these limitations. Hence, Spirit cannot realize itself in the natural individual. Concept can only be fully manifest in an individual not bound by such finite limits.

III. Since the finite limitations and relations of natural individuals prevent them from manifesting Concept, the individuals in which Concept can appear adequately must somehow overcome such finitude. The objects of art do so by manifesting in each of their parts the whole of the Concept. Just as the life of the animal is present in each of its parts, so too the Concept appears in each part of the art object. This is possible because the artist casts aside material features that do not represent the soul, such as blemishes and skin pores, in order to portray the essence of a subject's soul,[25] and because each part of the work of art is essentially connected with every other part and all together manifest Concept. That no element of an artwork expresses or, at least, should express anything other than the Absolute makes the artwork complete and self-contained. As such, it manifests freedom and acquires a kind of life, not the life that is the unity of soul and matter but the life that is the unity of Concept and its actuality, a more thoroughgoing unity than the former.

Thus, though nature fails to be adequately beautiful, it serves not only as the first manifestation of beauty, but also as the opposite of art, and, as the category of life, as the defining principle of art. The dialectic of beauty, like other dialectics of Spirit, works by identifying with something that turns out, on further reflection, to be an opposite and then incorporating this opposite into a richer whole. The three chapters discussed here use life, first as a logical category, to define beauty, then as a category of nature to grasp beauty in nature, and finally as a category of spirit to grasp the beauty of art.

V. Beauty, System, and Particular Works of Art

The preceding presentation of the argument of the first three chapters of the *Aesthetics* has been necessarily sketchy. This material has seemed to most readers to be an exposition of a variety of perspectives on art and nature with little or no internal logic, and Hegel or his student auditors have, unfortunately, encouraged this misapprehension by failing to draw inferences rigorously and by failing to distinguish remarks from the main body of argument. Some of what seems to come from the blue actually derives from earlier portions of the system, and Hegel is entitled to draw upon them here. Even so, in my exposition, I have added details in order to clarify the transitions and to highlight their rigor.

It goes almost without saying that Hegel's reasoning does not have the *modus ponens* type of rigor to be found in much contemporary work—his conclusions and analysis are simply too rich for this anemic principle of inference. It is also true that the reasoning here differs from that of other portions of his own system: there is little emphasis on internal contradictions or on conceptual transformations to new spheres. We would expect the reasoning of the *Aesthetics* to reflect its subject matter, and on the analysis proposed here, it does. As Absolute Idea that manifests itself as life, beauty is composed of categories from the end of the *Logic*. Like these categories, beauty is defined in relation to its parts. Thus, the proper mode of examining beauty and the aesthetic categories that succeed it is to consider their parts in respect of each other in order to ask whether all the parts are adequate to the whole. That is, the mode or reasoning in the *Aesthetics* depends on treating each category as properly self-contained and considering whether it truly meets this criterion.

It cannot be coincidental that this is also the right way to consider a particular work of art: it should be a self-contained whole whose every part manifests the self-conscious principle of unity. As usual, Hegel treats ideas *about* a subject in the same way that he would treat the ideas *within* the subject.

It is fashionable to criticize Hegel's aesthetics as overly conceptualized, overly romantic, or simply outmoded. I have not attempted to confront those criticisms here. Instead, I have focused on the kinds of conceptual categories it treats, how it treats them, and how the treatment fits into his system. I have argued that it is a rigorous part of the system. As such it must stand or fall with that system.

Notes

1. G. W. F. Hegel, *Vorlesungen über die Ästhetik, Werke in zwanzig Bänden,* ed. E. Moldenhauer and K. M. Michel, 20 vols. and Index (Frankfurt am Main: Suhrkamp Verlag, 1969ff), 13:18–19; English translation, G. W. F. Hegel, *Aesthetics: Lectures on Fine Art,* trans. T. M. Knox, 2 vols. (Oxford: Clarendon Press, 1975), 1:5–6. Further references will be given in the form: *Werke,* 13:18–19; *A,* 1:5–6.
2. *Werke,* 13:127–28; *A,* 1:91–92.
3. *Werke,* 13:136–38; *A,* 1:98–100.
4. *Werke,* 13:138–39; *A,* 1:100–101.
5. *Werke,* 13:104–6; *A,* 1:73–75. Later quotations in this paragraph are from this text.
6. *Werke,* 13:106; *A,* 1:75.
7. *Werke,* 13:138; *A,* 1:100.
8. *Werke,* 13:145; *A,* 1:106.
9. G. W. F. Hegel, *Wissenschaft der Logik II. Erster Teil: Die objektive Logik. Zweites Buch. Zweiter Teil: Die subjektive Logik, Werke in zwanzig Bänden,* ed. E. Moldenhauer and K. M. Michel, 6:471–72. English translation, G. W. F. Hegel, *Hegel's Science of Logic,* trans. A. V. Miller (London: George Allen and Unwin, 1969), 762–63. Further references will be given in the form: *Logik, Werke,* 6:471–72; Miller, 762–63.) Unless otherwise indicated, quotations in this paragraph of my text are from the Miller translation of this passage. For consistency, though, I substitute "Concept" for Miller's "Notion."
10. *Logik, Werke,* 6:472–73; Miller, 763.
11. *Werke,* 13:145; *A,* 1:106.
12. *Logik, Werke,* 6:474; Miller, 764. *Werke,*13:148–49; *A,* 1:109.
13. *Werke,* 13:161; *A,* 1:119.
14. *Werke,* 13:162–64; *A,* 1:120–21.
15. *Logik, Werke,* 6:476; Miller, 766.
16. *Metaphysics* Z.10.1035b24–27; 11.1036b30–32.
17. *Werke,* 13:174; *A,* 1:129–30.
18. *Werke,* 13:167; *A,* 1:123.
19. A principle of "organic unity" is commonly ascribed to Hegel; e.g., Robert Wicks, "Hegel's Aesthetics: An Overview," in *The Cambridge Companion to Hegel,* ed. F. Beiser (Cambridge: Cambridge University Press, 1993), 367–68. My discussion here shows why this is right.
20. Stephen Houlgate, *Freedom, Truth and History* (London: Routledge, 1991), 130, speaks of art's giving "concrete, living expression to the often unseen harmony and unity within life."
21. *Logik, Werke,* 6:468; Miller, 759–60.
22. *Werke,* 13:157; *A,* 1:116.
23. *Werke,* 13:145; *A,* 1:106.
24. *Werke,* 13:147–49; *A,* 1:108–10.
25. Robert Wicks speaks of the "idealization" of art and quotes this passage, "Hegel's Aesthetics," 366–67. He does not try to explain the basis for Hegel having this aesthetic preference.

About the Contributors

William Desmond is Professor of Philosophy and Director of the *International Program* of Philosophy at the Institute of Philosophy, Catholic University of Leuven, Belgium. Among his books are *Arts and the Absolute* and most recently, *Being and the Between* and *Perplexity and Ultimacy*. He is a past-President of the Hegel Society of America.

Carl Rapp is Professor of English at the University of Georgia. His books include *William Carlos Williams and Romantic Idealism* and, more recently, *Fleeing the Universal: The Critique of Post-Rational Criticism.* His articles have appeared in *The Southern Review, The Georgia Review, Critical Review,* and *Modern Age.*

Brian K. Etter is Associate Professor in Humanities at Kettering University, formerly GMI Engineering and Management Institute, in Flint, Michigan. He has published on Hegel and the arts in *The Owl of Minerva,* and is currently working on a book on Hegelian aesthetics.

Jere Surber is Professor of Philosophy and Cultural Studies at the University of Denver. Among his recent publications are *Language and German Idealism: Fichte's Linguistic Thought, Culture and Critique: An Introduction to the Critical Discourses of Cultural Studies,* and *Metacritique: The Linguistic Challenge to German Idealism.*

Stephen Houlgate is Professor of Philosophy at the University of Warwick. He is the author of *Hegel, Nietzsche and the Criticism of Metaphysics* and *Freedom, Truth, and History: An Introduction to Hegel's Philosophy,* as well as numerous articles on Hegel, Kant and Nietzsche. He is also the editor of *The Hegel Reader* and *Hegel and the Philosophy of Nature.* He served as Vice-President of the Hegel Society of America from 1992 to 1994 and as President from 1994 to 1996. He is currently editor of the *Bulletin of the Hegel Society of Great Britain.*

David Kolb is Charles A. Dana Professor of Philosophy at Bates College. He is the author of *The Critique of Pure Modernity, Postmodern Sophistications, Socrates in the Labyrinth,* and the editor of *New Perspectives on Hegel's Philosophy of Religion.* He has published essays on topics in the history of philosophy, on postmodernism in architecture, and on philosophy and nonlinear writing.

Richard Dien Winfield is Professor of Philosophy at the University of Georgia. He is author of *Reason and Justice, The Just Economy, Overcoming Foundations: Studies in Systematic Philosophy, Freedom and Modernity, Law in Civil So-*

ciety, Systematic Aesthetics, Stylistics: Rethinking the Artforms after Hegel, and *The Just Family.*

STEPHEN C. LAW is Professor of Humanities and Philosophy at the University of Central Oklahoma, in Edmond, where he serves as the head of the department. The work included in this volume is an outgrowth of his 1986 dissertation, *In Risu Veritas,* which analyzed the evolution of Greek and Roman comedy in terms of Hegelian aesthetics.

JUDITH NORMAN is an Assistant Professor of Philosophy at Trinity University in San Antonio, Texas. She has written articles on Fichte, Schelling, and the Nietzsche/Wagner relationship, and is currently translating *Beyond Good and Evil.*

MARTIN GAMMON is a Post-Doctoral Research Fellow in the Philosophy Department at Yale University, and is presently completing a book on the foundations of Kant's aesthetic theory. He has taught at Stanford University and the University of California, Berkeley. He has published on German aesthetics in the *Journal of the History of Philosophy,* the *Review of Metaphysics,* and *Kant-Studien.*

ANDREW FIALA received his Ph.D. from Vanderbilt University. He has subsequently taught philosophy at Vanderbilt University and Belmont University, and is currently teaching ancient history at the University School of Nashville. In addition to his interest in Hegel and Nineteenth Century Philosophy, he has done work in environmental ethics and political philosophy.

EDWARD HALPER is Professor of Philosophy at the University of Georgia. He is the author of *One and Many in Aristotle's Metaphysics: The Central Books* (1989), *Form and Reason: Essays in Metaphysics* (1993), and numerous papers in philosophy journals. Most of his published work is in ancient philosophy.

WILLIAM MAKER is Professor of Philosophy and Chair of the Philosophy and Religion Department at Clemson University. He is the editor of *Hegel on Economics and Freedom* and the author of *Philosophy Without Foundations: Rethinking Hegel,* and has published numerous articles on Hegel and contemporary philosophy. He was Vice-President of the Hegel Society of America from 1994 to 1996.

Index